CREATIVITY AND DEVELOPMENT

STRETCHING THE IMAGINATION
Representation and Transformation in Mental Imagery
C. Cornoldi, R. Logie, M. Brandimonte, G. Kaufmann, D. Reisberg

MODELS OF VISUOSPATIAL COGNITION
M. de Vega, M. J. Intons-Peterson, P. N. Johnson-Laird, M. Denis, M. Marschark

WORKING MEMORY AND HUMAN COGNITION
J. T. E. Richardson, R. W. Engle, L. Hasher, R. H. Logie, E. R. Stoltzfus, R. T. Zacks

RELATIONS OF LANGUAGE AND THOUGHT
The View from Sign Language and Deaf Children
M. Marschark, P. Siple, D. Lillo-Martin, R. Campbell, V. Everhart

GENDER DIFFERENCES IN HUMAN COGNITION
P. J. Caplan, M. Crawford, J. S. Hyde, J. T. E. Richardson

FIGURATIVE LANGUAGE AND THOUGHT
A. Katz, C. Cacciari, R. W. Gibbs, M. Turner

COGNITION AND EMOTION
E. Eich, J. F. Kihlstrom, G. H. Bower, J. P. Forgas, P. M. Niedenthal

BECOMING A WORD LEARNER
A Debate on Lexical Acquisition
R. M. Golinkoff, K. Hirsh–Pasek, L. Bloom, L. B. Smith,
A. L. Woodward, N. Akhtar, M. Tomasello, and G. J. Hollich

MEMORY FOR ACTION
A Distinct Form of Episodic Memory?
H. D. Zimmer, R. Cohen, M. J. Guynn, J. Engelkamp, R. Kormi-Nouri, M. A. Foley

CREATIVITY AND DEVELOPMENT
R. K. Sawyer, V. John-Steiner, S. Moran, R. J. Sternberg,
D. H. Feldman, J. Nakamura, M. Csikszentmihalyi

CREATIVITY AND DEVELOPMENT

R. KEITH SAWYER
VERA JOHN-STEINER
SEANA MORAN
ROBERT J. STERNBERG
DAVID HENRY FELDMAN
JEANNE NAKAMURA
MIHALY CSIKSZENTMIHALYI

OXFORD
UNIVERSITY PRESS

2003

OXFORD

UNIVERSITY PRESS

Oxford   New York

Auckland   Bangkok   Buenos Aires   Cape Town   Chennai
Dar es Salaam   Delhi   Hong Kong   Istanbul   Karachi   Kolkata
Kuala Lumpur   Madrid   Melbourne   Mexico City   Mumbai   Nairobi
São Paulo   Shanghai   Taipei   Tokyo   Toronto

Copyright © 2003 by Oxford University Press, Inc.

Published by Oxford University Press, Inc.
198 Madison Avenue, New York, New York 10016

www.oup.com

Oxford is a registered trademark of Oxford University Press

Library of Congress Cataloging-in-Publication Data
Creativity and development / R. Keith Sawyer . . . [et al.].
p. cm. — (Counterpoints)
Includes bibliographical references and index.
ISBN 0-19-514899-1; ISBN 0-19-514900-9 (pbk.)
1. Creative thinking. 2. Creative ability. 3. Developmental psychology.
I. Sawyer, R. Keith (Robert Keith) II. Counterpoints (Oxford University Press)
BF408.C7545 2003
153.3'5—dc21   2002151878

1 3 5 7 9 8 6 4 2

Printed in the United States of America
on acid-free paper

To Howard E. Gruber

Piaget, working with children, found that the growth of their ideas is a process spread over years. Now that we are learning about adult creative work in this new way, we can compare two radically different development processes that have some important points in common. Each will illuminate the other.

—HEG

Contents

Authors

R. KEITH SAWYER is Associate Professor of Education at Washington University in St. Louis. His research focuses on improvisational creativity, everyday conversation, and emergence in collaborating groups. He is the author of more than 30 articles and of four books related to creativity and development, including *Pretend play as improvisation* (1997) and *Group creativity* (2003).

VERA JOHN-STEINER is Regent's Professor of Education at the University of New Mexico. She is a scholar of developmental psychology, linguistics, and creativity, and an influential editor and interpreter of Russian psychologist Lev Vygotsky. She is the author of *Notebooks of the mind* (1985) and *Creative collaboration* (2000).

SEANA MORAN has worked with Professor John-Steiner for several years. She is currently an advanced doctoral student working with Professor Howard Gardner at Harvard University, focusing on the development of commitment in domain-transforming creative work.

ROBERT J. STERNBERG is IBM Professor of Psychology and Education at Yale University. He is one of the most widely published psychologists in the world, and his research interests span a range of topics. He is perhaps best known for his studies of intelligence and creativity; his books on creativity include *Developing creativity in students* (1996) and *The creativity conundrum* (2002). He is the editor of *Handbook of creativity* (1999).

DAVID HENRY FELDMAN is Professor of the Eliot-Pearson Department of Child Development at Tufts University. Author or editor of eight books and many articles, Dr. Feldman is an expert on cognitive development, developmental theory, and creativity. His 1986 book on child prodigies (with Lynn Goldsmith), *Nature's gambit*, earned Dr. Feldman the Distinguished Scholar of the Year award from the National Association for Gifted Children. He is coauthor of the 1994 book *Changing the world: A framework for the study of creativity*.

JEANNE NAKAMURA is Research Director of the Quality of Life Research Center at Claremont Graduate University. Her research and writing examine engagement and other aspects of positive experience, creativity, and the social context of good work in the professions, focusing on mentoring and apprenticeship. She is coauthor of *Engaged youth* (2001).

MIHALY CSIKSZENTMIHALYI is C. S. and D. J. Davidson Professor of Psychology and Management at Claremont Graduate University. The author or editor of many books and hundreds of scientific articles, Dr. Csikszentmihalyi is the author of *Flow: The psychology of optimal experience* (1990) and *Creativity: Flow and the psychology of discovery and invention* (1996). Dr. Csikszentmihalyi has also published extensively on his research with talent, creativity, and success in adolescence and in adults.

CREATIVITY AND DEVELOPMENT

Introduction

R. Keith Sawyer

This book is an exploration of the connections between creativity and development. These connections are rarely studied, because the fields of creativity research and developmental psychology have proceeded independently—conducted by different scholars and in different paradigms. Creativity research is typically conducted on adults, often by personality or social psychologists; in the *Creativity Research Journal*, there is rarely anything about children or development. Developmental psychologists likewise rarely study creativity in development; for example, at the biggest recent academic conferences on child development—the 1999 and 2001 Society for Research in Child Development (SRCD) meetings—there were only a handful of papers related to creativity.

Even though there has been no sustained attempt to bring theories of creativity and development together, there have nonetheless been many implicit and hidden connections between them. By identifying these connections, we intend this book to be of interest to both creativity researchers and developmental psychologists. Creativity researchers will learn that the much larger field of developmental psychology offers a body of theory and methodology that can be used in the study of creativity. At the same time, developmental researchers will be exposed to the tradition of research in creativity and will gain new perspectives on some long-standing issues in developmental psychology.

I begin this introduction by reviewing some commonly noted connections between creativity and development. I then distinguish our approach in this volume by noting that our unifying focus is *process* and *the dynamics of the emergence of novelty* over time. This focus leads to three themes; I discuss each of these and then briefly describe how each chapter speaks to those themes.

Throughout recorded history, scholars have noted similarities between artistic creativity and children. These similarities have led many scholars to suggest

3

that artistic activity and children's play are related and perhaps somehow tap into the same inner source. In the centuries prior to the modern era, this inner source was often conceived of as divine inspiration, and children were thought to be closer to God. German idealists such as Schiller (1793–1794/1968) associated the creative impulse with children's play, and almost since the beginning of formal schooling, idealists and romanticists alike have criticized overly structured classroom schooling for squashing children's natural creative ability. Many twentieth-century psychologists have also observed parallels between creativity and children's play. For example, Freud thought the artist was like a child at play: "He creates a world of his own, or, rather, re-arranges the things of his world in a new way which pleases him" (Freud, 1907/1989, p. 437). For Freud, fantasy worlds are created by both the child and the artist from the same motivating impulse: the desire to satisfy an unfulfilled wish (p. 439).

The belief that children are more creative than adults has taken on the status of an unexamined cultural myth. Are children really more creative? We examine this belief in chapter 6, and we conclude that the question cannot be answered except within a more subtle and sophisticated view of creativity, a view that is elaborated here in chapters 1 through 5.

A second way to study the connection between development and creativity is to study the development *of* creativity (Feldman, 1999). For example, in the 1970s, there were several studies suggesting that children who engaged in more pretend play scored higher on measures of divergent thinking (Dansky, 1980; Hutt & Bhavnani, 1976; Johnson, 1976; Li, 1978). Although the experimental evidence is equivocal (Pellegrini, 1992, p. 25), many scholars nonetheless believe that pretend play is an early childhood precursor to creativity (Russ, 1996; Sawyer, 1997; Singer & Singer, 1990; Smolucha, 1992). In a recent cross-cultural study of play, Haight (1999) compared caregiver-child pretend play in China and in the United States and found that pretend play in the two countries is different, and that the style of play corresponds to the type of creativity that each culture emphasizes. Chinese culture values structures and cultural frameworks, whereas U.S. culture values individual novelty and divergent thinking (pp. 143–144). Corresponding to this opposition, Chinese caregivers initiate pretend play as a way of teaching good behavior, especially of teaching routine interactions; U.S. caregivers initiate play particularly in the improvisational negotiation of interpersonal interactions (p. 141). These findings suggest that children may be socialized into culturally valued styles of creativity at a young age.

Similarly, a long tradition of research has studied the development of artistic ability in children and the role of the arts in education. Much of this research has been conducted by educational researchers, who are interested in determining the best way to integrate arts education into the curriculum. These researchers argue that early education in the arts can contribute unique developmental benefits to children—general skills related to creativity such as higher level thinking, analytic ability, problem solving, reflexive thinking, and self-regulation (Eisner, 1998).

A FOCUS ON PROCESS

Clearly, we are not the first to note that there are connections between creativity and development. However, observations like the above remain at a relatively broad-brush level; the substantive theoretical connections between developmental theory and creativity theory have barely been explored. The key insight driving this volume is that development and creativity are both *processes*. From the early twentieth century to the present, both creativity and development have been conceived of as processes of emergence in complex systems; this focus is shared among approaches ranging from Piagetian developmental theory to Csikszentmihalyi's systems model of creativity.

The process approach is a second wave in creativity research that developed only in the 1980s. The first wave of creativity research, from the 1950s through the 1970s, was heavily influenced by personality psychology, and focused on developing psychometric instruments and identifying the component traits of creativity in different domains. By the 1970s, the personality approach was largely thought to have reached its limit. One of the primary motivations of this research was to develop metrics that could identify exceptional creative talent in childhood, to select individuals that would be more likely to succeed in occupations demanding creativity; however, this research program was disappointed when longitudinal studies found few consistent relationships between measures of children's personality traits and creative success in adult life. Long before the renewed interest in creativity in the 1950s and 1960s, the Terman studies—which identified high-IQ children in the 1920s and tracked their development into adulthood—likewise proved something of a disappointment, because although a high percentage of subjects became successful professionals and scientists, few of them manifested exceptional creative performance in adult life.

In the 1970s and 1980s, a second wave of creativity researchers responded to these disappointments by arguing for a shift in focus from personality to process. This shift was inspired by the ascendance of cognitive psychology, which, in the 1970s, led psychology as a discipline away from a focus on personality and individual differences toward a focus on those mental processes that underlie not only exceptional ability, but also everyday problem-solving and decision-making skills. The coauthors of this volume are some of the most influential figures in this shift to the process approach.

Piagetian theory and method spread throughout U.S. developmental psychology in the 1960s and 1970s. Piagetian theory was also fundamentally concerned with developmental processes—the microgenetic details of how the interaction between a child's schema and the environment could drive the emergence of schemas characteristic of the next stage of development. Although Piaget's model has been increasingly criticized in the 1980s and 1990s, these criticisms are themselves couched in the language of developmental process, and Piaget's legacy is that contemporary developmental psychology is now centrally concerned with processes.

Thus, during the same time periods, creativity theory and developmental theory became fundamentally concerned with process. No doubt there were many common influences and hidden cross-fertilization. However, developmental theorists are rarely familiar with theories of the creative process proposed by creativity researchers, and creativity theorists are rarely familiar with the latest theories about developmental process. This mutual neglect is hard to explain, because there are many substantive connections between theories of the creativity process and theories of developmental process. For example, the core insight of constructivism—a long-established developmental paradigm associated with both Piaget and Vygotsky—is that development is a process in which children participate in the creation of their own knowledge. Likewise, much of creativity theory has been based on staged models that are fundamentally developmental. Piaget (1971) himself noted parallels between the processes of creativity and development: "The real problem is how to explain novelties. I think that novelties, i.e., creations, constantly intervene in development" (p. 192). Piaget claimed that his theory of development was a theory of genetic epistemology and, as such, applied both to individual development and to the historical development of scientific fields (see chapter 1).

In the chapters in this volume, prominent scholars explore these theoretical connections between creativity and development. The chapters explore both the nature of creative processes in development and the developmental nature of creative processes. All of the authors are established in both developmental psychology and creativity research. Because there has been so little work addressing both topics, it would be nearly impossible to write a comprehensive volume that covered every potential connection. Rather, the authors each draw on their decades of research and focus on distinct but complementary approaches to these topics.

The uniquely collaborative nature of Oxford's Counterpoints series allowed the authors to engage in a dialogue, addressing the key issues and potential benefits of making connections between creativity and development. In chapters 1 through 5, the authors apply their own well-known perspectives to explore connections between creativity and development. Then, in chapter 6, the authors come together to participate in a dialogue inspired by the key themes running through all of the chapters.

THEMES OF THIS VOLUME

This book is based on the observation that both creativity and development are processes that occur in complex systems, in which later stages or changes emerge from the prior state of the system. This processual or dynamical perspective is the central focus of these chapters. This central focus then gave rise to three related themes.

First, studies of process have always been balanced by a complementary focus on the stable end points of process. In development, the end point of a developmental process is the next stage of development, and ultimately, an adult level of ability. In creativity, the end point of the process is the created product. Prior to the shift in both disciplines to a focus on process, both disciplines were more concerned with the end points of the process—consider the focus on stages and the ages of stage transition in Piagetian psychology, and consider the focus on properties of created products in creativity research. A focus on process still requires a consideration of the end points of the process, but now, the focus is on how the end point emerges from the process, typically by using detailed microgenetic studies of how the process unfolds from moment to moment.

Second, studies of both creative and developmental processes have focused on the dialectic interrelation between individual processes and social processes. Since the early 1980s, both sociocultural developmental psychology and socially oriented theories of creativity have increasingly studied both the individual and the social. Scholars of both development and creativity have increasingly emphasized that the individual must be considered to be an integral part of a complex social system, and that the relative contribution of individual and social context can only be fully understood by analyzing the processual dynamic whereby individuals interact. This *sociocultural* approach is opposed to a more static conception in which individual and context are both characterized by fixed variables and the relation is studied via statistical significance (Rogoff, 1998).

Third, the process perspective emphasizes the role of mediating artifacts in the process. This is manifest in the concern with *domains* and *domain specificity* in both creativity and development, because domains are complex symbol systems composed of mediating artifacts. Feldman (1974, 1980) and Gardner (1983) emphasized that development must be studied within its cognitive domain, and Csikszentmihalyi (1988) emphasized that creativity always occurs within a domain. John-Steiner's 1985 *Notebooks of the Mind* revealed the important role played by mediating symbols in creativity. Both Piaget and Vygotsky were centrally concerned with the contribution of mediating physical artifacts in development. Studies of developmental and creative process both consider the role played by mediating artifacts, whether physical objects (paintbrushes, canvas, laboratory equipment) or symbol systems (the languages and conventions of poetry or music).

CHAPTER SUMMARIES

The first (Sawyer's) chapter provides a broad overview for the volume, and we chose to order the next four chapters from early life to later life, starting with Moran and John-Steiner's Vygotskian perspective on the social dynamics of creativity (chapter 2) and ending with Nakamura and Csikszentmihalyi's focus on creativity in later life (chapter 5). In between, Sternberg's chapter emphasizes school-age children (chapter 3), and Feldman's chapter is a hybrid, focusing on the creative development of Howard Gardner's *multiple intelligence* theory at the same time that it applies that theory to children (chapter 4). In combination, the chapters provide a broad set of perspectives on our three themes.

Sawyer's chapter begins the volume by reviewing the history of creativity research and developmental psychology, focusing on their common emphasis on process and dynamics. He introduces the concept of *emergence* as a way of identifying commonalities in the processual approaches essential to both creativity theory and developmental theory. Sawyer shows that emergentist thinking has been influential since the foundation of developmental psychology in the late nineteenth century, and he traces the influence of emergentism in both creativity theory and developmental theory. To demonstrate emergent process in social settings, Sawyer presents an example of an improvisational theater dialogue from his own research (Sawyer, 2003). His chapter focuses on the first two themes of this volume, process-product and social-individual relations.

Sawyer's chapter briefly reviews emergentist elements in Vygotsky's writings, and Moran and John-Steiner further draw on Vygotsky's writings to contrast person-centered and social approaches to the study of creativity. Their chapter focuses on the second and third themes of this book: the social-individual relation and the mediation of material and symbolic artifacts. Their Vygotskian approach is fundamentally developmental and considers both individual creativity and the social dimension of creativity. Like Piaget, Vygotsky emphasized the role of material objects in development, for example, arguing that objects used in play act as pivots that drive the development of symbolic thought. Vygotsky's theory is often considered to be a more socially oriented variant of constructivism than Piaget's, because in Vygotskian theory, the child co-constructs knowledge through socially situated action.

Sternberg's contribution explicitly turns to development in educational contexts. In educational theory and practice, both creativity and development are central concerns, and his chapter focuses on our first theme, the relation between process and end point. For educators, the goal is an end point—a student who has mastered the intended abilities. Yet contemporary educational theory is based on the constructivist insight that children create their own knowledge. In this framework, educators must be centrally concerned with creative processes, because they cannot simply teach students knowledge but rather must create the environmental conditions that will enable children to construct their own knowledge. Sternberg draws on his *propulsion* and *investment* theories of creativity to propose practical recommendations for teachers interested in encouraging the development of students' creativity.

Feldman's chapter focuses on both childhood development and on later life processes by engaging in a case study of Gardner's multiple intelligence (MI) theory. Feldman focuses on the creative process that led to Gardner's creation of MI theory. Because this represents more than a decade of activity, this case study provides Feldman with an opportunity to examine the extended process that led to the development of a creative product. Feldman's discussion emphasizes the first two themes of this book: the creative process that leads to the creative product and the role of social interaction. This case study provides an excellent demonstration that creativity is at heart a developmental process; many significant creative innovations occur over long periods of an adult's life span and often correspond to significant developmental changes in the creator. At the same time, MI theory itself deeply integrates both developmental psychology and creativity concerns; the intelligences correspond to cognitive domains, and (in a number of publications) Gardner has emphasized that both creativity and child development must be considered within the context of the domain of activity.

Like Feldman, Nakamura and Csikszentmihalyi focus on the development of adult creativity and examine creativity and development in later life. How does aging affect creativity—not only negatively, but also positively? As they write, "Every biography of a creative person tries to explain the achievements of its subject in light of a more or less implicit dynamic theory of life-span development. The interest, curiosity, and enduring engagement of the artist or scientist are seen to follow from a series of meaningfully connected experiences stretching from childhood to maturity and old age." This discussion draws on Csikszentmihalyi's systems perspective and considers not only the psychology of the creative individual, but also the role of the cultural *domain* and of the social community, or *field*. Thus, this chapter emphasizes our second theme, the interaction of the social and the individual. The authors are particularly concerned with a broad life-span perspective: What sorts of personality traits are associated with sustained and continued creativity across a long life span? What sorts of people continue to create into old age?

As with all Counterpoints volumes, we conclude with a discussion that allows each author to engage the others, with the goal of drawing out common themes and divergences found in research on creativity and development. Our discussion centers on three questions:

Does society suppress children's natural creativity?

How can we balance social context and individual psychological process in creativity research?

Are there different domains in development and in creativity?

Our responses to these questions further explore the three themes of process and product, social context, and mediation. We are all enthusiastic about the potential importance of the issues discussed, and we hope that this volume proves to be only the first step in an increasing cross-fertilization of research in creativity and development.

REFERENCES

Csikszentmihalyi, M. (1988). Society, culture, and person: A systems view of creativity. In R. J. Sternberg (Ed.), *The nature of creativity* (pp. 325–339). New York: Cambridge University Press.

Dansky, J. L. (1980). Make-believe: A mediator of the relationship between play and associative fluency. *Child Development, 51,* 576–579.

Eisner, E. W. (1998). *The kind of school we need.* Portsmouth, NH: Heinemann.

Feldman, D. H. (1974). Universal to unique. In S. Rosner & L. E. Abt (Eds.), *Essays in creativity* (pp. 45–85). Croton-on-Hudson, NY: North River Press.

Feldman, D. H. (1980). *Beyond universals in cognitive development.* Norwood, NJ: Ablex.

Feldman, D. H. (1999). The development of creativity. In R. J. Sternberg (Ed.), *Handbook of creativity* (pp. 169–186). New York: Cambridge University Press.

Freud, S. (1989). Creative writers and day-dreaming. In P. Gay (Ed.), *The Freud reader* (pp. 436–443). New York: Norton. (Original work published 1907)

Gardner, H. (1983). *Frames of mind: The theory of multiple intelligences.* New York: Basic Books.

Haight, W. L. (1999). The pragmatics of caregiver-child pretending at home: Understanding culturally specific socialization practices. In A. Göncü (Ed.), *Children's engagement in the world: Sociocultural perspectives* (pp. 128–147). New York: Cambridge University Press.

Hutt, C., & Bhavnani, R. (1976). Predictions from play. In J. S. Bruner, A. Jolly, & K. Sylva (Eds.), *Play: Its role in development and evolution* (pp. 216–219). New York: Penguin.

John-Steiner, V. (1985). *Notebooks of the mind: Explorations of thinking.* Albuquerque: University of New Mexico Press.

Johnson, J. E. (1976). Relations of divergent thinking and intelligence test scores with social and nonsocial make-believe play of preschool children. *Child Development, 47,* 1200–1203.

Li, A. K. F. (1978). Effects of play on novel responses in kindergarten children. *Alberta Journal of Educational Research, 24*(1), 31–36.

Pellegrini, A. D. (1992). Rough-and-tumble play and social problem solving flexibility. *Creativity Research Journal, 5,* 13–26.

Piaget, J. (1971). Comment on Beilin's paper. In D. R. Green, M. P. Ford, & G. B. Flamer (Eds.), *Measurement and Piaget* (pp. 192–194). New York: McGraw-Hill.

Rogoff, B. (1998). Cognition as a collaborative process. In D. Kuhn & R. S. Siegler (Eds.), *Handbook of child psychology: Volume 2. Cognition, perception, and language* (5th ed., pp. 679–744). New York: Wiley.

Russ, S. W. (1996). Development of creative processes in children. In M. A. Runco (Ed.), *Creativity from childhood through adulthood: The developmental issues* (pp. 31–42). San Francisco: Jossey-Bass.

Sawyer, R. K. (1997). *Pretend play as improvisation: Conversation in the preschool classroom.* Norwood, NJ: Erlbaum.

Sawyer, R. K. (2003). *Improvised dialogues: Emergence and creativity in conversation.* Westport, CT: Greenwood.

Schiller, F. (1968). *On the aesthetic education of man, in a series of letters* (E. M. Wilkinson & L. A. Willoughby, Eds. and Trans.). Oxford, UK: Clarendon Press. (Original work published as *Über die aesthetische Erziehung des Menschen in einer Reihe von Briefen,* 1793–1794)

Singer, D. G., & Singer, J. L. (1990). *The house of make-believe: Play and the developing imagination.* Cambridge, MA: Harvard University Press.

Smolucha, F. C. (1992). The relevance of Vygotsky's theory of creative imagination for contemporary research on play. *Creativity Research Journal, 5*(1), 69–76.

CHAPTER ONE

Emergence in Creativity and Development

R. Keith Sawyer

In this chapter, I introduce our volume's focus on process in creativity and development. I explore parallels between the creative process of the artist or scientist and the developmental process that children undergo as they age and mature. For example, the core insight of constructivism—a long-established developmental paradigm associated with both Piaget and Vygotsky—is that children participate in the creation of their own knowledge. Likewise, much of creativity theory has been based on stage models that are fundamentally developmental. In many cases, these parallels lead to very similar theoretical issues being addressed in both fields but being studied and resolved in somewhat different ways. In this chapter, I review the history of theoretical development in creativity research and developmental psychology, and I demonstrate that the two fields share many concepts and theoretical frameworks. I show how each field could benefit from incorporating aspects of the other field's theoretical frameworks, and I identify several common issues facing contemporary researchers in both areas.

I first noticed these parallels soon after I began to teach three related courses at Washington University in St. Louis: educational psychology, play and development, and the psychology of creativity. Often, I taught two of these courses in the same semester. I found myself teaching Piaget's stage theory of development to a class on Monday and then analyzing stage theories of the creative process on Tuesday. It began to seem increasingly obvious that Piaget's constructivist theory of development was fundamentally a theory of creativity. Later, as I began a more thorough examination of Piaget's thought, I discovered that Piaget (1971a) himself had noted these parallels: "The real problem is how to explain novelties. I think that novelties, i.e., creations, constantly intervene in development" (p. 192). In fact, Piaget always claimed that his theory of development was a theory of "genetic epistemology" and, as such, applied both to individual development and to the historical development of scientific fields. In his three-volume 1950 work, *Introduction à l'épistémologie génétique* (never translated into English, although see Piaget, 1970/1972), Piaget analyzed the development of mathematics (Volume 1), physics (Volume 2), and biology (Volume 3) using his developmental concepts of equilibration, abstraction, generalization, accommodation and assimilation (see Messerly, 1996, chapter 3).[1]

My exploration of these parallels is guided by my empirical studies of the improvisational creativity of verbal performance (Sawyer, 1997, 2003). In about 1998, these studies led me to an exploration of the long history of the theoretical concept of *emergence*. In the early twentieth century, philosophers defined emergence as the creation of something new that was unpredictable, even given a full and complete knowledge of the world prior to its emergence. The concept was originally developed to address issues in the theory of biological evolution. At the same time that I studied this philosophical tradition, I began to explore emergentist thinking in developmental psychology (Sawyer, 2002a) and in creativity research (Sawyer, 1999). In this chapter, my guiding theme is that both development and creativity are emergent processes and that dominant theories in both areas have been deeply influenced by emergentist thinking in philosophy and biology.

The first U.S. psychologist to elaborate Piaget's parallel between creative insight and developmental transitions was David Henry Feldman (1974), who noted that "Piagetian stage-to-stage advance and creative accomplishments share certain common attributes" (p. 57). The crucial assumption of Piaget's theory of intellectual development is that new schemas are constructed by the child and that these schemas are not simply continuous accumulations of new knowledge, but represent complete reorganizations of thought. Piaget acknowledged that he had no good explanation for how these reorganizations occur, referring to it as "the great mystery of the stages" (1971b, p. 9) and noting that "the crux of my problem . . . is to try and explain how novelties are possible and how they are formed" (1971a, p. 194). In his seminal 1974 study of Darwin's creative process, Gruber explored the relation between Piagetian universal thought structures and Darwin's highly original ones, and he suggested that Darwin's thought structures were transformed through a Piagetian constructivist process (cf. Feldman, 1980; also see the end of this chapter).

In this chapter, I show that these parallels are merely the most recent manifestation of over a century of theoretical parallels. Theories of both creativity and development have strong emergentist foundations and thus have their origins in nineteenth-century thought. I identify these emergentist foundations and show how they have influenced theories of creativity and development.

EMERGENCE

The concept of emergence is a unifying thread underlying both creativity theory and developmental theory. Theories of emergence have influenced psychological theory since the beginning of the field in the late nineteenth century (Sawyer, 2002a). Emergentism in psychology has its roots in nineteenth-century *organicism*: the theory that the organism is different from the sum of its parts and that it depends on the structural arrangement of the parts. Social organicism—the notion that society formed an integrated unity similar in some sense to that of living organisms—can be traced to classical social philosophy, but the publication of Darwin's account of evolution gave new energy to social organismic theories (see Giddens, 1970, p. 172). In the nineteenth century, organicism was prominent in German social philosophy; influential advocates included Schäffle and Lilienfeld. These theories influenced German psychologists including Wundt and the early gestaltists.

The nineteenth century was characterized by a preoccupation with evolution, and organicist metaphors almost always incorporated evolutionary themes. Evolutionary and organicist thinking were strong influences on psychology's founders. For example, many neurological theories proposed that the nervous system was composed of different levels that represented different levels of evolutionary development. Ernst Haeckel's famous "biogenetic law" stated that "ontogeny is the short and rapid repetition of phylogeny" (cited in Sulloway, 1979, p. 199), thus suggesting that the development of a child recapitulates the history of the species. Such ideas would later be explicitly invoked by Freud, Piaget, and Werner.

Theories of emergence and evolution were the focus of an influential group of British philosophers and evolutionary biologists just after World War I, a group that has been called the "British emergentists" (McLaughlin, 1992). Influential figures from this period include Broad (1925), Morgan (1923), and Whitehead (1926). The philosopher Broad (1925) defined emergentism in terms of irreducibility and nondeducibility: "The characteristic behavior of the whole *could* not, even in theory, be deduced from the most complete knowledge of the behavior of its components, taken separately or in other combinations" (p. 59). In spite of irreducibility, emergentists were materialists, holding that only physical matter existed and thus rejecting the vitalist belief in a nonmaterial life-giving substance. Because they were materialists, they held that emergent properties must *supervene* on microlevel properties. The supervenience account of emergentism requires that the behavior of the whole be determined by the nature and arrangement of its components. Even so, the emergentists rejected mechanistic theories which held that the behavior of the whole "could, in theory at least, be *deduced* from a sufficient knowledge of how the components behave in isolation or in other wholes of a simpler kind" (Broad, 1925, p. 59).

The emergentism of both Broad and Morgan involved several related claims (Kim, 1992; Teller, 1992):

- There are basic, nonemergent entities and properties, and these are material entities and their properties.
- Emergence is a process that occurs through time.
- When aggregates of basic entities attain a certain level of structural complexity, properties of the aggregate emerge. New stuff does not emerge; rather, it is properties of the higher level entities that emerges.
- What emerges are new levels of reality, corresponding to evolutionary or historical stages. In Morgan's account of "emergent evolution," the stages are matter, life, and mind. Other emergentists proposed more detailed systems of levels.
- Because these properties are properties of complex organizations of matter, they emerge only when the appropriate lower level material conditions are present.
- What emerges is novel; it did not exist before the process of emergence.
- What emerges is unpredictable, and could not have been known analytically before it emerged.
- Emergent properties are irreducible to properties of their lower level parts, even though they are determined by those parts.

Although first given explicit expression in the 1920s, these ideas derive from a current in nineteenth-century thought that has been called *evolutionary historicism* (Kitcher, 1992, p. 214). Nineteenth-century social and biological explanations were largely historical: A phenomenon was to be explained by offering an account of its development from earlier conditions (Kitcher, 1992, p. 66). Evolutionary historicism combined Hegel's dialectic theory of history, Darwin's evolutionary theory, and subsequent organicist metaphors. Hegel's model influenced the developmental psychologies of Freud, Werner, and Piaget; all three of these developmental theories incorporate the Hegelian idea that each stage of development bears within it the tensions and contradictions that propel development to the next stage (Brent, 1978). Evolutionary thought influenced the founding figures in developmental psychology, including Baldwin, Piaget, Werner, and Vygotsky (Morss, 1990; Siegler, 1996, pp. 22–26). Stage theories were also prominent in sociology, to a large extent independent of Darwin's work; Comte's theory of successive stages in historical development preceded Darwin (Comte, 1830–1842/1854), and Spencer's social evolutionary theory of stages was contemporary with Darwin.[2]

Morgan's final book, *The Emergence of Novelty* (1933), emphasized the importance of novelty in emergent evolution and in other developmental processes. For Morgan, emergent novelty "is some new pattern of relatedness.

In a sense, the 'items' of stuff are not new; and yet, in a sense, at each stage of substantial advance, the 'units' of stuff *are* new" (p. 33). Not only things are new, but also the laws that apply at the emergent stage: "There are, at successive stages of advance, new games in play, each with new rules of the game" (p. 39); knowing the lower level rules isn't enough to predict the higher level rules. Not only developmental stages but also the creative products of art and science are "instances of original novelty as emergent" (p. 103). Like Morgan, other 1920s thinkers argued that individual creative insights were emergent. In Mc-Dougall's 1929 account, the "creative synthesis" of individual minds was the only true emergence, because physical emergence always has the potential to be reductively explained with the progress of science (p. 122).

Because these thinkers drew on the same nineteenth-century influences as the founders of developmental psychology, they made observations associated today with figures such as Freud and Piaget. For example, Morgan (1933) claimed that thought proceeds in stages that are characterized by their distinctive mental structures: "In the recurrent development of each individual mind, there is, I believe, advance through new modes of organization to further novelty in organization" (p. 79). In other words, each stage of mental development emerges from the prior, and this process of emergence always involves a restructuring that is novel. Consequently, Morgan proposed a stage theory of development (p. 80), from *sentient* (before birth) to *perceptive* (0 to 36 months), to *reflective* (36 months onward). He referred to the study of cognitive development as both "mental evolution" and "genetic psychology" (p. 157), with *genetic* having the same emergentist connotations as Piaget's phrase *genetic epistemology*; in both cases, the term means that structures at each developmental stage emerge from interaction between the organism and its environment at the prior stage (p. 165).

The nineteenth-century notion that development proceeds in stages, and that each stage emerged from the prior stage, was second nature to both Freud and Piaget. Staged developmental concepts formed the backbone of Piaget's theory of cognitive development and of Freud's theory of affective development. At roughly the same time, writers on creativity such as Poincaré, Wallas, and Hadamard were proposing stage theories of the creative process. In developmental theory, the stages proceed over childhood, with each stage lasting several years; in creativity theory, the stages culminate in the production of a single creative work or creative thought. Thus, the latter stages were markedly shorter, lasting only a few months or even, in some cases, a few days.

Through the 1930s, the ideas of the British emergentists had a wide-ranging impact in psychology and the social sciences and were explicitly acknowledged as influences by theorists as diverse as Wolfgang Köhler, George Herbert Mead, and Talcott Parsons. Piaget never referenced these philosophers, and I am not claiming that Piaget read Morgan or even that Morgan was the first to notice the connections between creativity and development that have often been attributed to Piaget. Rather, my claim is that both Morgan and Piaget were working on issues that naturally presented themselves in the context of nineteenth-century evolutionary historicism, that these issues centered on the topic of emergence, and that the same themes were part of the intellectual background of early creativity theorists.

A theory of development or creativity as emergent is an intermediate position between two potential alternative explanations. First, one could explain the final state of the system by arguing that it is predetermined by the initial state of the system. In evolutionary biology, this position was known as *preformationism*, and this term was also frequently used in early twentieth-century developmental psychology; Piaget frequently used it in criticizing this view, which today corresponds to an overly simplistic conception of innatism (as criticized by Elman, Bates, Johnson, Karmiloff-Smith, & Parisi, 1996). In contrast, in emergentism, each stage emerges from activity and process at the prior stage and thus is a result of organism-environment interaction. Without this interaction, there would be no development. Thus, emergentism rejects a preformationist position that holds that the final state of the mature organism is present in the newborn.[3]

A second alternative to emergentism represents the empiricist pole; it explains development by arguing that the final state of the system is determined by the environment of the organism. Such a stance was common in sociology and in the radical empiricism of behaviorist psychology. Instead, emergentism holds that an explanation of the final state of the system requires an examination of the step-by-step interaction between organism and environment as it passes from stage to stage, because the state of the organism changes at each stage. Thus, the environment is not directly imposed on or internalized by the organism; rather, development results from a constructivist process of organism-environment interaction.

EMERGENCE IN COLLABORATING GROUPS

I originally began to study emergence theory as a way of helping me to understand collaborative group processes. In a series of studies, I have documented that collaborating groups have the key characteristics of emergence (Sawyer, 1997, 2001, 2003). I call this form of social group emergence "collaborative emergence." In collaborative emergence, novelty is a collective process. To demonstrate, here is a transcript of an improvised theater performance taken from a 1993 performance by Off-Off-Campus, a Chicago theater group. This is the first few seconds of dialogue from a scene that the actors knew should last about five minutes. The audience was asked to suggest a proverb, and the suggestion given was "Don't look a gift horse in the mouth."

Lights up. Dave is at stage right, Ellen at stage left. Dave begins gesturing to his right, talking to himself.

1	Dave	All the little glass figurines in my menagerie, The store of my dreams. Hundreds of thousands everywhere!	*Turns around to admire.*
2	Ellen		*Slowly walks toward Dave.*
3	Dave	Yes, can I help you?	*Turns and notices Ellen.*
4	Ellen	Um, I'm looking for uh, uh, a present?	*Ellen is looking down like a child, with her fingers in her mouth.*
5	Dave	A gift?	
6	Ellen	Yeah.	
7	Dave	I have a little donkey?	*Dave mimes the action of handing Ellen a donkey from the shelf.*
8	Ellen	Ah, that's . . . I was looking for something a little bit bigger . . .	
9	Dave	Oh.	*Returns item to shelf.*
10	Ellen	It's for my dad.	

By Turn 10, elements of the dramatic frame are starting to emerge. We know that Dave is a storekeeper, and Ellen is a young girl. We know that Ellen is buying a present for her dad and, because she is so young, probably needs help from the storekeeper. These dramatic elements have emerged from the creative contributions of both actors. Although each actor's incremental contributions to the frame can be identified, none of these turns fully determines the subsequent dialogue, and the emergent dramatic frame is not chosen, intended, or imposed by either of the actors.

It's important to emphasize that this emergent process cannot be reduced to actors' intentions in individual turns, because in many cases an actor cannot know the meaning of his or her own turn until the other actors have responded. In Turn 2, when Ellen walks toward Dave, her action has many potential meanings; for example, she could be a coworker, arriving late to work. Her action does not carry the meaning of a customer entering the store until after Dave's query in Turn 3. In improvised dialogues, many actions do not receive their full meaning until after the act has occurred; the complete meaning of a turn is dependent on the flow of the subsequent dialogue. This sort of retrospective interpretation is quite common in improvised dialogue, and it is one reason that the frame is analytically irreducible to the intentions or actions of participants in individual turns of dialogue (Sawyer, 2001b, 2003).

In each turn of dialogue, an actor proposes a new elaboration to the frame. But not all proposals are accepted; the other actors may decide they don't like the proposed change, they may attribute an unexpected meaning to it, or they may choose to modify it or elaborate it further. Only after the other actors have responded can we know whether or not an actor's proposal will become a part of the frame.

In improvisation as in everyday conversation, speakers proceed with the assumption that all turns of dialogue must be consistent with the frame. After Turn 4, because Ellen is now a young child and a customer, she cannot suddenly begin to act as a coworker; likewise, she cannot act as if she had a prior relationship with Dave, because his query in Turn 3 makes it clear that they have not met before. As the dialogue proceeds and the frame progressively emerges, each actor is increasingly constrained by the requirement to maintain coherence with the frame.

As the dialogue continues beyond Turn 10, we learn that Ellen is buying her dad a present because he has not been feeling well; in fact, he has been exhibiting psychotic behaviors. A third actor then enters the scene, enacting the character of Ellen's psychotic dad, and his condition is cured through some clever actions by the storekeeper. These dramatic elements—the characters, motivations, relationships, and plot trajectory—emerge from the collective interaction and creative contributions of all three actors.

The social process of creativity is analogous to collaborative improvisation; in both an improvised dialogue and a scientific discipline, creativity emerges from a complex interactional and social process (Sawyer, 1995). In the *systems model*—outlined by Csikszentmihalyi (1988b) and Gardner (1993)—the creative individual completes a creative product and then attempts to disseminate it to the broader community, or *field*. For example, a scientist may submit a manuscript to a journal to be considered for publication. The editors of the journal may decide to reject the manuscript, or they may send it to two or three scholars for peer review. This review process could also result in the rejection of the article. If the article—the individual's creative product—is rejected by this group of "gatekeeper" individuals, then it will never enter the *domain*, the shared body of accepted scientific knowledge.

Thus, in a sense, all creativity is an emergent process that involves a social group of individuals engaged in complex, unpredictable interactions (Sawyer, 1999). The systems model proposes that the analysis of creativity requires not only a psychological focus on the creative individual, but also a consideration of the social system. It is the entire system that creates, not the individual alone. Therefore an explanation of an improvisational performance requires a social level of analysis, a microinteractional analog of what occurs in the field of the systems model.

Many creativity researchers have observed that scientific insights often occur in collaborating groups (Csikszentmihalyi & Sawyer, 1995; John-Steiner,

2000). Ludwig Fleck (1935/1979), one of the earliest scholars of the history of science, was perhaps the first to comment on this socially emergent process: "A stimulating conversation between two persons" can result in the emergence of a "thought structure that belongs to neither of them alone" (p. 44). Based on this analogy, Fleck compared scientific work to "a soccer match, a conversation, or the playing of an orchestra," in that the result is not a summation of the participants' work but is "the coming into existence of a special form" (p. 99). These collaborative insights result from a social process of emergence.

THEORIES OF THE CREATIVE PROCESS

I have defined emergence, provided an example of collaborative emergence, and claimed that emergence is a key theoretical thread linking twentieth-century conceptions of creativity and development. I introduced this connection and demonstrated its plausibility by briefly discussing what Morgan and Piaget had to say about these connections.

To further elaborate these connections between creativity and development, I now delve more deeply into theories of both creativity and development. In this section, I discuss twentieth-century theories of creativity, and in the subsequent section, twentieth-century theories of development.

Creativity is notoriously difficult to define. Theorists have debated what the term means, and empirical researchers have employed different operationalizations of the term. For my purposes, I hold to a broad conception of creativity that has been widespread among creativity researchers since the 1970s: Creativity is "a socially recognized achievement in which there are novel products" (Barron & Harrington, 1981, p. 442). First of all, a creative idea or work must be *novel*. Yet novelty is not enough, because a novel idea may be ridiculous or nonsensical; many dreams are novel but rarely have any impact on the world after breakfast. In addition to novelty, to be creative an idea must be *appropriate*, recognized as socially valuable in some way to some community.

In the 1950s and 1960s, psychological studies of creators focused on their personalities and roughly fell under the aegis of personality or trait psychology. For example, creative individuals were found to be active, curious, and unconventional (Barron & Harrington, 1981). Beginning in the 1970s, the cognitive revolution began to influence creativity studies, with experimental methods being used to identify the internal cognitive processes associated with creativity, and with computer models that simulate the creative process (see chapters 5 to 9 in Sternberg, 1988). However, the individualistic trait conception of creativity tended to emphasize the generation of novelty and to neglect the appropriateness criterion. Feldman's 1974 article was an influential early argument for a focus on process rather than traits; he noted that the process approach is less individualistic than the trait approach, because it involves both individual and situation, organism and environment.

There are two substantive analogies between emergence theory and contemporary theories of the psychology of creativity (Sawyer, 1999). First, emergence theory of the 1920s was primarily an evolutionary theory, and many of the most influential contemporary theories of creativity are based on an evolutionary metaphor. The evolutionary approach to creativity is usually traced to Campbell (1960), who proposed that creativity was subject to the same three-stage process as evolution: blind variation, selective retention, and preservation and reproduction. Csikszentmihalyi followed Campbell in arguing that creativity was not a property of an individual, but a function of both the individual and the selective environment. Csikszentmihalyi's influential systems model (1988b) is also based on evolutionary metaphors, and includes three components analogous to Campbell's: the *creative individual,* who generates a novel product; the *field,* a social system of individuals in a discipline, that evaluates novel products and selects some of them according to established criteria; and a *domain*, an external body of work whose stable physical traits allow it to serve the function of preservation across time.

There is a second substantive comparison between emergence theory and the contemporary psychology of creativity: A creative insight is hypothesized to emerge from the subconscious mind of the creator. Morgan (1933) viewed emergence as "new modes of relatedness" that arise from a system of smaller, interacting entities; today, a novel creative insight is often considered to be a new configuration of mental elements, none of which are individually novel. The mathematician Henri Poincaré (1913/1982) described the emergence of an insight in a widely quoted passage: "One evening, contrary to my custom, I drank black coffee and could not sleep. Ideas rose in crowds; I felt them collide until pairs interlocked, so to speak, making a stable combination. By the next morning, I had established the existence of a class of Fuchsian functions" (p. 387). A contemporary example of such a theory is Simonton's cognitive model (1988), which proposes that the individual first internalizes *mental elements*—facts, theories, images, and information from the creative domain—and that these are stored in the brain; during a subconscious creative process, these mental elements combine into *chance configurations*, and although many of these novel configurations never make it into consciousness, some of them are stable enough to emerge and cause the subjective sensation of having an insight.

In sum, the contemporary conception of the creative process corresponds quite closely to concepts of emergence:

- Creativity is theorized as a process through time, rather than a static trait of individuals or of certain creative products.
- The creative product is novel.

• The creative product emerges from the combination of lower level elements, in combination in a complex system. In other words, no new substance is created, only combinations of elements in complex systems.

In the following sections, I elaborate on some specific emergentist aspects of contemporary creativity theory.

The Stages of the Creative Process

The mind being prepared beforehand with the principles most likely
for the purpose . . . incubates in patient thought over the problem, trying and rejecting, until at last the proper elements come together in the
view, and fall into their places in a fitting combination.
ALEXANDER BAIN, *The Senses and the Intellect*

In addition to the previously noted broad parallels between current conceptions of creativity and the history of emergentist thought, there is a more specific parallel. Throughout the history of creativity theory, creativity has been thought of as a staged process. Many contemporary creativity researchers attribute the insight that creativity proceeds in stages to Henri Poincaré (1913/1982) or Joseph Wallas (1926). In developing their stage theories, both of these theorists attributed the original description of the stages to the physiologist Hermann von Helmholtz. Yet, as the epigraph indicates, such ideas were widespread in the nineteenth century, well before Helmholtz.[4] In an address delivered near the end of his life in 1891, Helmholtz reflected on his own creative work and identified the same three stages that Bain proposed: an initial investigation, a period of rest, and then the emergence of the sudden, unexpected solution (Helmholtz, 1971, p. 474).

An influential elaboration of these ideas was presented by Poincaré in a talk before the *Société de Psychologie* in Paris. Hadamard—whom Poincaré nurtured, and who in 1912 was elected to the Academy of Sciences to succeed Poincaré—was present at the talk. He later built on the work of Poincaré and others to elaborate the stages and the role of the unconscious (in a book published in English in 1945, after he had emigrated to the United States). Based on an introspective analysis of his own mathematical insights, Poincaré (1913/1982) proposed that the creative process must begin with "a period of conscious work," which should then be followed by a rest period where the mind is focused on other activities. It is during this rest period that one receives "the appearance of sudden illumination," and this illumination is the result of "long, unconscious prior work" that was taking place during the rest period (p. 389) The illumination does not appear fully formed, but must be verified and elaborated by a subsequent period of conscious work.

Graham Wallas (1926), drawing on both Helmholtz and Poincaré, coined the names for the four stages that are in most widespread use today: *preparation, incubation, illumination,* and *verification* (p. 80). Preparation is the initial phase of preliminary work: collecting data and information, searching for related ideas, listening to suggestions. Incubation is a term for the frequently-observed delay between preparation and the moment of illumination; Wallas presumed that, during this period, the prepared material did not just sit in the mind passively but underwent some sort of internal elaboration and organization. Illumination is the subjective experience of having the idea, the moment of insight. By verification, Wallas meant both evaluation of the worth of the insight, and elaboration of its complete form (p. 81). The insight must be evaluated and verified by the conscious mind; not all insights are good ideas, and some of them don't pan out. Shortly after Wallas's book appeared, Catherine Patrick (e.g., 1937) conducted several studies of creative individuals and found broad evidence for these four stages.

A few stage theories are somewhat independent of this tradition; these tend to originate in practical studies of business creativity and innovation. For example, Joseph Rossman (1931/1964, p. 57) conducted a questionnaire study of 710 inventors and identified seven stages: (1) observation of a need or difficulty; (2) analysis of the need; (3) a survey of all available information; (4) a formulation of all objective solutions; (5) a critical analysis of these solutions, identifying advantages and disadvantages; (6) the insight or invention; and (7) experimentation to test the invention, and perfection of the final product. Rossman referred to the moment of insight of the invention in emergentist terms; it is "greater than the sum of the parts that have entered into it" (p. 61). But Rossman's stages place most of the creative work in conscious stages; particularly, Stages 4 and 5 seem to correspond to the configuration-and-selection aspect of Poincaré's unconscious. This shift in emphasis to conscious process is probably due to the fact that invention is more like problem solving than the more problem-finding types of creative insights; problem finding is likely to require longer incubation periods and a more significant role for the unconscious (Csikszentmihalyi & Sawyer, 1995).

The Unconscious Incubation Stage

In these stage models, the incubation stage is both the least understood and the most essential. The incubation stage is usually associated with the unconscious, or what is sometimes referred to as the preconscious or fringe consciousness (to reflect the fact that it is often just below the surface of awareness).[5] In incubation, elements are hypothesized to combine, and certain combinations are hypothesized to emerge into consciousness. Yet, the exact nature of these processes remains unknown. How do elements combine, and which combinations make it into conscious awareness?

One persistent explanation is that the combinations are random. Wallas (1926) ridiculed Poincaré's idea that the process of association could be directed by sensibility or beauty (pp. 75–78). Campbell (1960) argued that the process is blind or trial-and-error; the creative individual "just happened to be standing where lightning struck" (p. 390). Simonton's theory of chance configurations is explicitly grounded in Campbell's model. Scientific innovations arise when mental elements are combined through "chance permutations," although these may not be completely random (Simonton, 1988, pp. 6–8; also see Gruber, 1988).

Other theorists believe that incubation is directed in some way. Poincaré (1913/1982) was the first to claim that the subconscious mind does not randomly generate combinations but only generates combinations "which have to some extent the characteristics of useful combinations" (p. 386; also see pp. 390–391). Poincaré argued that this unconscious work is directed, with a sense of the domain of work (pp. 389–394); the unconscious possesses "esthetic sensibility" (p. 392). Poincaré noted that anyone could make new combinations from known entities, but the combinations that resulted would be "infinite in number and most of them absolutely without interest" (p. 386). In the mind of the inventor, "the sterile combinations do not even present themselves" (p. 386); rather, an "unconscious machine" generates good combinations because the conscious work of preparation has "mobilized" certain elements (p. 389). The combinations that become conscious are those that seem "beautiful" to the conscious mind (p. 391). If verification determines that an insight is false, "had it been true, [it] would have gratified our natural feeling for mathematical elegance" (p. 392).

Hadamard (1945) agreed with Poincaré: The ideas that emerge are those that are beautiful and that appeal to the creator's "emotional sensibility" (p. 31). The unconscious not only generates all of the combinations, but also has to select those that satisfy our sense of beauty. The conscious mind must still verify, because sometimes beautiful ideas are wrong (p. 57). Using Wallas's term, Hadamard suggested that the fringe-consciousness is "at the service of full consciousness" (p. 81) and can be called on when necessary.

Several psychoanalytic theorists have likewise proposed that the creative unconscious is guided by the conscious mind. Arieti (1976) studied the contributions of primary process (unconscious) and secondary process thinking to creativity, in what he called a "tertiary process." Rothenberg (1979) proposed that the combinations were "active, directed forms of cognition in which the creator intentionally and in distinct ways brings particular types of elements together" (p. 11); the elements are "integrated" rather than being "merely added or combined" (p. 12).

Cognitive psychologists have also argued that some criteria must be applied at the ideation stage. For example, Johnson-Laird (1987) argued on algorithmic grounds that constraints must be applied at the ideation stage; otherwise, the search space of ideas resulting from the ideation stage will be too large. Both Johnson-Laird and Sawyer (2002b) used the example of jazz improvisation in making this argument. Jazz improvisation is a real-time creative task; evaluation and ideation must proceed in parallel, because there is no opportunity for revision or selection during a live performance. Johnson-Laird referred to staged models with a constrained variation stage as "neo-Lamarckian" to contrast them with the random variation of Campbell's neo-Darwinian model.

Many researchers have noted that the unconscious process can be facilitated by taking time off from the problem. Wallas (1926) noted that incubation can be made to occur by either working on another problem, or by retreating from creative activity altogether (p. 86), for example by engaging in physical exercise (p. 89). This allows the mind to engage in a form of parallel processing; Hadamard (1945) noted that "the unconscious has the important property of being manifold; several and probably many things can and do occur in it simultaneously" (p. 23). This parallelism contrasts with the conscious mind, which can only focus on one thing at a time (also see Csikszentmihalyi & Sawyer, 1995). This multiplicity allows the unconscious to make many combinations simultaneously and in parallel.

There is one important alternative to the dominant combination-of-mental-elements approach to incubation. This is Wertheimer's (1945) gestalt theory of "productive thinking." For Wertheimer, the creative process involves a transformation from one whole situation (S1 in his notation) to another (S2). Wertheimer accounted for the motivation of the transformation in terms of holistic systemic properties of S1: "S1 contains structural strains and stresses that are resolved in S2," and he argued that the transformation springs directly from these structural troubles (p. 193). Structural features determine the transformation, not the goals of the individual (p. 196). These conceptual structures always tend to move toward "objectively better or adequate structure" (p. 198). Insights cannot be analyzed as elements combining, but rather must be analyzed as transformations in complex structures.

Piaget was one of the first to identify the key problem with gestaltism: Gestalts are irreducible and thus must always spring to mind as a totality. They cannot be analyzed in terms of the empirical origins of the elements that contribute to them. Gestalts are ahistorical; they are not thought of as the product of past interactions with an environment. A Piagetian schema, on the other hand, is dynamic and is always continuous with the prior schemas from which it emerged: "The schema is therefore a gestalt which has a history" (Piaget, 1936/1952b, p. 384). Schemas are elastic structures and continually modify themselves, whereas gestalt forms are static (cf. Flavell, 1963, pp. 72–75). Unlike gestalts, schemas "do not replace each other, but . . . are integrated into one another. The simplest ones become incorporated into later, more complex ones" (Piaget, 1971b, p. 7). As I discuss below, Piaget's theory of schema emergence has interesting similarities to element combination theories of unconscious incubation.

The Nature of the Creative Insight

In stage theories, the creative insight emerges from unconscious incubation. The creator experiences this emergence as an "Aha!" or "Eureka!" moment. As I showed previously, most creativity theories describe the mental process that leads up to this moment in terms familiar from emergence theory; the insight is a higher level holistic combination, configuration, or system of lower level elements, units, or ideas.

How do creative insights emerge from the incubation process? How do combinations form at all? Most serious contenders are variations of associationism, as first suggested by Bain. Bain (1855/1977) argued that creative novelty was "constructive association" and that the construction of "new combinations" (p. 573) is a form of "associating force" because "the new combinations grow out of elements already in the possession of the mind" (p. 572). Most creativity theories have proposed that a creative insight results in the mind of a creator when a set of more basic elements, none of them novel, is brought together to form a more complex cognitive structure. Like Morgan's account of emergence, no new substance is created; rather, novelty is a new mode of relatedness, a combination of elements into complex systems.

Subjective reports from creative individuals provide some support for these theories of creativity. Creativity researchers have long been familiar with the first-person accounts of scientists such as Poincaré and Kekulé. Einstein wrote in a letter to Hadamard that the "psychical entities which seem to serve as elements in thought are certain signs and more or less clear images which can be combined. . . . This combinatory play seems to be the essential feature in productive thought" (as cited in Hadamard, 1945, p. 142). Both Einstein and Poincaré referred to this process as associative. Wallas's (1926) theory of the associations that occur in the incubation stage is taken directly from early British associationism (e.g., see Wallas, pp. 61–65). The illumination is the "culmination of a successful train of association" (p. 94). As partial evidence for this claim, Wallas noted that some creators have a premonition that the insight is about to come; he called it "intimation" (p. 97).

One of the earliest modern statements of this theory of creativity was made by the psychologist Sarnoff Mednick (1962), who defined creative thinking to be "the forming of associative elements into new combinations." This associationist theory of creativity was based in the history of British associationist definitions from Locke to Bain (Mednick, 1962, p. 221). Mednick elaborated on associationism by proposing three distinct mechanisms of association: serendipity, similarity, and mediation. He identified several mental variables that contribute to the likelihood of creativity, including the organization of an individual's *associative hierarchy*, or what in the cognitive era of the 1970s would be called the "semantic network," the strength and structure of associations invoked by a given concept; the *number of associations* the individual has to the relevant elements of the problem; the individual's *cognitive style* (concrete vs. conceptual, visual vs. verbal); and the ways that individuals *select* the creative combination. For example, Mednick proposed that in problem-solving creativity, the selection criteria join the associative elements, whereas in problem-finding creativity, the task of selection also involves identifying relevant criteria (p. 225). Mednick contrasted his associative theory with theories that required connections based on "elaborate rules of logic, concept formation, or problem solving" (p. 227). He developed a psychometric test based on his theory and used the test to support several of his theoretical claims (Mednick & Mednick, 1965).

Many contemporary theories, including Rothenberg's and Simonton's, propose that creative insights result from combinations of mental elements; yet it is often unclear whether or not these models are associationist, because the details of the combinatory mechanism are rarely theorized. For example, Rothenberg's (1979) concept of "homospatial process" is one in which "discrete entities are fused and superimposed" while they "continue to interact and relate to one another" (p. 365). His theory is short on exactly how the distinct components interact with each other and join together in combination to form emergent wholes; instead, he simply observed that they are occupying the same space. The theory provided insufficient detail to determine how it was similar to or different from any other associationist theory. The same lack of detail characterizes Simonton's (1988) chance configurations. A complete theory of this process should include (a) a theory of the internal structure of preconscious cognition; (b) a structural theory of what mental elements and combinations are, and how elements combine; (c) a theory of what, if anything, motivates that preconscious process—of what elements come together in what protocombinations, and why.

Associationism provides another account of how the incubation stage might be guided, supporting arguments such as those of Poincaré (1913/1982, p. 393) and others that the ideation stage is not independent of evaluation. Mednick (1962) argued that the ideas generated are not unrelated, but instead reflect associative patterns. If incubation is not random, then the ideation stage is not completely independent of evaluation; this prefigured arguments such as those of Runco (1993) that evaluation processes must take place during divergent thought, beyond conscious awareness. Even if it is psychologically meaningful to distinguish ideation from evaluation, there is no compelling reason to insist that they cannot occur in parallel. Both types of thought may be constant, ongoing components of the creative mind.

Critiques of Stage Theories

For almost as long as there have been stage theories of creativity, there have been critics of stage theories. I have even found a textbook that criticized the stage conception (Lowenfeld & Brittain, 1987, p. 76). These critics accept that the researcher can identify distinct aspects of creative thought but argue that they occur in parallel rather than in series. This is a difference in emphasis rather than a diametric opposition; even Wallas (1926) noted that "in the daily stream of thought, these four different stages constantly overlap each other" (p. 81) and that when exploring a problem, "the mind may be unconsciously incubating on one aspect of it, while it is consciously employed in preparing for or verifying another aspect" (p. 82). Yet ultimately, Wallas felt that these four stages could "generally be distinguished from each other" (p. 82).

Vinacke's (1952) critique of stage theories (pp. 243–251), directed at Patrick and Rossman, was inspired by Wertheimer's holistic thinking; he proposed that, rather than looking for distinct stages, "it would be better to conceive of creative thinking in more holistic terms, a total pattern of behavior in which various processes overlap and interweave between the occurrence of the original stimulus and the formation of the final product" (p. 248). He reconceived the stages as "parallel processes" and argued that "it is necessary to conceive of creative thinking in terms of dynamic, interplaying activities rather than as more or less discrete stages" (p. 249). He noted that in many creative fields, especially fine art, there is a series of insights beginning with the first draft or sketch and continuing until the work is completed. He argued that incubation does not occur in a particular stage but operates to varying degrees throughout the creative process. For example, poems and plays do not emerge suddenly or completely but are gradually developed through a process of many incubations and insights.

The psychoanalytic theories of both Arieti and Rothenberg echoed Vinacke's criticism. Arieti (1976) noted that "complex works that can be divided into parts" involve a series of insights, with incubation occurring throughout the creative process. He concluded that the distinct phases exist only as abstractions (p. 18). Rothenberg (1979) argued that creation is not found in a single moment of insight but is "a long series of circumstances . . . often interrupted, reconstructed, and repeated" (p. 131). He criticized stage theories, arguing that "the temporal distinction made between inspiration and elaboration in the creative process is an incorrect one; these phases or functions alternate—sometimes extremely rapidly—from start to finish" (p. 346).

Guilford's (1967) "structure-of-intellect" model proposed a multifactor conception of intelligence based on five operations. From the most basic to the least, the operations are cognition, memory, divergent production, convergent production, and evaluation. Guilford was critical of staged conceptions such as Rossman's, arguing that all five operations proceed in parallel during the creative process, with "evaluation all along the way" (p. 329), although he acknowledged that there are probably higher levels of evaluative processes toward the end of the creative process.

Howard Gruber (1988) also criticized stage theories of creativity (pp. 47–49). He argued that each creative individual is likely to be unique and therefore that there are not likely to be general stages of creativity that apply universally. As evidence for his claim, Gruber (1974) appealed to his study of Darwin's creative process: "Darwin's achievement was realized not in a golden moment of insight but in the slower process of constructing an original point of view" (p. xiv). This criticism echoed those of Arieti and Rothenberg. Gruber applied Piagetian notions of schema transformation to Darwin's development of the theory of natural selection over a 2-year period, to argue that Darwin's theory could not simply be an isolated, sudden insight. For example, the principle of natural selection was well-known before Darwin; Darwin's creativity was not in the insight of natural selection but in his development of a conceptual schema within which natural selection could be perceived as an evolutionary force, whereas prior statements had conceived of it as a conservative force (Gruber, 1974, p. 7).

Although Gruber argued that Darwin's creative process was not staged, Gruber's application of Piagetian concepts seems to imply a staged conception of Darwin's creative process, because Piaget's theory is a stage theory. Gruber resolved this apparent contradiction by taking the somewhat unconventional position that Piaget's theory was not a stage theory (Gruber & Vonèche, 1977). This raises the question of what *would* count as a stage theory for Gruber. Gruber was probably reacting to comments by Piaget to the effect that the details of his stages were not as important as the fundamental processes of assimilation and accommodation (e.g., Piaget, 1945/1962, p. 291). Nonetheless, Piaget always insisted that development occurred in stages.

To further explore these conflicting accounts of the creative process, it is instructive to turn to developmental theory. Many developmental theories are based on stage conceptions, and there has been a great deal of theory surrounding the nature of stages, the number of stages, and how transitions between stages occur. Throughout the history of developmental psychology, these theories have been influenced by nineteenth-century emergentist and evolutionary theory.

THEORIES OF DEVELOPMENTAL PROCESS

Theories of development are partially defined by their rejection of the behaviorist concept of *learning*. The field of developmental psychology has always been based on nonbehaviorist assumptions; when behaviorists study similar phenomena, the endeavor is called *the psychology of learning* or *learning theory*. In the behaviorist conception, learning proceeds according to associationist mechanisms: The individual perceives two stimuli at the same time, or in succession, and after enough perceptions of the two stimuli in this relation, the mind begins to associate them. Forms of learning include habituation, classical conditioning, and operant conditioning.

In the behaviorist framework, learning is a linear, monotonic process: Skills and knowledge increase linearly with experience of the world. Learning can be explained in terms of experience, without incorporating theories of the internal mental models of individuals. In contrast, theories of development involve elements of either *maturationism* or *cognitivism*. Maturationism is the position that the organism is biologically determined to develop at a certain pace; cognitivism is the position that development cannot be explained without incorporating conceptions of the inner mental structures of the developing organism.

Although theories of the creative process retain elements of associationist thinking, such theories are typically based on stage models, and they assume that complex cognitive structures play an essential role in processes of creative insight. There are no stages or cognitive structures in learning theories, only in developmental theories, because stages can only result from qualitative transformations in internal mental structures. In fact, Piaget (1971a) equated novelty with stages: "If there are novelties, then, of course, there are stages. If there are no novelties, then the concept of stages is artificial" (p. 194).

In the following sections, I review theories of the developmental process proposed by Freud, Piaget, and Vygotsky. All three of these thinkers were socialized in the nineteenth-century intellectual environment of evolutionary historicism, all three were influenced by biological conceptions of evolution and development, and all three explicitly discussed artistic or scientific creativity in addition to their better known theories of developmental process.

Freud

I begin with Freud for two reasons. First, his ideas had a significant influence on creativity theory throughout the twentieth century; second, his ideas were a major influence on Piaget's developmental theory, and beginning with Freud will help to underscore the nineteenth-century origins of Piaget's thought.

Many recent scholars have observed that Freud is essentially a nineteenth-century thinker; his developmental theory was based on biological and evolutionary conceptions of development as staged and as emergent from a dialectic of successive tensions in each stage (Kitcher, 1992; Sulloway, 1979). In addition to the general influences of this nineteenth-century perspective, a wide range of direct influences has been documented.

In nineteenth-century evolutionary conceptions of biological development, the nervous system was thought to be composed of different levels that represented different stages of evolutionary development. Today, the best-known statement of this position is Haeckel's biogenetic law that "ontogeny recapitulates phylogeny." Sulloway (1979) argued that Haeckel's recapitulationism was a major influence on Freud (pp. 258–264). Freud read British neurologist John Hughlings Jackson, who developed an elaborate version of this theory in which the lower levels represented more primitive thought processes (Kitcher, 1992, p. 24). This formed the basis of Freud's famous distinction between primary and secondary process thought, and the basic psychological framework that could explain regression to a prior stage of development; regression could occur because the primitive structures survived alongside the more sophisticated, developmentally later mechanisms (Kitcher, 1992, p. 72). Thus, Freud's familiar stage theory of erotogenesis was an emergentist, nineteenth-century account. Each stage—oral, anal, genital, oedipal—provides the context within which the next stage can emerge (see Freud, 1917/1966, pp. 397–444, for a canonical statement).

In addition to these biological influences, Freud was familiar with Comte's staged theories of social history. Mill, an English admirer of Comte, was also well-known by Freud; for example, Freud translated four of Mill's essays into German (Kitcher, 1992, pp. 12–13). Freud read anthropologist Edward B. Tylor (1832–1917); Tylor, like Comte, proposed a social evolutionary model in which culture evolved through different levels of civilization. Like Wundt, Freud believed that knowing how civilization arose and developed would provide important clues to understanding the development of human intelligence (Kitcher, 1992, p. 21).

Thus Freud's theory of development was essentially emergentist, and he used this same theory to explain creativity. Freud located the creative impulse in repressed wishes, which were associated with primary process thought and unconscious thought. This theory of creativity remained influential late into the twentieth century (e.g., Arieti, 1976; Martindale, 1990; Rothenberg, 1979). In his most explicit statement on the topic, the essay "Creative Writers and Day-Dreaming," Freud proposed that the play of the child gradually transforms into adult fantasies, or daydreams (Freud, 1907/1989, p. 438). Daydreams are always motivated by unsatisfied wishes (p. 439). A neurosis is simply an "over-luxuriant" fantasy, and fantasies are the "immediate mental precursors" of neuroses (p. 440); in this way, Freud connected the creative impulse with his general theory of neurosis. For example, Freud wrote that "every child at play behaves like a creative writer, in that he creates a world of his own" (p. 437). Childhood is the source of fantasies and imagination, just as childhood is the source of most neuroses: "A strong experience in the present awakens in the creative writer a memory of an earlier experience (usually belonging to his childhood) from which there now proceeds a wish which finds its fulfillment in the creative work" (p. 442).

Piaget

One of the oldest oppositions in developmental theory is that between theorists who propose that development is a process of passive *transmission* to the child (either from the environment or from adult instruction) and those who propose that development is an active process in which the child *transforms* sense impressions and information from the external world. Transformationist theories view development as a creative process. Almost all twentieth-century theories of development, including behaviorism, psychoanalysis, and socioculturalism, accept some form of transformationist view (Lawrence & Valsiner, 1993), yet this perspective attained its most sophisticated expression in the constructivism of Jean Piaget.

Piaget's *genetic epistemology* was a direct outgrowth of the nineteenth-century currents that I identified previously. Piaget called his theory "constructivist," emphasizing that the child invents rather than discovers new ideas. For Piaget, the ideas do not exist out in the world waiting to be discovered; rather, each child invents them for himself. Yet, the child's construction is not free and undirected; rather, the functioning of the logic of each stage determines the structure of the stage that follows (Gruber & Vonèche, 1977, p. xxxvii).

Piaget's genetic psychology was opposed to the reductionist atomism of behaviorist associationism (see Taylor, 1985, p. 140). The contrast with associationism is that once a child has successfully constructed a fundamental schema—such as number, equivalence, or conservation—the child's thought is fundamentally transformed; the presence of that new schema then influences the manner in which the child apprehends the world from that point forward. Thus, development is not linear; it proceeds in stepwise, staged fashion.

Piaget's experiments demonstrated that perception was influenced by the cognitive schemas of the child. Thus perception was not unmediated by thought, as empiricist associationism claimed; rather, perception was foundationally guided by the categories of thought. It was in this limited sense that Piaget was a neo-Kantian, although like Durkheim (1912/1915), Piaget rejected the idealism of Kant and argued that the categories of thought were not a priori. Whereas Durkheim argued that the categories were socially constructed, Piaget proposed that they were constructed by the child in the course of development.[6]

Piaget's constructivism was emergentist; schemas at one stage emerge from the interaction between activity and schemas at the prior stage. His empirical research focused on the detailed incremental mechanisms of this emergence. By providing bottom-up explanations of the emergence of mental schemas through time, Piaget rejected the claim of the gestaltists that higher level phenomena could be analyzed and explained without reference to their components or to the history of their emergence.

Conceptions of development as staged derive from nineteenth-century biological thought, and Piaget was always explicit about the biological motivations behind his theory (Messerly, 1996). His degrees were in the biology of mollusks, and even late in his career, he said that schemas "have essentially a biological meaning, in the sense that the order of the stages is constant and sequential. Each stage is necessary for the following one" (1971b, p. 7). These nineteenth-century concepts also influenced Piaget through Freud. After Piaget received his Ph.D. in biology, he spent 8 months in analysis in Geneva before moving to Paris to study pathological psychology with mental patients. Piaget (1945/1962) acknowledged a series of parallels between Freud's theory of affective development and his own theory of intellectual development: "The two fundamental facts discovered by Freud and his school are: firstly that infantile affectivity passes through well-defined stages, and secondly that there is an underlying continuity, i.e., that at each level the child unconsciously assimilates present affective situations to earlier ones, even to those most remote. These facts are all the more interesting from our point of view in that they are completely in line with those of intellectual development" (p. 185).

Piaget and Freud shared a nineteenth-century focus on biological emergentism, which included a belief in biological explanations of mental phenomena, a focus on structures that result from the adaptation of an organism to its environment, a search for stages of these structures and transitional forms between them, and a focus throughout on homeostasis of the organism.[7] Their common emergentism accounts for many of the parallels between the theories of Piaget and Freud: (a) Each stage involves a shift from object fixation to generalized, symbolic fixation; (b) each stage has an inherent tension that propels development to the next stage; (c) after a transition to the next stage, the prior stage remains in the subconscious mind, latent, and there is occasional reversion to the prior stage; (d) equilibrium results from the tension between assimilation and accommodation, which Piaget explicitly acknowledged was modeled directly on Freud's contrast between the reality principle and the pleasure principle; and (e) this tension results in the symbol becoming detached from its referent. (In Freud, this process results in dreams, paraphrases, and neuroses; in Piaget, in symbolic thought). For two versions of Piaget's stage theory of development that have these characteristics, see particularly 1923/1955 and 1945/1962; for his comments on Freud and psychoanalysis, see particularly 1945/1962, pp. 182–212, and 1936/1952b, pp. 383–384.[8]

Piaget always emphasized that it was the dynamic process of emergence, and not the specifics of particular stages, that were most essential to his theory (1945/1962, p. 291; also see Gruber & Vonèche, 1977, p. xxvi). For example, a close reading of Piaget's 1945/1962) account of how symbolic thought develops during play reveals the ways that the tension between assimilation and accommodation at each stage propels the transition to the next stage (pp. 182–212). Thus, for Piaget, the transition to the next stage always involves a moment of emergence. Piaget (1971a) did not believe that these stages and their ordering were innate or preformed; although the ordering of the stages was the same in every individual, it could only be determined by documenting processes of emergence through time, and it could not be found in the genetic code of the individual. All that must be innate is a very general ability to coordinate the actions that are needed to jump-start the whole developmental process (Piaget, 1968/1970, pp. 61–68; see Gruber & Vonèche, 1977, p. xxxv).

There is a history of controversy about whether Piaget is an elementarist or a holist, and this relates directly to his status as an emergence theorist. Van der Veer (1996) and Kitchener (1985) both claimed that Piaget's structures were additive and thus not emergent, in contrast to gestalt structures, which were nonadditive. The schema is the product of past interactions, and therefore it is "a gestalt which has a history" (Piaget, 1936/1952b, p. 384). Thus, although his schemas are additive, they are always seen as evolving structures, and lower level structures are constrained by higher level emergent structures (see Gruber & Vonèche, 1977, p. xxxii). Kitchener (1985) concluded that Piaget rejected emergence, because the whole is reducible to the relations between the parts, and thus the composition is reversible (p. 291).

Yet, although the 1920s emergentists were antireductionists, nineteenth-century biological emergentism more generally was not incompatible with reductionism, because in a sense the emergent later forms are reductively explained in terms of the dynamical relations and processes of the earlier forms (see Wimsatt, 1997). Piaget referred to himself as a "relationist," and his discussion makes clear that this is a form of emergentism; Piaget is emergentist because he places his position between reductionist atomism and holism (e.g., see Piaget, 1967, p. 1228). Piaget (1968/1970) rejected the antireductionism of holists such as the gestaltists (pp. 8–9) and accepted that wholes or cognitive schemas are additively composed of elements and their relations; in his view, this process is a continual dynamic and occurs through time, such that a schema cannot be reduced to its elements at a given time but must be explained in terms of its origin from elements in the past. For this reason, schemas *as wholes* are analytically prior to their elements, in that they have causal downward effects over those elements (p. 7).

Vygotsky

Like Piaget, Vygotsky rejected behaviorist conceptions of learning and maturationist conceptions of development (1978, chapter 6). He identified three possible relations between learning and (maturationist) development. First, learning does not influence development; rather, the ability to learn from the world is determined by the developmental level of the child, and this level is determined by endogenous biological factors. Vygotsky placed Piaget's theory in this category (p. 80), but this misrepresented the emergentist nature of Piaget's theory; see the similar critique by Beilin (1971) and Piaget's response (1971a). Second, learning and development can be viewed as identical processes. Vygotsky placed behaviorism in this category. Third, learning and development can mutually influence each other. Vygotsky placed Koffka's gestaltism in this category; Koffka proposed that development is based on both the maturation of the nervous system and on experience of the external environment.

Vygotsky rejected all three of these positions to propose his theory of the *zone of proximal development*. Like Koffka, he agreed that learning and development are related. Learning must be "matched" with the child's developmental level (Vygotsky, 1978, p. 85). Vygotsky's innovation was to elaborate the notion of developmental level by defining it as a "zone": the difference between the child's "actual developmental level," as determined by independent problem solving, and the level of "potential development," as determined by problem solving under the guidance of someone more capable. These latter represent "functions that have not yet matured but are in the process of maturation" (p. 86). Thus, a child can only learn things that are appropriate to his developmental level.

Thus the relation between learning and development was that "learning awakens a variety of internal developmental processes" and that "the developmental process lags behind the learning process" (Vygotsky, 1978, p. 90). At its root, this perspective is not that different from Piaget's, because in both—contrary to Vygotsky's interpretation of Piaget—interaction with the external world drives development.[9]

Because Vygotsky's works were composed primarily between 1924 and 1934, it is not surprising that he was influenced by the same emergentist conceptions as Piaget. Like the gestaltists, Vygotsky rejected the reductionist atomism of both behaviorism and introspectionism (Vygotsky, 1965/1971, p. 18; also see Cole & Scribner, 1978, p. 5, and Wertsch, 1985, p. 4). Although he was heavily influenced by the gestaltists, Vygotsky agreed with Piaget that they did not explain the origins of complex mental phenomena. Whereas Piaget explained mental schemas by documenting their emergence from individual-environment interaction, Vygotsky drew on several strands of nineteenth-century sociological theory in proposing that irreducible psychological wholes originated in collective life; his belief in the social origins of higher psychological processes was influenced by both Marx and by the Durkheimian school of French sociology (see Cole & Scribner, 1978, p. 6).

EMERGENTISM AND CONNECTIONS BETWEEN CREATIVITY AND DEVELOPMENT

In the preceding two sections, I reviewed theories in creativity and development. I focused on the elements of twentieth-century theories that are emergentist, and I argued that these elements are central to the dominant theories of both creativity and development.

Based on this brief discussion, in the following sections I consider some additional connections between creativity and development that are revealed by the emergentist perspective. My purpose in these discussions is to show that a comparison of theories in these two areas has the potential to provide insights and new perspectives to researchers in both areas. I show that, in some cases, developmentalists and creativity researchers are grappling with similar issues and considering analogous hypotheses. At times they take similar paths, at other times different paths, to resolving these issues. I argue that theories in these fields face common issues because they are both theories of emergence.

Process Versus Product

Emergence requires a focus on process rather than on end product. A shift to process has been characteristic of recent work on both creativity and development. Socioculturalists such as Rogoff (1990) and Cole (1996) emphasized the focus on developmental process and on microgenetic studies, in contrast to prior developmental work that focused on end points of development. Creativity researchers such as Feldman, Getzels, and Csikszentmihalyi have been influential in shifting the focus from an emphasis on creative products to the creative process. Consequently, both fields have been faced with parallel sets of issues: What is the relationship between processes and products? How do products evolve and change during the process—for example, the gradual redrafting and editing that slowly accumulate into a finished book?

For example, my own studies of group improvisation (Sawyer, 2003) reveal a collaborative creative process that could not, even in theory, be analyzed as a creative product. To understand why, compare an improvisational performance to a scripted theater performance (cf. Sawyer, 2001a). A traditional scripted play is composed and prepared by a single creative individual, the playwright. The staging and dramaturgical preparation for a given performance are typically controlled by the director. The actors are thus controlled by two different creative individuals: their words, stage entrances, and emotional expressions by the playwright; their stances, physical positions, and interpretation by the director. As a result of our literate tradition, many people consider a play to be represented by the script, a creative product that results from the creative process of the playwright. Many plays are studied in English literature departments, using similar techniques to those used for texts such as poems and novels; the performative and processual aspects of the play are thus neglected.

An improvisational performance is radically different, because the actors do not start with a text. There is no creative product that is being performed or executed. Instead, the creative process occurs on stage, between the actors, in front of the audience. The goal of this collective creative process is not to generate a creative product; there is no resulting product, as there is with the creative process of individuals such as painters, composers, and playwrights. Instead, the goal of the performance is the process itself; the process is the product. Consequently, studies of improvisational performance must be foundationally focused on its processual, emergent qualities.

Emergentist approaches to development are also processually focused. Perhaps more than any other contemporary developmentalists, the socioculturalists continue Piaget's emphasis on the processes of development, rather than focusing on a detailed structural description of the individual stages that represent static developmental states. Although many standard readings of Piaget emphasize his stages and their properties, his own writings emphasized the processual dynamics of assimilation and accommodation that led to the emergence of new schemas. It is this emphasis that led some Piagetian scholars to deny that Piaget is primarily a stage theorist (e.g., Gruber and Vonèche, 1977).

For those focused on developmental process, a promising research methodology is the *microgenetic method*, in which the child is closely observed as his or her psychological structures are changing, and frequent samples of children's mental states are obtained throughout the process. Most of the early developmental psychologists who were influenced by nineteenth-century evolutionary naturalism used some form of microgenetic method, including Werner, Piaget, and Vygotsky. Werner first used the term "microgenesis" to describe the extremely short processes of development that occur during the performance of a single task (Werner, 1940, p. 37; see also Flavell & Draguns, 1957). A microgenetic focus is a focus on process through time; such a focus is necessary to understand the dialectic between organism and environment that results in emergence. Piaget was engaged in a form of microgenetic research: his close analyses of his own children from day to day as they engaged in specific tasks. From Vygotsky's work onward, Soviet developmental psychology has emphasized microgenetic or "microstructural" methods (Zinchenko & Gordon, 1979; see Wertsch & Stone, 1978). Microgenetic studies of parent-child dyads have revealed evidence for Vygotsky's zone of proximal development, or what

Bruner (1983) called "scaffolding": At the beginning of the task situation, the parent and child interact to jointly solve the task, and toward the end, the child gradually takes over more of the responsibility for the task.

One consistent finding of microgenetic studies of cognitive development is that children do not ordinarily substitute a more advanced strategy for a simpler one (Kuhn, 1995). Older strategies continue to be used even after they are clearly seen to be less effective. A second consistent finding is that children generally think about a problem in many ways at once. This cognitive variability is most evident during a period of rapid change (Alibali & Goldin-Meadow, 1993). The implications of such findings for creativity theory are that the different stages of the creative process are probably not completely distinct. As even most stage theorists acknowledge, the stages are somewhat artificial constructs, and there is likely to be overlap among them. However, creativity theorists have not done much detailed empirical work to study the exact nature of these overlaps, or the exact microgenesis of the steps that lead from one stage to another, with as much detail as these developmental studies of cognitive change. Part of the problem is that the creative process is hard to re-create in the laboratory and typically occurs on a longer timescale than the cognitive transitions studied by developmentalists.

Timescales

Development has been conceived of as occurring on many different timescales. The shortest timescale is change during a single task: Werner and his colleagues studied transitions that took less than a second (e.g., Werner, 1940). The longest timescale is the cultural-historical; this approach includes nineteenth-century theories of social development such as those of Comte, Spencer, and Tylor, as well as the more practice-based theories of Vygotsky and Soviet psychology (see Wertsch and Stone, 1978). Of course, perhaps the longest timescale is that of biological evolution, the nineteenth-century developmental theory that first gave rise to emergentist thinking. Most developmental research takes place in an in-between territory—the study of ontogenesis, or the development of the single organism across successive tasks and many types of psychological events (cf. Rogoff, 1998).

Creativity research is also characterized by a range of timescales. Csikszentmihalyi and Sawyer (1995) proposed that big C Creativity required a long time span, and little c creativity could occur within a shorter time span. In their account, a more revolutionary insight required a longer period of preparation and incubation, both because more elements of information had to be gathered during preparation, and because more combinations would have to be attempted by the preconscious before the insight would emerge. In contrast, the small insights of everyday creativity require fewer internalized elements and a shorter period of trial and error before an appropriate combination emerges.

Some psychologists have explicitly compared the stages of creativity to the stages of problem solving, a form of microgenetic study (Flavell & Draguns, 1957, p. 201; Guilford, 1967). Artificial intelligence models of creativity largely assume that creativity is a form of problem solving (e.g., Boden, 1991); consequently, these models draw on general theories of the microgenesis of problem solving. Klahr (2000) was the latest in a long artificial-intelligence tradition of considering scientific discovery to be a special case of everyday problem solving. His main influences included Herbert Simon and Allen Newell, two developers of one of the first artificial intelligence (AI) systems, the General Problem Solver (Newell & Simon, 1972; also see Klahr & Simon, 1999). In Klahr's (2000) view, both scientific discovery and general problem solving are forms of "constrained search in problem spaces" (p. 201). In response, many creativity researchers have argued that creativity involves both problem solving and *problem finding* and have argued that artificial intelligence models are inadequate for modeling the latter (Csikszentmihalyi, 1988a). Unfortunately, creativity theorists have not yet developed theories of problem finding that would be suitable for computational modeling.

Long-timescale cultural-historical changes have been studied for many years by historians of art and science. Some creativity researchers have begun to apply the quantitative methods of historiometrics (e.g., Martindale, 1990; Simonton, 1988). Evolutionary models have been influential in creativity research at least since Donald Campbell's seminal 1960 article that proposed variation-selection-reproduction as a model of creativity. Campbell also argued that the same three-stage model could be used to describe learning; he held to a trial-and-error learning theory (p. 382). Siegler's recent developmental theory (1996) was based on this three-stage evolutionary metaphor, although Siegler rejected Campbell's hypothesis that variation is blind, instead proposing that it is directed through various mechanisms (pp. 24–25). And of course, Campbell was an early precursor of the amorphous field of memetics, which has explored cultural variation and retention using evolutionary models (e.g., Csikszentmihalyi, 1993; Dennett, 1995).

Thus both creativity and development can be studied on multiple timescales. Rather than arguing that one or another timescale is the proper one for study, in both fields we need a combination of research projects. To get a complete picture of development, developmentalists realize that they need to understand the second-to-second changes of microgenesis, the life-span changes of ontogenesis, and the cultural-historical changes that result in different contexts and end points of development. Different methodologies are required for each form of study; microgenesis can be studied experimentally, ontogenesis requires longitudinal or cross-sectional methods, and cultural-historical study requires both historical study and the comparative methods of ethnography.

Likewise, a complete picture of creativity will require analysis at multiple timescales. Many creativity researchers have taken a life-span developmental approach (e.g. Simonton, 1988; Gardner, 1993). Other researchers (e.g., Csik-szentmihalyi, 1996) have focused on the day-to-day work processes of creative individuals, a mid-range approach. The microgenesis of the creative process has been neglected (although see Getzels & Csikszentmihalyi, 1976). Those re-searchers who created experimental tasks to measure divergent thinking ability also focused on a short timescale of analysis, but one that was not microgenetic, because it measured only the number of ideas accumulated by the end of the task, and it only analyzed a single stage of the creative process. Thus, one area of promising future study would be microgenetic analysis of the creative process.

Creativity and the Life Span

Most theories of the creative process examine the process that leads to a single creative product, and in most creativity theories, this process is hypothesized to have two broad stages. In the first, new ideas are generated, and in the second, the good ideas are selected from those generated in the first stage. These two stages correspond to Campbell's (1960) blind variation and selective retention, to Guilford's divergent and convergent thinking (Guilford, 1967), and to Freudian theories of primary process and secondary process thinking (Kris, 1952).

Stage models of development are generally more complex; there are more stages, and each stage may have substages (as in Piaget's theory). For example, Klahr's model (2000) is an elaborate hierarchical stage model, with the three main stages—search hypotheses, test hypotheses, and evaluate evidence—each broken down into substages, and some of those substages further separated into sub-substages (p. 37). Creativity theory could benefit from a close considera-tion of the life-span and stage theories of developmentalists. For example, they could learn to think about creativity as a longer term process, one in which indi-vidual creative products are only small pieces of the whole story rather than the point of the story, as Gruber (1988) argued in proposing his "networks of enter-prise" model. For example, developmentalists have focused on how small in-cremental changes gradually accumulate to result in a major stage transition, the prototype being Piaget's close case studies of his children.

The idea that the generation of a product involves two stages, with ideation preceding convergent thought, overly simplifies the complexity and hard work of most creativity; in most cases, creators experience small insights throughout

a day's work, with each small insight followed by a period of conscious elaboration. These only gradually accumulate to result in a finished work, as a result
of a process of hard work and intellectual labor of the creator. Many influential
studies have demonstrated the complexity of creativity by focusing on what
could be called the ontogenesis of the creative product—biographical studies of
the day-to-day development of creative products over months and years. The
seminal study of this type is Gruber's (1974) close reading of Darwin's journals.
Creativity researchers are still fleshing out theories about these long-term
processes: how long creative periods are sustained and how one multiyear period is succeeded by a shift to another research question or another style of visual representation (cf. Csikszentmihalyi & Nakamura, this volume; Gruber,
1988).

For example, Howard Gardner and others observed a "10-year rule": There
seem to be 10-year gaps between major significant works. Gardner (1993) interpreted this as evidence that it takes 10 years to internalize the domain. Elliott
Jacques (1965), in the famous paper that coined the term *midlife crisis*, identified two distinct types of creativity associated with early adulthood and later life
(and separated by the midlife crisis at approximately age 35). The early creativity is "hot-from-the-fire," "intense and spontaneous, and comes out ready-
made" (p. 503). In contrast, creativity in later adulthood is a "sculpted creativity." There is a longer period between the first inspiration and the final creative
product; the inspiration comes more slowly, rather than in a sudden burst; and
the creator spends much more time "forming and fashioning" the product, in a
process of sculpting that results in "externally emergent creation" (p. 503).

The study of life-span creativity would be a form of emergentist study, but
with emergence processes occurring over the longer timescale of an entire career, rather than over the timescale of a single creative task or product.

The Unconscious in Development and Creativity

Many schools of twentieth-century art were based on the idea that art involves
the revelation of unconscious material, including expressionism, dadaism, and
surrealism. Both Freud and Piaget considered the role of the unconscious in
both creativity and development. Freud's definitions of *primary process* and
secondary process thinking were developed to describe developmental
processes; however, these concepts have often been applied to creativity. According to Freud, the creative insight emerges into consciousness from primary
process or subconscious processes. Freud drew continuities between creativity
and daydreams, fantasy, and full-fledged neuroses (1907/1989). This led many
subsequent theorists to connect creativity with other manifestations of primary
process thought, such as dreams and children's play.

Piaget's (1945/1962) book about these connections was one of the most ambitious. He argued that symbolic thought as manifest in children's play is not qualitatively different from the unconscious symbolic thought discussed by Freud, that "children's dreams seem to be closely related to symbolic play" (p. 182), and that adult dreams are, as well (p. 209). Therefore, regarding children, he disagreed with Freud's claim that symbolic play was discontinuous with unconscious thought; rather, Piaget argued that the symbolism associated with Freud's unconscious was outwardly manifested in symbolic play, and that often, it could be demonstrated that children were consciously aware of what they were doing. Piaget also noted that Freud's theory of symbolism was dependent on classic associationism and thus that Freud denied that symbolic thought is a constructive activity (p. 189).[10]

Freudian-influenced psychoanalytic thinkers have continued to apply these Freudian developmental concepts to the creative process. Many influential thinkers have argued that creativity involves both primary processes and secondary processes. The first theorist to move in this direction was Ernst Kris (1952), who argued that the creator was an individual who could manage some degree of conscious ego control over his own primary process thought, using it in service of his work. In this sense, creativity is a product of the preconscious rather than the unconscious: "A part of the work is done in preconscious elaboration, the result of which comes into consciousness in sudden advances," and the insight is "observation impregnated with previous preconscious experiences" (p. 296).

Whereas Freud's emphasis on the connection between creativity and primary process led to a hypothesized link between creativity and madness, Kris's ideas imply that the creative individual requires a rather sophisticated balance between primary and secondary process thinking that would be hard to maintain in the presence of mental illness. Rothenberg (1979) denied that creative people are more likely to be mentally ill than anyone else; he claimed that the creative process is "an advanced type of secondary process" rather than primary process (p. 42) and that it is "not only *not* primitive but [is] consistently more advanced and adaptive than ordinary waking thought" (p. 43). He rejected the idea that there is unconscious incubation that results in a surprise of insight (p. 130).

Although psychoanalysis has not played a significant role in the post-1980s resurgence of creativity research, the phenomenon to be explained remains the same as that first identified by Freud: the relation between the preconscious and the conscious. The preconscious is different from the unconscious in that it can easily become conscious, given the proper conditions. In contrast, the unconscious cannot become conscious without considerable effort. These relationships are central to several influential contemporary theories, even those that are not explicitly psychoanalytic (e.g., Martindale, 1990; Simonton, 1988).

Stage Transitions and Novelty

The processes that lead to the emergence of the next stage are the central unresolved questions in both creativity research and developmental psychology. In developmental stage theories such as those of Freud and Piaget, the child is propelled to the next stage by a disturbance in the equilibrium of the prior stage. For Piaget, disequilibrium was caused when the dominant schemas of a stage could no longer successfully assimilate external experiences. Piaget's empirical work documented the microgenesis of the emergence of the next stage from the logical necessity of the clash between the current schema and environmental interaction. Piaget also documented the process of development within a stage—which was typically a transition from a more concrete to a more abstract set of schemas.

Some developmentalists have proposed that there is something like an incubation period between developmental stages, because it takes time for individuals "to appropriate the complex knowledge that they co-construct during social interaction" (Azmitia, 1998, p. 240). Complex ideas must ferment or percolate in our unconscious until they fully develop and begin to influence cognitive performance. These ideas are reinforced by experimental studies that have documented extended periods of stage transition during which multiple schemas and strategies are active (Siegler, 1996). In Siegler's evolutionary model, development is a process of age-related changes in the repertoire of cognitive strategies and in the preference for and ability to use different cognitive strategies. Siegler's *overlapping waves approach* proposed that the child has multiple strategies available at any one time, and that these strategies compete; over time, the more effective strategies are increasingly used, in a process of selection that Siegler (1998) explicitly compared to biological evolution (p. 92). With time, the more successful strategies thrive and become more frequent, and the less successful strategies fade away. Siegler also hypothesized that children can create or discover new strategies, but he admitted that his theory is weakest in explaining the emergence of novelty, our concern here (p. 96).

Note the similarities between Siegler's (1998) non-stage version of development and the criticisms of stage theories of creativity (pp. 28–29). For example, Guilford (1967, p. 329) made a point similar to that of Siegler; he accepted that there are different aspects to the creative process—his five operations correspond closely to the four-stage model—he argued, however, that all operations are present simultaneously, but with various operations coming to dominate as the creative process proceeds.

Late in his life, Piaget noted that the most serious unresolved problem was the issue of novelty—how a child makes the transition to the next stage. Like Piaget, many other developmentalists have argued that we have very little knowledge of what happens during stage transitions. Beginning in the 1970s and inspired by the growth of cognitive psychology, advocates of cognitive models of development claimed that they could provide new conceptual tools with which to understand the transition mechanisms of development (e.g., Case, 1985; Simon & Halford, 1995). Many of these scholars argued that Piagetian theory was largely focused on structures and thus neglected the processes of development (e.g., Case, 1985, p. 410; Klahr, 1982, p. 80), although a more recent line of Piagetian scholarship has argued that these are mischaracterizations of Piaget. As I demonstrated above, Piaget was at root a theorist of developmental process. Case's (1985) information-processing model was neo-Piagetian in that it retained four universal stages, although it tended to shift Piaget's theory away from an emergence theory and toward a maturational theory; Case argued that stage transitions were dependent on biologically determined increases in working memory capacity.

Creativity researchers might benefit from developmental studies of how a stage emerges from a prior developmental stage. Piaget's close empirical studies documented, in great incremental detail, how a cognitive schema emerged from an interaction between a prior cognitive schema and physical objects. Creativity researchers could learn from the complex and varied theories proposed by developmentalists for how the transformation from one stage to another occurs; for the most part, creativity theorists don't have very sophisticated theories of these stage transitions. For example, they don't have very good theories about why or when a transition from divergent to convergent thinking takes place.

Cognitivists hypothesize that children increasingly *encode* features of the environment, helping them to perceive the critical features of a situation more rapidly and to determine what is relevant to a problem or task. Encoding has obvious parallels with the creative process, because it involves discrimination, differentiation, identification of critical features, and the formation of mental models (Siegler, 1998, p. 323). In creativity terms, encoding is the process whereby mental elements are formed. An adequate developmental theory of the process of encoding will of necessity be a theory of creativity, because the emergence of a new encoding is a creative process.

Creativity theories are weak in the explicit theorization of mental elements and how they combine into higher level configurations. Researchers could draw on cognitivist theories of cognitive structure, semantic networks, and mental associations to provide more rigor to such theories.

Domain Specificity

In the 1970s, 1980s, and 1990s, developmentalists increasingly found evidence that children seem to progress through Piagetian stages at different rates in different realms of cognitive competence (Callanan, 1999, p. 150). Piaget's theory was foundationally based on the claims that the stages are general properties of the child's cognition and that when a child transitions to the next stage, the mental schemas of that stage will be manifest in all activities of the child, regardless of the topic, sensory modality, or social context. Feldman (1974, 1980) coined the term "domain" to describe a culturally-derived symbolic system associated with a given realm of creative activity.

This critique of Piaget was a claim for the *domain specificity* of cognitive development. This claim was readily accepted by creativity researchers, because of the failure of trait psychology and factor analysis studies of the creative personality in the 1960s. In the 1960s, personality studies of creativity resulted in the development of several tests to measure a "creativity quotient," or the several factors that were hypothesized to contribute to creativity. However, this research was generally considered to have failed because it was unable to predict actual creative performance in specific domains of creative endeavor.

Beginning in the 1970s, many researchers began to argue that creativity was domain-specific (Feldman, 1974, 1980; John-Steiner, 1985; Csikszentmihalyi, 1988b). In the first argument for this position, Feldman (1974) explicitly opposed this notion to the trait conception of creativity. Feldman's (1986) work on prodigies showed that the prodigial ability is domain-specific. John-Steiner's (1985) studies of creativity showed that creativity requires fluency in the language, symbols, and tools of a domain. Domain-specific conceptions of creativity attained their widest dissemination in Gardner's (1983) influential theory of *multiple intelligences*, which he has applied both as a general theory of development and to creative individuals (see Feldman, this volume).

Why are individuals creative in only one domain? Most theorists believe this is because a large number of mental elements must be internalized before the individual is capable of generating a novel creative combination. Most domains of creative activity have a long history of prior activity—for example, the periods of twentieth-century painting, or the history of empirical research in particle physics. Without first internalizing this domain, an individual does not have the raw material with which to create novel combinations. Similar ideas have long been influential in the history and philosophy of science. Fleck (1935/1979) wrote of how the "thought style" of a scientific discipline "constrains the individual by determining 'what can be thought in no other way'" (p. 99). He also noted that if two people belong to different "thought collectives," they cannot have the exactly same thought (p. 100). A variant of Fleck's ideas, Kuhn's *paradigm* (1960), became influential in the 1960s and 1970s and no doubt indirectly contributed to theories of creative domains.

A concern with the physical and symbolic tools that are used by individuals is found in both fields. Wertsch (1998) drew on Vygotsky in analyzing "mediated action" in development; John-Steiner (1985), also drawing inspiration from Vygotsky, studied how "languages" affect the creative process. Regarding domain specificity, creativity theory might be able to inform developmental theory, because creativity theorists have spent a great deal of effort identifying the language of a domain of creative activity, how that language is internalized by creative individuals, and how they can generate novel combinations in that language. The issue of exactly what domains exist in the child, and how development proceeds in these distinct domains, remains unresolved in developmental psychology.

Internalization of the Domain

The existence of creative domains—complex symbol systems representing the attainments of past creative individuals—forces us to confront issues of internalization, appropriation, and mastery. Vygotsky argued that development involved a process of internalization (Lawrence & Valsiner, 1993). Some sociocultural psychologists have rejected the term *internalization*, arguing that it implies a passive child absorbing information from the environment without transformation or creative construction. Socioculturalists, like constructivists, insist on a transformation view of development rather than a transmission view. From a constructivist perspective, the child does not internalize information passively, but rather constructs information endogenously as a by-product of interaction with the environment.

For example, Wertsch (1993) argued that better terms for internalization would be appropriation or mastery. Rogoff (1998) argued that there is no sense at all in which the child can be said to internalize, appropriate, or master anything; such concepts imply a boundary between the child and the social environment. In contrast, Rogoff argued that the child and the social world are inextricably linked, such that it doesn't make sense to speak of information or knowledge crossing over a boundary from the environment to the child, as implied by the term *internalization* (Sawyer, 2002c).

Although all creativity theorists agree that an important part of the creative process is the internalization of the language and symbols of the domain that occurs in the preparation stage, they do not claim that this is sufficient for creativity; it is only a prerequisite. Creativity results when the individual somehow combines these internalized elements and generates some new configuration. Thus creativity theory provides a subtly different perspective on internalization. Creativity researchers accept that much knowledge is internalized in a rather passive and direct way; the student of physics must learn Maxwell's equations and Einstein's theories as they already are, and this process does not have to be creative. Nonetheless, once the existing elements of the domain are internalized, novel combinations can be formed. Thus, creativity theory retains a conception of internalization that is compatible with creative construction and novelty.

By analogy, the child could be said to internalize many elements and components of knowledge in some domain, and this internalization could be compatible with a transformative, constructivist view of development. After internalization, the child has to go through some sort of integrative or transformative process in which those elements or components are placed into a structure or framework of knowledge. This is similar to the information-processing theory that the child encodes and "automatizes" knowledge into increasingly complex combinations.

Some socioculturalists claim that there is no role for internalization in development, and that constructive appropriation is always taking place. This observation can be applied to the creative process as well. Creative people rarely simply internalize; they often transform and appropriate, even as they are gathering new knowledge. An artist walking through a gallery views paintings very selectively, looking for ideas or inspirations that can solve creative problems with which he or she is currently working. This can lead the artist to see something in a painting that its creator may not have intended or been aware of. For a scientist reading a historical work by a long-dead theorist, it is a commonplace to read into the work those perspectives or issues with which the reader is currently working. In neither case does the creative individual first simply internalize the work and then transform it; the transformation is a part of the original perception.

Piaget's notion of the schema is a proposal that the child executes a process similar to that of the scientist; the schema causes a child to perceive the world in certain ways, whether or not it is accurate, as in the famous fluid conservation experiments. The analogy to creativity theory is with the internalized creative domain, or paradigm; the domain functions like a working schema that guides how the creator perceives new works by other artists or scientists (cf. Carey, 1986). Piaget has been criticized for considering the child to be a "little scientist" (Kuhn, 1989); yet even the cognitive scientist David Klahr, who is critical of Piaget, developed computational models that he then applied to both developmental processes and scientific discovery (Klahr, 2000).

In sum, the common issues in creativity and development are the relations between a cognitive schema and the new knowledge that is apprehended from the world. How is the perception of the new knowledge influenced by the current schema? How can the schema be changed by the new knowledge? The construction of a new schema roughly corresponds to a Kuhnian scientific revolution, when the old paradigm is completely replaced by a new domain, a new language, or a new way of thinking. Having a transformative creative insight is like advancing to a new developmental stage. In contrast, normal science corresponds to development within a stage. After having an insight, the creative individual might spend years executing or implementing that insight, and this corresponds to a child's cognitive processing during the period in a single developmental stage.

The Social and the Individual

The role of social interaction first entered creativity research in the early 1960s, with the influential publications of Osborn and Gordon. Osborn (1953) coined the term *brainstorming* and emphasized the importance of group interaction in developing ideas. Gordon's *synectics* (1961) was based on the claim that group thinking is always superior to individual thinking. Although influential, these claims were not based on empirical evidence; many attempts to compare individual performance to group performance find that individuals generate more ideas, more original ideas, and better ideas than groups do (e.g., Larey & Paulus, 1999; Taylor, Berry, & Block, 1958).

Sociological studies of scientific discovery have long downplayed psychological factors, preferring to identify the social properties associated with creations, for example, by studying the incidence of multiple invention and the sociological processes whereby novel ideas or theories are accepted or rejected by a discipline. This approach came to prominence in the 1960s, when Kuhn's 1960 book led to a burst of activity in the history of ideas. Sociologists argue that discovery can be analyzed as a sociological-historical process. One empirical path toward demonstrating this has been the studies of *multiple discovery*, which sociologists argue are evidence that the insight should be attributed to collective properties of the scientific discipline rather than to psychological processes in any individual scientist (but see Simonton, 1988).

Such sociological theories often propose that scientific disciplines develop in stages. For example, Nicholas Mullins (1983) proposed a four-stage model of the growth of a scientific specialization. In the first stage, the founding figures produce their innovations but remain on the fringe of the dominant paradigm. There is only an informal group around the leading figure(s). In the second stage, layers of networks begin to connect numbers of people. In the third stage, other centers are colonized and distinct clusters begin to form. A focus on jobs, publications, and meetings becomes important; secondary works explaining the paradigm begin to appear. Structurally, the group divides into a core of less than 25 people, and a periphery. In the fourth and final stage, the specialty paradigm has attained maturity. The founding figure may move on, but organizational structures are in place; new research using the ideas develops outside the primary clusters (an index that the work has become routine), and textbooks appear. According to Mullins, this process takes between 8 and 25 years (pp. 320–321).

In the 1980s, developmental researchers known as socioculturalists began to examine how groups develop through time. Some ethnographers (for example, Kevin Dunbar and Ed Hutchins) began to examine how groups create novelty by studying workgroups. Rather than focusing on specific individuals in the group, they treated the group itself as an entity that develops through time, in successive stages, and as a result of interaction with its environment. More in keeping with Vygotsky than with Piaget, socioculturalists such as Rogoff proposed a social version of constructivism, arguing that knowledge is emergent from a social process. This was continuous with the Piagetian tradition of constructivism, because it emphasized "the active role of children and of their social partners" (Rogoff, 1990, p. 197). But Rogoff made the stronger sociological claim that children not only create their own knowledge but also "are active in creating culture" as well (p. 198).

Rogoff (1990) briefly discussed adult creativity within the sociocultural framework. First, the creative process "builds on the technologies already available, within existing institutions. A creative idea is in some sense a reformulation of existing ideas" (p. 198). This, of course, is the familiar *domain* from contemporary creativity theory: the collection of symbols, symbol systems, and artifacts that must be internalized as the raw material of the creative process. Second, Rogoff noted that creativity always occurs within a social context of apprentices, colleagues, coworkers, and evaluators.

In the late 1980s, in parallel with this sociocultural movement in developmental psychology, creativity researchers began to emphasize the need to move beyond a psychological study of the individual creator. Among creativity researchers, this recent development is often attributed to an article published by Mike Csikszentmihalyi in 1988, in which he proposed the "systems view" of creativity. The creative system is a social system that includes three elements: the *individual*, the social institution or *field*, and the cultural symbol system or *domain* (p. 325). This tripartite model was also used by Howard Gardner in a chapter in the same 1988 volume, and he has drawn on it heavily in several books about creativity (e.g., Gardner, 1993). Rogoff's first book appeared in 1990, soon after the 1988 statements of the systems model by Csikszentmihalyi and Gardner.

There are close connections between socioculturalism and contemporary creativity theory; it is interesting that the shift from an individual to a social perspective occurred almost simultaneously in both developmental psychology and in creativity theory. The full story of this shift is a task for the history of ideas and is beyond the scope of this chapter. However, both Csikszentmihalyi and Gardner developed their socially oriented theories of creativity while in interdisciplinary institutional settings that placed them in close contact with both cultural anthropologists and developmental psychologists; Csikszentmihalyi was in the Committee on Human Development at the University of Chicago, where the cultural psychologist Richard Shweder was based, and Gardner was based in the Harvard Graduate School of Education's Department of Human Development, with the cultural anthropologist Robert Levine. Shweder and Levine were both closely associated with the socioculturalists during this time.

Thus, at about the same time, both developmental psychology and creativity research shifted from a purely individualistic level of analysis to increasingly incorporate a social level of analysis. Many creativity researchers now focus on how individual and social factors combine during the creative process (cf. John-Steiner, 1993, p. 103). This requires the researcher to decide on an appropriate level of analysis for the phenomenon. If both individual and social levels are involved, what is the nature of the relationships and causal connections between these levels? Are there similar developmental processes at both levels of analysis? In fact, these are long-standing issues in sociological theory. Particularly in the last two decades, theorists of the *micro-macro link* have attempted to reconcile the reductionism of methodological individualism and various antireductionisms such as sociological realism and sociological holism (Sawyer, 2001b).[11]

The failure to explicitly address these sociological considerations has led to lacunae in socially-oriented creativity theories: The exact nature of the individual-social relationship is not fully elaborated, and the ontological status of the social is not directly addressed (Sawyer, 2001b, 2002a). These issues are widely debated among socioculturalists but remain unresolved. Fleck (1935/1979) said that a thought style "constrains the individual by determining 'what can be thought in no other way'" (p. 99), using Durkheimian language regarding social facts; but psychologists who study creativity are, perhaps by style and nature, averse to formulations that explicitly state that the individual is constrained by social forces.

Throughout the history of sociology, and in several influential contemporary theories, the micro-macro link has been conceived of as a relation of emergence. Social properties are thought to emerge from the collective actions and interactions of the component individuals of the system (Sawyer, 2001b). In many of these theories of emergence, the social properties are thought to then take on some causal powers, such that individuals can be causally influenced by social properties, even though those social properties emerged from the actions of those same individuals. Such theories can provide a useful framework within which to conceptualize socially oriented theories of creativity.

CONCLUSION

The above review of emergentist elements in both creativity and developmental theory shows that studies of creativity could provide insights into developmental processes; likewise, developmental psychology could provide a valuable set of data and techniques for creativity researchers. Yet, in spite of these similarities, the fields are different in some fundamental ways.

Modern creativity research began as a branch of personality psychology, with Guilford's 1950 presidential address to the American Psychological Association (APA). This talk emphasized a factorial model of personality traits and focused on scientific and technological creativity. Guilford's comments seemed remarkably prescient when the Soviets beat the Americans into orbit with the launch of Sputnik in October 1957. The U.S. response was a mobilization in the schools to attempt to identify and nurture scientific talent and creativity. During the 1960s, a wide variety of metrics and tests were developed by creativity psychologists. These tests were meant to be applied to children in school contexts to determine who had the most creative potential, particularly in science and math. In the 1970s, in response to perceived weaknesses with the personality approach, psychologists increasingly began to examine creative processes.

The study of developmental processes has an older history, with its roots in the late nineteenth-century psychology of G. Stanley Hall and James Mark Baldwin. Developmental psychology continued with Piaget in Switzerland, Vygotsky in the Soviet Union, and Dewey in the United States. Developmental psychology grew rapidly after World War II and is now one of the largest nonmedical research sciences. For example, the major conference for developmentalists, the biannual Society for Research in Child Development (SRCD), typically draws well over 5,000 scholars, whereas there are so few creativity researchers that they have no annual conference.

Thus there is an obvious asymmetry between these two fields. Developmental psychology is a large field with a lot of resources, grant money, and institutional structures of support, whereas creativity research has never quite established itself as a research field in its own right. Creativity research does not yet have a textbook, indicating that it has not yet become a mature specialty paradigm (Mullins, 1983). Job ads often specify their search for developmental psychologists, but I have never seen a job ad for a creativity researcher. Creativity researchers in psychology tend to study creativity as a secondary endeavor, making their livings by studying some other topic.

As a result of this asymmetry, it is perhaps unavoidable that when creativity researchers and developmentalists talk shop, the developmentalists will have more to say—more experiments to report on, more theories to discuss, and more articulated theories. Yet developmentalists can also benefit from the unique focus of creativity researchers. The greatest potential benefit to developmentalists lies in conceptions of the developmental process—in the unresolved questions of how novelty occurs in development and how children make the constructive and creative transition to the next conceptual stage.

Piaget intended his genetic epistemology to apply to both ontogenetic development and to scientific development, and I have drawn several parallels between creative and developmental processes. These parallels have been debated before. In an afterword to Feldman's 1980 book, Gruber took issue with similar parallels drawn by Feldman (1974, 1980) that Feldman had partially attributed to Gruber's 1974 study of Darwin. Instead of claiming credit for the idea that creativity and development were similar processes, Gruber argued that there were many differences between creative insight and developmental stage transitions (Gruber, 1980). In response to Feldman's claim that Piaget's disequilibration model applies to both ordinary development and to creativity, Gruber countered by arguing that creativity is "purposeful work," whereas ordinary development is not (p. 177). Creative work does not result from a single step, but from "the concatenation and articulation of a complex set of interrelated moves" (p. 178). In this context, it is relevant to note that Gruber was generally opposed to creativity theories that focus on a single important moment of insight (Gruber, 1981).

Gruber (1980) argued that the creative process is guided by the creative person's sense of purpose. Piaget's disequilibrium model cannot account for this sort of directionality, because for Piaget, development proceeds without the influence of intentions toward remote goals (p. 178). The transition to the next stage is thus an unintended effect of the child doing something for another reason entirely (p. 179).

In his response, Feldman (1980) agreed that creativity and development are not identical; in fact, he proposed a "universal to unique" continuum to account for these differences. In response to Gruber's insistence that the creative process is directed, Feldman noted that creative individuals aren't always aware of their goals, and that much creative work proceeds without a final end product in sight.

The lesson of this debate is that the parallels between the processes of creativity and development are not simple and direct. There are many parallels, but these must be closely examined to ascertain that they are more than surface similarities, and to determine what, if any, substantive implications they have for research in either field. This book is a continuation of the debate between these two important scholars. And, like that debate, it is a continuation of themes and issues that were first addressed in the nineteenth century.

NOTES

While completing this chapter, I was supported in part by a National Academy of Education Spencer Postdoctoral Fellowship.

1. Creativity was a familiar topic in the Geneva school of Piaget's era. Two of Piaget's predecessors in Geneva, Claparède and Flournoy, collaborated on one of the first studies of creativity, published in 1902 and 1904 (see Hadamard, 1945, pp. 8, 137). De Saussure was also concerned with these issues (see Hadamard, 1945, pp. 128, 131).

2. Morss (1990) has documented the influence of these and other non-Darwinian evolutionary concepts on the key founders of developmental psychology, including Hall, Baldwin, Freud, Piaget, and Werner.

3. Beilin (1971) argued that Piaget's emergentism was essentially a maturationist and preformationist position, because the organism goes through the same stages re-

gardless of the external environment. He noted that a purely environmentalist position would allow for a wide range of developmental paths, varying with the environment, and would also allow *reversibility* (rejected by Piaget) if the environment changed in a certain way. In his response, Piaget (1971a) accepted that there were elements of maturationism in his position. However, he insisted that he was not preformationist because the stages emerged during development and were not present in the organism at birth.

4. For other nineteenth-century precedents, see Campbell, 1960, pp. 385–387.

5. Wallas first applied the term *fringe consciousness* to creativity (1926, pp. 95–96); the term *fringe* is taken from William James (1890, Vol. 1, pp. 258–264; see Hadamard, 1945, p. 25).

6. Although all Piaget scholars have noted the relation to Kant, none of them have noted the connection to Durkheim's epistemology. This may be because Piaget himself only occasionally noted the influence of Durkheim (although see Piaget, 1952a, pp. 240–242; 1995, pp. 39–40). Durkheim (1912/1915) was the first to argue that Kantian a priori categories were constructed contingently in the individual (see Rawls, 1996); in his case, the categories derived from emergent social forms, whereas in Piaget's case, the categories emerged from organism-environment interaction.

7. See Morss, 1990, and Litowitz, 1999. For purposes of my argument, it is not necessary to determine the exact lineage of influence, because I have claimed that such ideas were widespread and deeply ingrained in nineteenth-century thought. There are competing hypotheses; this shared influence could derive from Darwin or Spencer (or, in the case of Piaget, Baldwin, who was influenced by Spencer). Freud's debt to Darwin has been documented by Kitcher (1992) and Ritvo (1990). Others have criticized the idea that Darwin was a significant influence on Piaget, instead attributing the biological influences to other nineteenth-century evolutionary theorists such as Spencer (Ghiselin, 1986).

8. Note however that Piaget clarified that his stages were described in terms of overall structures, whereas Freud's were in terms of dominant characteristics, such that all of the characteristics exist at all stages (Piaget, 1971b, p. 2).

9. For an exploration of Vygotsky's writings on creativity, see Moran and John-Steiner, this volume.

10. Rothenberg's (1979) psychoanalytic theory of "homospatial thinking" also seems influenced by associationism; see p. 27.

11. Socioculturalists often attribute micro-macro thinking to the Soviet Marxian psychologist Lev Vygotsky. However, Vygotsky represents only one figure in a long sociological tradition of thinking about micro-macro relations; in this broader view, his theories are not qualitatively different from those of Marx. Vygotsky has not played any role in contemporary sociological theory, although Marx remains indirectly relevant, through the practice theories of Giddens and Bourdieu.

REFERENCES

Alibali, M. W., & Goldin-Meadow, S. (1993). Gesture-speech mismatch and mechanisms of learning: What the hands reveal about a child's state of mind. *Cognitive Psychology, 25,* 468–523.

Arieti, S. (1976). *Creativity: The magic synthesis.* New York: Basic Books.

Azmitia, M. (1998). Dissolving boundaries between collective and individual representations: A welcome contribution to developmental psychology. *Human Development, 41,* 239–244.

Bain, A. (1977). *The senses and the intellect.* Washington, DC: University Publications of America. (Reprint of 1855 edition published by John W. Parker and Son, London)

Barron, F., & Harrington, D. M. (1981). Creativity, intelligence, and personality. *Annual Review of Psychology, 32,* 439–476.

Beilin, H. (1971). Developmental stages and developmental processes. In D. R. Green, M. P. Ford, & G. B. Flamer (Eds.), *Measurement and Piaget* (pp. 172–189). New York: McGraw-Hill.

Boden, M. (1991). *The creative mind: Myths and mechanisms.* New York: Basic Books.

Brent, S. B. (1978). Individual specialization, collective adaptation and rate of environmental change. *Human Development, 21,* 21–33.

Broad, C. D. (1925). *The mind and its place in nature.* New York: Harcourt, Brace.

Bruner, J. (1983). *Child's talk: Learning to use language.* New York: Norton.

Callanan, M. A. (1999). Culture, cognition, and biology: Contexts for the developing mind. *Human Development, 42,* 149–158.

Campbell, D. T. (1960). Blind variation and selective retention in scientific discovery. *Psychological Review, 67,* 380–400.

Carey, S. (1986). Cognitive science and science education. *American Psychologist, 41*(10), 1123–1130.

Case, R. (1985). *Intellectual development: Birth to adulthood.* Orlando, FL: Academic Press.

Cole, M. (1996). *Cultural psychology: A once and future discipline.* Cambridge, MA: Harvard University Press.

Cole, M., & Scribner, S. (1978). Introduction. In M. Cole, V. John-Steiner, S. Scribner, & E. Souberman (Eds.), *Mind in society: The development of higher psychological processes* (pp. 1–14). Cambridge, MA: Harvard University Press.

Comte, A. (1854). *The positive philosophy of Auguste Comte* (Harriet Martineau, Trans.). New York: D. Appleton. (Original work published in six volumes, in French, from 1830 to 1842.)

Csikszentmihalyi, M. (1988a). Motivation and creativity: Toward a synthesis of structural and energistic approaches to cognition. *New Ideas in Psychology, 6*(2), 159–176.

Csikszentmihalyi, M. (1988b). Society, culture, and person: A systems view of creativity. In R. J. Sternberg (Ed.), *The nature of creativity* (pp. 325–339). New York: Cambridge University Press.

Csikszentmihalyi, M. (1993). *The evolving self: A psychology for the third millennium.* New York: HarperCollins.

Csikszentmihalyi, M., & Sawyer, R. K. (1995). Creative insight: The social dimension of a solitary moment. In R. J. Sternberg & J. E. Davidson (Eds.), *The nature of insight* (pp. 329–363). Cambridge: MIT Press.

Csikszentmihalyi, M. (1996). *Creativity: Flow and the psychology of discovery and invention.* New York: HarperCollins.

Dennett, D. (1995). *Darwin's dangerous idea: Evolution and the meanings of life.* New York: Simon & Schuster.

Dunbar, K. (1995). How scientists really reason: Scientific reasoning in real-world laboratories. In R. J. Sternberg & J. E. Davidson (Eds.), *The nature of insight* (pp. 365–395). Cambridge: MIT Press.

Durkheim, E. (1915). *The elementary forms of the religious life.* New York: Free Press. (Original work published as *Les Formes élémentaires de la vie religieuse: le système totémique en Australie,* Paris: Alcan, 1912)

Elman, J. L., Bates, E. A., Johnson, M. H., Karmiloff-Smith, A., Parisi, D., & Plunkett, K. (1996). *Rethinking innateness: A connectionist perspective on development.* Cambridge: MIT Press.

Feldman, D. H. (1974). Universal to unique. In S. Rosner & L. E. Abt (Eds.), *Essays in creativity* (pp. 45–85). Croton-on-Hudson, NY: North River Press.

Feldman, D. H. (1980). *Beyond universals in cognitive development.* Norwood, NJ: Ablex.

Feldman, D. H. (1986). *Nature's gambit: Child prodigies and the development of human potential.* New York: Basic Books.

Flavell, J. H. (1963). *The developmental psychology of Jean Piaget.* Princeton, NJ: D. Van Nostrand.

Flavell, J. H., & Draguns, J. (1957). A microgenetic approach to perception and thought. *Psychological Bulletin, 54*(3), 197–217.

Fleck, L. (1979). *Genesis and development of a scientific fact.* Chicago: University of Chicago. (Original work published as *Entstehung und Entwicklung einer wissenschaftlichen Tatsache: Einfürung in die Lehre vom Denkstil und Denkkollektiv,* Basel: Benno Schwabe, 1935)

Freud, S. (1989). Creative writers and day-dreaming. In P. Gay (Ed.), *The Freud reader* (pp. 436–443). New York: Norton. (Original work published 1907)

Freud, S. (1966). *Introductory lectures on psycho-analysis.* New York: Norton. (Paper originally presented December 6, 1907; original work published 1917)

Gardner, H. (1983). *Frames of mind: The theory of multiple intelligences.* New York: Basic Books.

Gardner, H. (1993). *Creating minds.* New York: Basic Books.

Getzels, J. W., & Csikszentmihalyi, M. (1976). *The creative vision.* New York: Wiley.

Ghiselin, M. T. (1986). The assimilation of Darwinism in developmental psychology. *Human Development, 29,* 12–21.

Giddens, A. (1970). Durkheim as a review critic. *Sociological Review, 18,* 171–196.

Gordon, W. J. J. (1961). *Synectics: The development of creative capacity.* New York: Harper.

Gruber, H. E. (1974). *Darwin on man: A psychological study of scientific creativity.* Chicago: University of Chicago.

Gruber, H. E. (1980). Afterword. In D. H. Feldman, *Beyond universals in cognitive development* (pp. 175–180). Norwood, NJ: Ablex.

Gruber, H. E. (1988). The evolving systems approach to creative work. *Creativity Research Journal, 1,* 27–51.

Gruber, H. E., & Vonèche, J. J. (1977). Introduction. In H. E. Gruber & J. J. Vonèche (Eds.), *The essential Piaget* (pp. xvii–xl). New York: Basic Books.

Guilford, J. P. (1950). Creativity. *The American Psychologist, 5*(9), 444–454.

Guilford, J. P. (1967). *The nature of human intelligence*. New York: McGraw-Hill.

Hadamard, J. (1945). *The psychology of invention in the mathematical field*. Princeton, NJ: Princeton University Press.

Helmholtz, H. von. (1971). An autobiographical sketch: An address delivered on the occasion of his Jubilee in Berlin, 1891. In R. Kahl (Ed.), *Selected writings of Hermann von Helmholtz* (pp. 466–478). Middletown, CT: Wesleyan University Press.

Hutchins, E. (1995). *Cognition in the wild*. Cambridge: MIT Press.

Jacques, E. (1965). Death and the mid-life crisis. *International Journal of Psychoanalysis, 46,* 502–515.

James, W. (1890). *The principles of psychology*. New York: H. Holt.

John-Steiner, V. (1985). *Notebooks of the mind: Explorations of thinking*. Albuquerque: University of New Mexico Press.

John-Steiner, V. (1993). Creative lives, creative tensions. *Creativity Research Journal, 5*(1), 99–108.

John-Steiner, V. (2000). *Creative collaboration*. New York: Oxford University Press.

Johnson-Laird, P. N. (1987). Reasoning, imagining, and creating. *Bulletin of the British Psychological Society, 40,* 121–129.

Kim, J. (1992). "Downward causation" in emergentism and nonreductive physicalism. In A. Beckermann, H. Flohr, & J. Kim (Eds.), *Emergence or reduction? Essays on the prospects of nonreductive physicalism* (pp. 119–138). New York: Walter de Gruyter.

Kitchener, R. F. (1985). Holistic structuralism, elementarism and Piaget's theory of "relationism." *Human Development, 28,* 281–294.

Kitcher, P. (1992). *Freud's dream: A complete interdisciplinary science of mind*. Cambridge: MIT Press.

Klahr, D. (1982). Nonmonotone assessment of monotone development: An information processing analysis. In S. Strauss (Ed.), *U-shaped behavioral growth* (pp. 63–86). New York: Academic Press.

Klahr, D. (2000). *Exploring science: The cognition and development of discovery processes*. Cambridge: MIT Press.

Klahr, D., & Simon, H. A. (1999). Studies of scientific discovery: Complementary approaches and convergent findings. *Psychological Bulletin, 125*(5), 524–543.

Kris, E. (1952). *Psychoanalytic explorations in art*. New York: International Universities Press.

Kuhn, D. (1989). Children and adults as intuitive scientists. *Psychological Review, 96,* 674–689.

Kuhn, D. (1995). Microgenetic study of change: What has it told us? *Psychological Science, 6,* 133–139.

Kuhn, T. S. (1960). *The structure of scientific revolutions*. Cambridge: MIT Press.

Larey, T. S., & Paulus, P. B. (1999). Group preference and convergent tendencies in small groups: A content analysis of group brainstorming performance. *Creativity Research Journal, 12*(3), 175–184.

Lawrence, J. A., & Valsiner, J. (1993). Conceptual roots of internalization: From transmission to transformation. *Human Development, 36,* 150–167.

Litowitz, B. E. (1999). Freud and Piaget: *Une fois de plus. Genetic Epistemologist, 27*(4). Retrieved January 18, 2003, from http://www.piaget.org/GE/1999/GE-27-4.html

Lowenfeld, V., & Brittain, W. L. (1987). *Creative and mental growth* (8th ed.). Upper Saddle River, NJ: Prentice Hall.

Martindale, C. (1990). *The clockwork muse: The predictability of artistic change.* New York: Basic Books.

McDougall, W. (1929). *Modern materialism and emergent evolution.* London: Methuen.

McLaughlin, B. P. (1992). The rise and fall of British emergentism. In A. Beckermann, H. Flohr, & J. Kim (Eds.), *Emergence or reduction? Essays on the prospects of nonreductive physicalism* (pp. 49–93). Berlin: Walter de Gruyter.

Mednick, S. A. (1962). The associative basis of the creative process. *Psychological Review, 69*(3), 220–232.

Mednick, S. A., & Mednick, M. T. (1965). *The associative basis of the creative process* (Cooperative Research Project No. 1073). Ann Arbor: University of Michigan.

Messerly, J. G. (1996). *Piaget's conception of evolution: Beyond Darwin and Lamarck.* Lanham, MD: Rowman & Littlefield.

Morgan, C. L. (1923). *Emergent evolution.* London: Williams and Norgate. (Originally presented as the 1922 Gifford Lectures at the University of St. Andrews, Scotland)

Morgan, C. L. (1933). *The emergence of novelty.* London: Williams & Norgate.

Morss, J. R. (1990). *The biologising of childhood: Developmental psychology and the Darwinian myth.* Hillsdale, NJ: Erlbaum.

Mullins, N. C. (1983). Theories and theory groups revisited. In R. Collins (Ed.), *Sociological theory 1983* (pp. 319–337). San Francisco: Jossey-Bass.

Newell, A., & Simon, H. A. (1972). *Human problem solving.* Englewood Cliffs, NJ: Prentice Hall.

Osborn, A. F. (1953). *Applied imagination.* Buffalo, NY: Creative Education Foundation Press.

Patrick, C. (1937). Creative thought in artists. *Journal of Psychology, 4*, 35–73.

Piaget, J. (1950). *Introduction a' l'épistémologie génétique.* Paris: Presses Universitaires de France.

Piaget, J. (1952a). Jean Piaget. In E. G. Boring, H. S. Langfeld, H. Werner, & R. M. Yerkes (Eds.), *A history of psychology in autobiography* (pp. 237–256). Worcester, MA: Clark University Press.

Piaget, J. (1952b). *The origins of intelligence in children.* New York: International Universities Press. (Original work published as *La naissance d'intelligence chez l'enfant*, Neuchâtel, France: Delachaux & Niestlé, 1936)

Piaget, J. (1955). *The language and thought of the child* (M. Gabain, Trans.). Cleveland: World Publishing Company. (Original work published as *Le langage et la pensée chez l'enfant*, Neuchâtel, France: Delachaux & Niestlé, 1923)

Piaget, J. (1962). *Play, dreams, and imitation in childhood* (C. Gattegno & F. M. Hodgson, Trans.). New York: Norton and Company. (Original work published as *La formation du symbole chez l'enfant: Imitation, jeu et rêve, image et représentation*, Neuchâtel: Delachaux & Niestlé, 1945)

Piaget, J. (1967). Les tendances communes aux "Épistémologies internes" des diverses sciences. In J. Piaget (Ed.), *Logique et connaissance scientifique* (pp. 1226–1271). Paris: Éditions Gallimard.

Piaget, J. (1970). *Structuralism*. New York: Basic Books. (Original work published 1968)

Piaget, J. (1971a). Comment on Beilin's paper. In D. R. Green, M. P. Ford, & G. B. Flamer (Eds.), *Measurement and Piaget* (pp. 192–194). New York: McGraw-Hill.

Piaget, J. (1971b). The theory of stages in cognitive development. In D. R. Green, M. P. Ford, & G. B. Flamer (Eds.), *Measurement and Piaget* (pp. 1–11). New York: McGraw-Hill.

Piaget, J. (1972). *The principles of genetic epistemology*. New York: Basic Books. (Original work published as *L'Épistémologie génétique*, Paris: Presses Universitaires de France, 1970)

Piaget, J. (1995). *Sociological studies*. New York: Routledge.

Poincaré, H. (1982). *The foundations of science*. Washington, DC: University Press of America. (Original work published 1913)

Rawls, A. W. (1996). Durkheim's epistemology: The neglected argument. *American Journal of Sociology, 102*(2), 430–482.

Ritvo, L. B. (1990). *Darwin's influence on Freud: A tale of two sciences*. New Haven, CT: Yale University Press.

Rogoff, B. (1990). *Apprenticeship in thinking: Cognitive development in social context*. New York: Oxford University Press.

Rogoff, B. (1998). Cognition as a collaborative process. In D. Kuhn & R. S. Siegler (Eds.), *Handbook of child psychology, 5th edition, Volume 2: Cognition, perception, and language* (pp. 679–744). New York: Wiley.

Rossman, J. (1964). *Industrial creativity: The psychology of the inventor*. New Hyde Park, NY: University Books. (Original work published 1931)

Rothenberg, A. (1979). *The emerging goddess: The creative process in art, science, and other fields*. Chicago: University of Chicago Press.

Runco, M. A. (1993). *Critical creative thought*. Paper presented at the Wallace Symposium, University of Kansas, Lawrence, May 1993.

Sawyer, R. K. (1995). Creativity as mediated action: A comparison of improvisational performance and product creativity. *Mind, Culture, and Activity, 2,* 172–191.

Sawyer, R. K. (1997). *Pretend play as improvisation: Conversation in the preschool classroom*. Mahwah, NJ: Erlbaum.

Sawyer, R. K. (1999). The emergence of creativity. *Philosophical Psychology, 12*(4), 447–469.

Sawyer, R. K. (2001a). *Creating conversations: Improvisation in everyday discourse*. Cresskill, NJ: Hampton Press.

Sawyer, R. K. (2001b). Emergence in sociology: Contemporary philosophy of mind and some implications for sociological theory. *American Journal of Sociology, 107,* 551–585.

Sawyer, R. K. (2002a). Emergence in psychology: Lessons from the history of nonreductionist science. *Human Development, 45,* 2–28.

Sawyer, R. K. (2002b). Evaluative processes during group improvisational performance. In M. A. Runco (Ed.), *Critical creative processes* (pp. 303–327). Cresskill, NJ: Hampton Press.

Sawyer, R. K. (2002c). Unresolved tensions in sociocultural theory: Analogies with contemporary sociological debates. *Culture & Psychology, 8*(3), 283–305.

Sawyer, R. K. (2003). *Improvised dialogues: Emergence and creativity in conversation.* Westport, CT: Greenwood.

Siegler, R. S. (1996). *Emerging minds: The process of change in children's thinking.* New York: Oxford University Press.

Siegler, R. S. (1998). *Children's thinking* (3rd ed.). Upper Saddle River, NJ: Prentice Hall.

Simon, T. J., & Halford, G. S. (Eds.). (1995). *Developing cognitive competence: New approaches to process modeling.* Hillsdale, NJ: Erlbaum.

Simonton, D. K. (1988). *Scientific genius: A psychology of science.* New York: Cambridge University Press.

Sternberg, R. J. (Ed.). (1988). *The nature of creativity.* New York: Cambridge University Press.

Sulloway, F. J. (1979). *Freud, biologist of the mind: Beyond the psychoanalytic legacy.* New York: Basic Books.

Taylor, C. (1985). What is involved in a genetic psychology? In C. Taylor (Ed.), *Human agency and language* (pp. 139–163). New York: Cambridge University Press.

Taylor, D. W., Berry, P. C., & Block, C. H. (1958). Does group participation when using brainstorming facilitate or inhibit creative thinking? *Administrative Science Quarterly, 3*(1), 23–47.

Teller, P. (1992). A contemporary look at emergence. In A. Beckermann, H. Flohr, & J. Kim (Eds.), *Emergence or reduction? Essays on the prospects of nonreductive physicalism* (pp. 139–153). Berlin: Walter de Gruyter.

van der Veer, R. (1996). Structure and development: Reflections by Vygotsky. In A. Tryphon & J. Vonèche (Eds.), *Piaget-Vygotsky: The social genesis of thought* (pp. 45–56). Hove, UK: Psychology Press.

Vinacke, W. E. (1952). *The psychology of thinking.* New York: McGraw-Hill.

Vygotsky, L. S. (1971). *The psychology of art* (Scripta Technica, Inc., Trans.). Cambridge: MIT Press. (Original work published as *Psikhologiia iskusstva,* 1965)

Vygotsky, L. S. (1978). *Mind in society: The development of higher psychological processes* (M. Cole, V. John-Steiner, S. Scribner, & E. Souberman, Eds.). Cambridge, MA: Harvard University Press.

Wallas, G. (1926). *The art of thought.* New York: Harcourt, Brace, & World.

Werner, H. (1940). *Comparative psychology of mental development.* New York: Harper & Brothers.

Wertheimer, M. (1945). *Productive thinking.* New York: Harper & Brothers.

Wertsch, J. V. (1985). Introduction. In J. V. Wertsch (Ed.), *Culture, communication, and cognition: Vygotskian perspectives* (pp. 1–18). New York: Cambridge University Press.

Wertsch, J. V. (1993). Commentary. *Human Development, 36,* 168–171.

Wertsch, J. V. (1998). *Mind as action.* New York: Oxford University Press.

Wertsch, J. V., & Stone, C. A. (1978). Microgenesis as a tool for developmental analysis. *Quarterly Newsletter of the Laboratory for Comparative Human Cognition, 1*(1), 8–10.

Whitehead, A. N. (1926). *Science and the modern world*. New York: Macmillan.

Wimsatt, W. C. (1997). Aggregativity: Reductive heuristics for finding emergence. *Philosophy of Science, 64*(Proceedings), S372–S384.

Zinchenko, V. P., & Gordon, V. M. (1979). Methodological problems in the psychological analysis of activity. In J. V. Wertsch (Ed.), *The concept of activity in Soviet psychology* (pp. 72–133). Armonk, NY: M. E. Sharpe.

CHAPTER TWO

Creativity in the Making

Vygotsky's Contemporary Contribution to the Dialectic of Development and Creativity

Seana Moran and Vera John-Steiner

In representing creativity as a social as well as an individual process, L. S. Vygotsky introduced some of the most critical new notions that characterize current systems approaches. Although his contributions are best known in developmental psychology and education, his ideas regarding the growth of creative imagination, the changing impacts of creative activities on individuals over their life spans, and how creativity works in expanding individual and cultural meaning are timely to creativity studies.

Vygotsky died of tuberculosis at age 38, leaving many of his manuscripts unpublished. In addition, his writings were suppressed for more than 20 years in the Soviet Union under Stalin and were further neglected in the West as a consequence of the Cold War. But once his work became more broadly available with the publication of *Thought and Language* (1934/1962), it was acknowledged as an important contribution to the cognitive revolution.

Vygotsky's career was framed by work on creativity, starting with his study of the aesthetic reaction in literary works, *The Psychology of Art* (1965/1971), which was accepted as his dissertation in 1925 but was not published during his lifetime. In this early work, he first formulated his important principle that creative work is profoundly social: "Art is the social within us, and even if its action is performed by a single individual it does not mean that its essence is individual. . . . Art is the social technique of emotion, a tool of society which brings the most intimate and personal aspects of our being into the circle of social life. . . . It would be more correct to say that emotion becomes personal when every one of us experiences a work of art: It becomes personal without ceasing to be social" (p. 249).

In these words, Vygotsky captured a powerful synthesis between aspects of experience that are usually separated, issues he returned to later in his career. For example, in a short paper written a couple of years before he died, "On the Problem of the Psychology of the Actor's Creative Work" (1936/1999a), he revisited these issues of aesthetics, experience, and emotion as social phenomena. Whereas his work on creativity is fragmentary, when placed in the broader framework of his theoretical approach, it provides a challenging point of view, which has been largely ignored by both creativity and cultural-historical theorists.

In this chapter, we propose that Vygotsky's work provides an opportunity to both focus and expand the scope of creativity research. In applying his dialectical approach to this domain, he viewed the creative process as interaction, tension, transformation, and synthesis over the parallel timescales of the creative act, the creative life, and historical cultural development. Rather than studying structures that already have been completed and stabilized, he was interested in the origins and interrelationship of functions. In this emphasis on the transformational construction of the new, we find a powerful commonality between Vygotsky's theoretical perspective and emerging complex systems approaches that have arisen with computer modeling (Van Geert, 1994). Vygotsky's approach also shares some important features with Csikszentmihalyi's (1988) systems model, as they both recognize the critical role of social processes in creativity. In stressing the transformation of interpersonal activities into intrapersonal ones, Vygotsky provided the dynamic mechanisms for how the three nodes of Csikszentmihalyi's model—the individual, the domain, and the field—affect each other. In addition, the value of an expanded Vygotskian theory of creativity is reflected in adding time to the multidirectional connections between the individual's mind, the symbolic knowledge base of the domain, and the social and cultural processes of the field.

Therefore, although more than 70 years old, Vygotsky's work is contemporary. His ideas are particularly appropriate for this Counterpoints volume because they present a sophisticated and dynamic understanding of the interweaving of individual and social processes in creative endeavors. He both complements and supports some other approaches presented in this volume, particularly in his emphasis on the development of new ideas, artworks, and scientific undertakings as emergent social and psychological functional systems. In order to argue this position more systematically, we approach Vygotskian and contemporary Western theories dialectically, culminating in an integration that can serve as a springboard for future research. We share Vygotsky's view that creativity is fundamental to the development of all individuals, and through the study of the interweaving of creativity and development, people's true natures are revealed.

THE DIALECTIC OF DEVELOPMENT AND CREATIVITY

Development never ends its creative work.
    LEV VYGOTSKY, "The Problem of Age"

We argue that development and creativity are dialectically interrelated processes. Vygotsky conceived of developmental and creative processes as *internalization* or appropriation of cultural tools and social interaction. Internalization is not just copying but rather a transformation or reorganization of incoming information and mental structures based on the individual's characteristics and existing knowledge. He mostly studied internalization in childhood, when it is most apparent, although it is a significant aspect of lifelong learning and development. The dynamic form that results from this process is the individual personality—the embodied social mind—composed of interfunctional psychological systems. A personality is a characteristic way of behaving that constrains future activity.

What is usually referred to as *creativity* in Western psychology involves *externalization* in Vygotsky's and his followers' thinking. Externalization is the construction and synthesis of emotion-based meanings and cognitive symbols. Once expressed, these meanings and symbols are embodied in cultural artifacts—creative products—that endure over time to be used by future generations. The dynamic constructions that result from externalization are materialized meanings, composed of shared ideas, beliefs, knowledge, emotions, and culture.

Therefore, the two social processes, internalization and externalization, and the two symbol-based forms, personality and culture, are in dialectical tension with each other. This tension provides fertile ground for the growth of new ideas and creative products. Internalization is not the grafting of a culture onto a personality but an engagement with existing cultural resources, which leads to newly realized aspects of the self. Externalization is the basis for domain-changing creative transformations that expand the culture. This internal/external movement becomes cyclical, connecting past to future, and the results of these processes over time contribute to a community's history and culture. Creativity, then, depends on development, and development depends on creativity.

The two are interdependent. Figure 2.1 provides a visual map of this relationship. It is a schematic representation of these complex and cyclical connections and serves as a signpost for our own thinking.

In this chapter, we provide a brief review of Vygotsky's cultural-historical theory and methodology, then show how Vygotsky applied his general developmental framework to the formation of the creative imagination. We discuss how Vygotsky conceptualized the creative process in terms of the sharing of emotion and the development of meaning, and how the experience of this cycle of creative development can lead to commitment and a creative personality. Then we portray the important role of historical time in Vygotsky's notions of creativity. We conclude by expanding Vygotsky's approach to collaborations and linking some of the implications of Vygotsky's approach to possible future directions in creativity research.

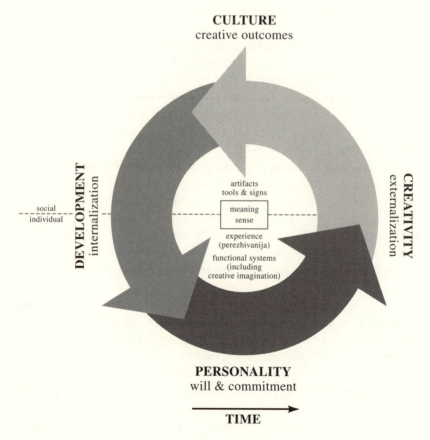

FIGURE 2.1. A visual representation of Vygotsky's dialectical conception of development and creativity

VYGOTSKY'S DEVELOPMENTAL FRAMEWORK

To study something historically means to study it in the process of
change. . . . To encompass in research the process of a given thing's
development in all its phases and changes—from birth to death—
fundamentally means to discover its nature.

LEV VYGOTSKY, *Mind in Society*

Vygotsky's framework is referred to as cultural-historical theory. Within this
theory, he emphasized that development is a social process, mediated through
signs and tools, that forms and integrates psychological functional systems that
change over time. This path is not necessarily linear or smooth: "Our concept of
development implies a rejection of the frequently held view that cognitive development results from the gradual accumulation of separate changes. We believe that child development is a complex dialectical process characterized by
periodicity, unevenness in the development of different functions, metamor-
phosis or qualitative transformation of one form into the other, intertwining of
external and internal factors, and adaptive processes that overcome impedi-
ments that the child encounters" (Vygotsky, 1978, p. 73).

Learning and development are not processes undertaken alone: A person
"represents the totality of social relations internalized and made into functions
of the individual and forms of his structure" (Vygotsky, 1960/1997b, p. 106).
They proceed through the ongoing dialectical tensions and transformations of
social processes. Children's past achievements and new cultural symbolic capacities become the springboard for their future growth. Vygotsky did not sub-
scribe to the Cartesian dichotomies underlying most Western psychological research. Instead, Vygotsky focused on the *relationships* between phenomena and
the *processes* by which those relationships change over time. His main interest
lay in origins, turning points, syntheses, transformations, and interactions of social, psychological, and cultural phenomena.

A central argument of Vygotsky's theory is that all mental functions are first
experienced socially. People come to know about the world through transforming the information they receive from the speech and action of others; they co-
construct knowledge based on these experiences. One of Vygotsky's best-known
concepts is the zone of proximal development, through which a less skilled person learns in collaboration with more skilled individuals. In fact, according to
Vygotsky (1931/1998b), it is only through knowing others that one comes to
know oneself: "If the thought of the child did not meet with the thoughts of others, the child would never become conscious of himself" (p. 72). Vygotsky's genetic law of development states that internalized joint activity underlies the development of psychological systems. Individuals synthesize diverse influences,
which become the basis for their new concepts and cognitive strategies.

This internalization is culturally mediated: "The central fact of our psychology is the fact of mediation" (Vygotsky, 1968/1997f, p. 138). Vygotsky discussed two primary forms of mediation: tools and signs. Tools make changes in external objects, whereas signs make changes in mental processes. He also mentioned artifacts, which are objects that contain past knowledge and experience. As children, we quickly learn to interact with the world indirectly through different sign systems, especially through language. According to Vygotsky, this ability forms the basis for the development of higher mental functions. Higher mental functions are based in culture; they are not aggregates of more elementary, biological functions, but complex wholes that must be studied at their own level of analysis: "Culture creates special forms of behavior, it modifies the activity of mental functions, it constructs new superstructures in the developing system of human behavior" (Vygotsky, 1960/1997b, p. 18). Thus, the focus of Vygotsky's study is the means, the functions, and the processes of becoming within a social, cultural milieu (Vygotsky, 1960/1997b).

These higher mental functions are never completed, but rather continue to develop and interact with other higher mental functions as the child grows into adolescence and adulthood. Through these interactions, a person forms psychological functional systems, or "complex connections that develop between different functions" (Vygotsky, 1982/1997e, p. 92). What develops, then, are not just the functions themselves, but the relationships between them. This development leads to increased flexibility and complexity of thought: "Each step in the child's achievement of a more profound penetration of reality is linked with his continued liberation from earlier, more primitive forms of cognition" (Vygotsky, 1960/1987, p. 349). At first, children need external objects and other people to help regulate their behavior, but later can do so using only internal, symbolic, psychological functions (Vygotsky, 1978, p. 73).

Change over time is key to Vygotsky's framework. He viewed the human mind dynamically, whether within particular activities, over a person's life span, or within a changing social and cultural milieu. These three timescales—social activity, individual life, and history—represent parallel interacting levels at which both development and creativity operate. Furthermore, development and creativity are future oriented. Through the transformation of social interaction and the use of cultural tools and signs, people free themselves from the constraints of the present environment and take control of their own futures. Thus, past experience influences but does not determine what people do; in reorganizing the known, individuals anticipate future needs and goals. In this way, they can be simultaneously experts—based on past experience—and novices in planning the future. There is no end to development: It is an open system. Thus, development is not an unfolding of maturational processes, but the continual reformation of complex relationships that arise over time as a result of the interdependence of the individual and the social world.

VYGOTSKY'S METHODOLOGY

The search for method becomes one of the most important problems
of the entire enterprise of understanding the uniquely human forms of
psychological activity. In this case, the method is simultaneously prerequisite and product, the tool and the result of the study.

LEV VYGOTSKY, *Mind in Society*

The study of change was the primary objective of Vygotskian methodology. To accomplish this objective, Vygotsky (1978) proposed that "the aim of psychological analysis is . . . (1) process analysis as opposed to object analysis; (2) analysis that reveals real, causal or dynamic relations as opposed to enumerations of a process's outer features, that is, explanatory, not descriptive analysis; and (3) developmental analysis that returns to the source and reconstructs all the points in the development of a given structure" (p. 65). One of the experimental approaches devised by Vygotsky was the method of double stimulation. Its aim was to tease apart the developmental process, "to alter the automatic, mechanized, fossilized character of the higher forms of behavior and to turn it back to its source" (Vygotsky, 1978, p. 64). He achieved this objective by first presenting a simple stimulus, then presenting a second (mediating) stimulus whose role was to help participants organize their responses. In this way, he discovered how children create their own mediating signs to help them successfully master certain operations; he also discovered how children acquire word meanings. Although this method was simple, it provided a way to provoke changes that occur right "before one's eyes" (Vygotsky, 1978, p. 61). Even though Vygotsky used traditional experimental methods, he discovered how children invent their own mediational methods. It is this aspect of his thinking that prepared the way for studies of innovative and creative behaviors by Vygotskian scholars (Smolucha, 1992).

In an examination of cross-cultural variations in thinking and reasoning, Vygotsky and his colleague, Alexander Luria, planned an ambitious study in Central Asia. The motivation for such an inquiry drew from their desire to study cognition as it occurs in changing sociocultural settings rather than separated from life in an experimental laboratory. Vygotsky was too ill to join the expedition, so Luria conducted research on problem solving, self-awareness, and reasoning. In studying imagination, he found that isolated farmers remained rooted in their practical experience, whereas those with some education were ready for new expressions of knowledge while still limiting their reliance on imagined situations (Luria, 1976, pp. 134–143). More contemporary studies of creativity among nonindustrial people describe many further examples of sustained innovation and the construction of the new (Cole, 1996; Greenfield, in press; Scribner, 1977).

Vygotsky (1960/1997b) emphasized connections rather than separation and simplification. His methods, therefore, aimed to study creativity and development *in the making* by "converting thing into movement, fossil into process" (p. 71). In this way, he could examine the developmental interrelationships of the social environment, humanly crafted artifacts, and individual cognitive and emotional processes.

THE DEVELOPMENT OF THE CREATIVE IMAGINATION

Imagination is a transforming, creative activity directed from the concrete toward a new concrete . . . with the help of abstraction.
   LEV VYGOTSKY, "Imagination and Creativity in the Adolescent"

Based on this developmental framework and methodology, Vygotsky put forth a theory of how the creative imagination develops as a higher mental function, in two papers and a lecture: "Imagination and Creativity in Childhood" in 1930 (1930/1998c); "Imagination and Creativity in the Adolescent" in 1931 (1931/1998d); and "Imagination and Its Development in Childhood" in 1932 (1960/1987). Creative imagination introduces "something new into the flow of our impressions, the transformation of these impressions such that something new, an image that did not previously exist, emerges" (Vygotsky, 1960/1987, p. 339). Vygotsky asserted that creative imagination is necessary for effective functioning in society. That is, people with a less developed creative imagination cannot remove themselves from the immediate stimuli of the environment:

> We saw that the zero point of imagination . . . appears in the following way—the individual is in a state where he is unable to abstract himself from a concrete situation, unable to change it creatively, to regroup signs to free one's self from under its influence. (Vygotsky, 1931/1998d, p. 152)

The creative imagination makes people more adept at manipulating signs and psychological tools and, therefore, at adapting to their social environments (Vygotsky, 1960/1997b).

Vygotsky theorized that children first learn to create and manipulate symbols and signs during play. Then children's pretend play and object substitution become internalized as fantasy or imagination as inner speech develops. In adolescence, creative imagination results when imagination and thinking in concepts become conjoined, which, in adulthood, can mature into artistic and scientific creativity.

Childhood Play

By dragging a child into a topsy-turvy world, we help his intellect
work, because the child becomes interested in creating such a topsy-
turvy world for himself in order to become more effectively the master
of the laws governing the real world.

LEV VYGOTSKY, *The Psychology of Art*

Vygotsky thought that children first learn to create, manipulate, and give meaning to signs and symbols through play. Play also allows them to tease out relationships, try on and practice different roles, and exercise their growing capabilities (Vygotsky, 1984/1999b). As with other cultural behavior, pretend play
starts with social interaction with adults: Somebody first shows a child how a
banana can be a phone, or how a broom can be a dancing partner (Smolucha &
Smolucha, 1986). At first, children imitate what they have seen or heard or done
before. Over time and experience, they become more adventurous, as make-believe objects move further from their real-world characters. As children reach
school age, goals and rules become a focus of play, and play becomes an early
mechanism for self-mastery: "A child's greatest self-control occurs in play"
(Vygotsky, 1978, p. 99). In fact, through play, children can scaffold their own
learning, creating a zone of proximal development between their present level
of achievement and their more competent future selves. By practicing skills or
trying out ideas within a play situation, children become better able to handle
real situations (Sawyer, 1997).

Vygotsky's conception of play parallels that of Piaget, who saw play as a
symbolic capacity-building process that leads to creative imagination (Ayman-
Nolley, 1999). However, whereas Vygotsky asserted that imagination was internalized play developed in conjunction with others, Piaget (1962) suggested
that play was externalized imagination that spontaneously arises in playing
alone. Smolucha found some evidence to support both Vygotsky's theory and
Piaget's: Children do perform spontaneous object substitutions as early as 12
months, but most substitutions occur during their second year through pretend
play initiated by caregivers (Smolucha & Smolucha, 1986). Other researchers
also support Vygotsky's notion that play is associated with later creativity, especially with divergent thinking (Russ, Robins, & Christiano, 1999; Singer &
Singer, 1990). Most of these studies, however, are correlational and cognitive,
and they usually do not share Vygotsky's developmental perspective. Rather,
they tend to look at the co-occurrence of play and creativity only within a single
age group.

Adolescent Fantasy

No accurate cognition of reality is possible without a certain element of imagination, a certain flight from the immediate, concrete, solitary impression in which this reality is presented in the elementary acts of consciousness.

LEV VYGOTSKY, "Imagination and Its Development in Childhood"

Play becomes internalized as fantasy. Fantasy entails a new relationship between visual and verbal phenomena as well as concrete and abstract thought. An object no longer has to be present for children to consider it as part of their activities. Emotion-infused mental images and inner speech replace physical objects and actions as a child's focus of attention (Smolucha & Smolucha, 1986; Vygotsky, 1930/1998c). However, fantasy is not exclusively visual but can incorporate all the senses (Vygotsky, 1930/1998c).

During adolescence, two forms of fantasy develop: subjective and objective fantasy. These become woven together, through further development, in adult creativity. Subjective fantasy orients toward desire fulfillment and private inner life: "The adolescent, with the help of fantasy, illuminates and clarifies himself and turns his emotions, his tendencies into a creative image" (Vygotsky, 1931/1998d, p. 165). In fact, Vygotsky viewed subjective fantasy as a key force in personal transformation. Young people rely on it to shape and master their own emotions. Although Vygotsky criticized Freud's ideas regarding the relationship of wish fulfillment and creativity, Freud's influence on Vygotsky becomes apparent in his construct of subjective fantasy. Objective fantasy, on the other hand, is used in understanding and constructing external reality; its application contributes to cultural transformation. Through objective fantasy, adolescents, as well as adults, anticipate and plan their future behavior, helping to construct the culture of which they are a part (Vygotsky, 1930/1998c).

These two forms of fantasy are conjoined: "Objective expression is colored with bright emotional tones, but even subjective fantasies are frequently observed in the area of objective creativity" (Vygotsky, 1931/1998d, p. 165). Adolescents learn to balance these two kinds of fantasy; they become increasingly reflective and critical about their own imaginative products. The forms of these products change also: Artworks produced in childhood and early adolescence are often syncretic, fusing different styles and techniques in a single product. With further development, creative endeavors come to reflect conventional forms and intentional stylistic elements (Smolucha, 1992; Vygotsky, 1960/1987).

Vygotsky's theory (1931/1998a) anticipated later researchers' findings of a decline in creative productivity due to social influence around puberty: "In the process of an adolescent's development, at its most critical stage, there is usually a decline in school progress, a weakening of formerly established habits, particularly when productive work of a creative nature unfolds before the child" (p. 13). For example, Gardner (1994) and Winner (1982) found that adolescents may draw less because they are more aware of objective cultural standards and therefore more critical of their own work. As subjective and objective fantasy intertwine in a more sophisticated manner, old ways of thinking succumb to new, and young creators may narrow their areas of interest based on social input (Vygotsky, 1931/1998a). Thus, adolescence is the age of mastering one's internal world and "the age of growing into culture" (Vygotsky, 1983/1997a, p. 251).

Imagination and Thinking in Concepts

In creative imagination, the emotional and intellectual aspects of the adolescent's behavior find a complex synthesis.

LEV VYGOTSKY, "Imagination and Creativity in the Adolescent"

Creative imagination emerges when fantasy becomes infused with thinking in concepts. Then, imagination and the ability to abstract and categorize become integrated into a functional system (Vygotsky, 1931/1998d). Whereas Piaget (Piaget & Inhelder, 1969) based concept formation on direct sensorimotor interaction with objects, for Vygotsky, the key to concept formation was semantic mediation (Vygotsky, 1934/1962). Thinking in concepts does not emerge fully formed, but develops through trial and error, the use of subjective criteria, sensory connections, and finally logical connections. This ability continues to grow throughout a person's life span; however, Vygotsky focused on adolescence when it first develops in all its complexity.

A concept is fully formed when adolescents or adults can use it in their own words successfully in a communicative setting; when they understand its many connections to other concepts. However, it is only in late adolescence and early adulthood that people can objectify and reflect on the concept (Vygotsky, 1934/1962). This reflective function is assisted by the imagination. A person must be able to be in an oppositional, critical, or reflective relationship with reality in order to fully internalize a concept's meaning. The imagination provides the capacity for this type of critical relationship.

Thus, Vygotsky traced the origins of the creative imagination to children's symbolic play. Once play is internalized, it forms the basis of fantasy, which develops further when linked to inner speech. In adolescence, imagination is fueled by the intense needs and emotions of the young person, but it also becomes closely linked to thinking concepts—as Vygotsky remarked, it becomes "intellectualized."

THE DEVELOPMENT OF A CREATIVE PRODUCT

Creativity exists not only where it creates great historical works, but
also everywhere human imagination combines, changes, and creates
anything new.

    LEV VYGOTSKY, "Imagination and Creativity in Childhood"

The development of the creative imagination, then, is based on what is usually considered creative activity: pretend play, fantasy, and the making of creative products. In accordance with Vygotsky's developmental and dialectic
perspective, he viewed creativity not as a trait nor a genetically determined
stable property limited to special people. In fact, he never studied "creative
people" in the sense of people who had made a transformative contribution to
art, science, or invention. Rather, he viewed creativity as a growing, positive
capability of all healthily functioning individuals. Vygotsky would have
probably agreed with Feldman (1994) that creativity is a "transformational
imperative" in everyone. Creativity transforms both the creator, through the
personal experience of the process, and others, through the impact of new
knowledge and innovative artifacts disseminated through culture. By engaging in creative activity, people weave together the transformation of the
known and the new into social forms. What makes this activity particularly
salient is the sharing of emotions and the transformative power of jointly negotiated meaning making.

Emotion

Art systematizes a very special sphere in the psyche of social man—
his emotions.

    LEV VYGOTSKY, *The Psychology of Art*

Vygotsky (1965/1971) thought that emotion motivates imagination, thinking,
meaning making, and the understanding and use of signs: "All psychological
systems which attempt to explain art are nothing but various combinations of
the theories of imagination and emotion" (p. 200). Through the embodiment
of creative process and subjective experience into objective form and meaning, creativity makes the emotions of the artist and audience public in a systematic way, and it achieves an aesthetic effect from the tensions between
form and meaning. Society thus uses art as a means to bring intimacy into the
social realm. In *The Psychology of Art*, Vygotsky (1965/1971) wrote that art
"introduces the effects of passion, violates inner equilibrium, changes will in a
new sense, and stirs feelings, emotions, passions and vices without which so-

ciety would remain in an inert and motionless state" (p. 249). In viewing the role of art in this manner, he explored the mobilizing and cathartic effects of creativity and the placing of these feelings into the social realm. He further wrote that "art is the organization of our future behavior. It is a requirement that may never be fulfilled but that forces us to strive beyond our life toward all that lies beyond it" (p. 253). Creativity's emotional energy drives us toward future possibilities.

Therefore, underpinning creativity is the conscious awareness of the interaction of one's own and others' subjective, emotional experiences. The sharing of emotions through art does not mean that each individual experiences that emotion in the same manner; each internalizes the experience through his or her own lens and background. Emotion may start out simply as a bodily reaction, but it takes on new, productive functions in the context of cultural mediation (Vygotsky, 1959/1987). In fact, emotion operates under the social and cultural norms of the person's time: "Complex emotions emerge only historically. They are combinations of relationships that develop under the conditions of historical life" (Vygotsky, 1982/1997e, p. 103).

Vygotsky (1936/1999a) continued this line of thinking in a short essay on the psychological "paradox of the actor" first noted by Diderot (1773/1936). Actors embody feelings that become what the entire audience feels. But these embodied feelings are not necessarily the actors' real feelings; the actors do not live through or subjectively experience the emotions they convey. Still, these emotions are interpreted as real by the audience (see Sawyer, in press). Vygotsky surmised that understanding this phenomenon lies at the intersection of the qualities of the actors and the general psychological and ideological patterns prevalent in a particular culture at a specific historical period: in the interaction of personality and culture. The actor draws from "idealized passions" of his or her culture that are similar to the conventional literary or artistic forms on which novelists and sculptors draw. The art of the actors is the crystallization of these social passions in dialectic with the audience.

Vygotsky's thinking parallels the early studies of Gardner (1994), which emphasized art as an exchange between creator, performer, viewer, and critic. Through a Vygotskian lens, this exchange could be a resonance between ways in which these different roles create meaning from the artwork, as described later in this chapter. Through imagination, emotion is invested in and separated from the art object or performance by each participant in the aesthetic encounter. Leontiev (1990) followed up on this idea by asserting that objects become "colored" with personal meaning and that art reflects this subjective transformation.

Meaning and Sense

New systems are not just linked with social signs but also with ideol-
ogy and meanings which function in the consciousness of people.
                    LEV VYGOTSKY, "On Psychological Systems"

Through signs, people can create secondary mental stimuli that mediate their
own and others' interaction with people and objects: People can give things
meaning. According to Vygotsky (1930/1997d, p. 111; 1968/1997f), meaning
relates emotion to activity and activity to emotion via a complex process of
shared understanding. Meaning is the socially agreed-on definition of something—the dictionary definition for a word, for example. Creativity involves
bringing something new into the realm of social meaning. Vygotsky used the
term *sense* to refer to how this something new emerges. Sense is "the sum of all
the psychological events aroused in our consciousness by the word" (Vygotsky,
1934/1962, p. 149). It can fluctuate over time, from person to person, and across
situations. It includes meanings no longer used and possible future meanings;
connotations and metaphorical connections; and latent properties of the sign or
object. For example, the sense of a literary work's title becomes deepened by
the text, which is the context that enriches it. Through the interaction of the title
and other words in the text, it acquires new significance, a broader sense.

Creative thought, then, starts as an imaginary sense of how things might be,
which is expressed in an ongoing dialectic between the general categories of the
culture and the specific materials and emotional experiences with which the individual works (Prawat, 1999; Vygotsky, 1936/1999a). Creative work builds on
the fluidity and personal influences of sense. For example, an artist's subjective
experience can be combined with different senses of his or her medium and
symbol system and externalized as an artifact whose social meaning is intersub-
jectively negotiated (John-Steiner, 2000). This expansion of meaning into sense
could correspond to Guilford's (1970) divergent thinking, and the acceptance of
the new meaning into intersubjective agreement parallels both Wallas's (1926)
notion of verification and Csikszentmihalyi's (1988) "gatekeeper" field functions. The subtle use of sense when brought into the social sphere through art is
part of the challenge creative people face as they build new relationships and
externalize their own understanding.

Vygotsky's writings on meaning focused on language. His exploration of
the psychology of art relied heavily on his analysis of *Hamlet* and many other
literary examples (Vygotsky, 1965/1971). The power of words (in bridging
time and space, personal and social experience, and the past and the present) is
well understood by creativity researchers. As Csikszentmihalyi (1996) noted:
"The first narrative stories telling of real or imaginary events, the myths and
campfire stories of our ancestors, extended dramatically the range of human

experience through imagination" (p. 238). As mentioned above, inner speech is a critical component in the development and use of fantasy during adolescence. When Vygotsky traced language from its external, communicative manifestations to its most condensed inner representation, he concluded that inner speech "is to a large extent thinking in pure meanings. It is a dynamic, shifting, unstable thing" (Vygotsky, 1934/1962, p. 249). Inner speech, then, is the condensation of meaning derived from social interaction. It is related to our own experience, to form a more intricately interconnected web of understanding of oneself and one's world.

In *Thought and Language*, Vygotsky (1934/1962) used an example from Tolstoy's *Anna Karenina* to capture the condensed nature of inner speech and the depth of understanding that it requires to follow another's telegrams of thought. In elaborating on the role of inner speech in creative activity, John-Steiner (1997) proposed that "inner speech writing," such as that found in Virginia Woolf's journals, are cryptic forms of creative thought that help individuals plan, organize, and transform their ideas: "Creative thinking is that search for meaning which encompasses rapid bursts of ideas embedded in the sustained thought activities of the thinker. There is a continuing interaction between generative thought, which is often condensed, fluctuating, and unstable and communicated thought, which is expanded and organized for maximum impact" (p. 218). Inner speech assists the person in creating new meanings.

Although Vygotsky focused on language, he realized that it is not the only symbol system to which this meaning-making process applies. In "The Instrumental Method in Psychology" (1997c) he elaborated on the many domains available: "The following may serve as examples of psychological tools and their complex systems: language, different forms of numeration and counting, mnemotechnic techniques, algebraic symbolism, works of art, writing, schemes, diagrams, maps, blueprints, all sorts of conventional signs, etc." (p. 85). John-Steiner (1995) called this array of psychological tools and artifacts "cognitive pluralism." Particular types of thought develop depending on what activities people participate in, how they represent experiences, and which situations they prefer (John-Steiner, 1997). Therefore, they can develop and create in many different ways, depending on what the culture has available to match their talents and goals. There are usually many thinking styles present in a given culture (Wertsch, 1991). However, it should be noted that domains and thought processes are not synonymous: Different kinds of psychological systems can be used in a variety of domains. As John-Steiner (1997) and Gardner (1983, 1993) pointed out, a dancer could be primarily a musical or a geometric thinker; a scientist could be strong in either algorithmic or spatial thinking or both.

Therefore, the creative process builds on the externalization of emotions, imagination, concepts, and the varied meanings and senses of words as they are synthesized and transformed into creative products. This systematic process of cultural development changes the interfunctional relationships of social and psychological systems over time.

THE DEVELOPMENT OF A CREATIVE PERSONALITY

The dynamic of the personality is drama.
LEV VYGOTSKY, "The Problem of the
Cultural Development of the Child"

Through the use of creative imagination and the personal experience of developmental internalization and creative externalization, a personality forms and transforms. A personality is a characteristic way of behaving brought about by increasing, conscious mastery of these processes. This mastery, in turn, regulates further behavior. Therefore, Vygotsky (1960/1997b) emphasized the changing process of personality formation rather than the personality as a set of stable traits: "The transformation from outside inward transforms the process itself, changes its structure and functions" (p. 106). A personality develops over one's life span through struggle and continuous change, internally and in tandem with the environment; the stage on which this drama unfolds is the individual mind within a cultural-historical context (Vygotsky, 1929/1994a). Depending on their experiences, some individuals can develop personalities that become characteristically creative.

Experience

The essential factors which explain the influence of environment on
the psychological development of children, and on the development of
their conscious personalities, are made up of their emotional experiences [*perezhivanija*].
LEV VYGOTSKY, "The Problem of the Environment"

The basis of personality development is a person's experience. Although the role of experience in cognitive development is widely discussed among students of Vygotsky, his exploration of it in emotion and personality are less well-known. In "The Problem of the Environment," Vygotsky (1935/1994b) describes the concept of *perezhivanija* (p. 339). This word refers to subjective experience or living through an event. Vygotsky (1935/1994b) thought that psychologists need to find the particular "prism" that determines the role and influence of the environment, or "how a child becomes aware of, interprets, [and] emotionally relates to a certain event" (p. 341). The developing individual internalizes the impact and meaning of the *experience* of an event.

Perezhivanija is an important part of the transformative mechanisms of internalization and externalization; it is a reason that social culture and individual personality are not exact replicas of each other. Because one person may emotionally experience an event, artwork, object, or sign differently from another person, that event, artwork, object, or sign will have a different influence on each of these individuals. As a result, these individuals will follow different developmental trajectories over their life spans. An event's objective meaning has little relevance; what is important, developmentally and creatively, is the meaning from the point of view of the person as influenced by social context. Perezhivanija is the relationship between people and their environments; this prism leads to different colorings of life for different people, which leads to different personalities.

Personality Development

We shall never understand fully the human personality if we are to look at it statically as a sum of phenomena, of acts, and the like, without an integral biographical plan of personality, without a main line of development which transforms the history of man's life from a row of disconnected and separate episodes into a connected, integral, life-long process.

LEV VYGOTSKY, "The Dynamics of Child Character"

Vygotsky's (1983/1997a) conception of the personality is not as broad as that of some contemporary theorists: "We will not include here all the traits of the individual that distinguish it from a number of other individualities, that make up its uniqueness or relate it to one specific type or another. . . . The personality is a social concept. . . . It is not innate but arises as a result of cultural development because 'personality' is a historical concept. It encompasses unity of behavior that is marked by the trait of mastery" (p. 242). Personality is the process, based on one's distinct interactional pattern of higher mental functions, of mastering one's experiences in the world and using those experiences for future development.

Increasing mastery allows for better allocation of one's psychological and social resources toward goals, decision making, and self-reflection: "Intention is a type of process of controlling one's own behavior by creating appropriate situations and connections" (Vygotsky, 1983/1997g, p. 211). In a seeming contradiction, we observe two related developments in the formation of personality: As people become more social and more effective in society, they also become more thoroughly individuated. Each person is a subset of human possibilities, because he or she can only appropriate a fraction of culturally provided possibilities. As people developmentally integrate and master these possibilities, they construct their personalities.

Mastery also has a more subjective component, that of personal transformation. For example, the more positively people experience creative activities, the more creativity becomes a part of their personalities. Over time, they gain more recognized patterns and more formal systems of concepts to draw from and to transform into creative, cultural products within their chosen domains. Creativity, then, not only transforms objective materials into creative products; it also transforms the creator: "In fulfilling the activity, the subjects also change and develop themselves. The transforming and purposeful character of activity allows the subject to step beyond the frames of a given situation and to see it in a wider historical and societal context. It makes it possible for the subject to find means that go beyond the possibilities given" (Engestrom, Miettinen, & Punamaki, 1999, p. 39). In fact, Vygotsky (1931/1998d) went so far as to suggest that personal transformation is perhaps one goal of creativity: "It is for oneself, in the mind, that poems and novels are produced, dramas and tragedies are acted out, and elegies and sonnets are composed" (p. 165). Creativity creates the self as well as external artifacts.

In the midst of rapid historical and cultural change, creative individuals need to sustain their sense of integrity and determination. As Vygotsky saw this process, continuity is maintained as fragments of existence are integrated into life narratives. Vygotsky's ideas of personality development are similar to Howard Gruber's (1989) evolving systems theory of creativity, which emphasizes the construction of a creative life based on the ways people make a sustained commitment to their creative tasks. Gruber argued that the interaction between work and personal integrity is guided by a "network of enterprises." In a Vygotskian framework, we speak of a lifelong "zone of proximal development." Past acts, current experiences, and future plans expand and mobilize the resources of creative individuals. Through their experiences playing with materials and ideas, using their creative imaginations, and seeking distant teachers through cultural artifacts, creators scaffold further possibilities for themselves. Creativity forms a lifelong zone of proximal development that contributes to the sustained development of a creative personality.

THE DEVELOPMENT OF CULTURE

Every inventor, even a genius, is always the outgrowth of his time and environment. His creativity stems from those needs that were created before him, and rests upon those possibilities that, again, exist outside of him.
     LEV VYGOTSKY, "Imagination and Creativity in Childhood"

Creativity results in the proliferation of culture: "In the process of historical development, social man changes the methods and devices of his behavior . . . and develops and creates new forms of behavior—specifically cultural" (Vygotsky,

1960/1997b, p. 18). How a culture changes historically—via institutions, technologies, semiotic tools, and variations in values, beliefs, and practices—impacts people's thinking, literacy, numeracy, art, and other capabilities. Because creativity produces an artifact with which others can interact, it crystallizes subjective experience for others. Existing tools and symbols are the fossilized thought and ideas of people who have come before in history. When these tools and symbols do not serve current needs, new ones can be created (Vygotsky, 1960/1997b). Thus, cultural development progresses and is both supported and constrained by the possibilities of a particular historical time.

Historical Time as Support

The application of psychological tools enhances and immensely extends the possibilities of behavior by making the results of the work of geniuses available to everyone.

LEV VYGOTSKY, "The Instrumental Method in Psychology"

Internalization of what is already available in one's culture and society is the foundation for what a person can later contribute (Scribner, 1985). In fact, Vygotsky (1935/1994b) suggested that the environment is not a setting but a "source of development of these specifically human traits and attributes, most importantly because these historically evolved traits of human personality . . . exist in the environment, but the only way they can be found in each individual human being is on the strength of his being a member of a certain social group, and that he represents a certain historical unit living at a certain historical period and in certain historical circumstances" (p. 352).

Signs, tools, and artifacts develop over time and are only incompletely determined at a given point in history (John-Steiner, 1995). Historical conditions dynamically create new contexts and opportunities for development and creativity. John-Steiner (2000) notes that certain innovations within a domain, such as music, cannot occur until the supporting tools (in this case, instruments) are available to allow it, and changes in tools can dramatically alter how a domain progresses. For example, Vygotsky (1965/1971) showed how Shakespeare's and other authors' creativity is based on selecting and combining certain elements within socially accepted standards and aesthetic tastes of their time. New tools, signs, and artifacts provide the gradient on which even more tools, signs, and artifacts can be created in the future. Because historical context is always changing, there can be no universal representation of these developmental dynamics (John-Steiner & Mahn, 1996).

This line of thinking also parallels historiometric research, which uses aggregate data to determine which historical periods, geographical locations, and sociocultural circumstances have best nurtured creativity in Western civilization. Simonton (1997) found that "the coming and going of great creative genius in various times and places can be better attributed to changes in the cultural, social, political, and economic circumstances that determine the extent to which the resulting milieu nurtures the development of creative potential and the expression of that developed potential" (p. 3). One of his most intriguing assertions is that the zeitgeist—or spirit of the times—influences and perhaps even determines creativity. Simonton suggests that the designation of greatness goes to those who best fulfill the expectations of their age. Getzels and Csikszentmihalyi's (1976) study came to a similar conclusion: The most successful painters, 10 years after art school, were those whose methods corresponded to the institutionally valued styles of that historical period. Through a Vygotskian lens, we can explain these results: The most eminent are those creators who best utilize the social and cultural tools and best fit with the social and cultural expectations of their time.

Historical Time as Constraint

Creativity is an historically continuous process in which every next
form is determined by its preceding ones.
        LEV VYGOTSKY, "Imagination and Creativity in Childhood"

Creators, then, are of their time; also, their creativity is made apparent by their products' juxtaposition to other "reference" products from past and present creators. In his theory of expansive learning, Engestrom (1987, 1996) represents Vygotsky's developmental-creativity processes in terms of activity that becomes increasingly disruptive. Once internal contradictions can no longer be ignored, internalization turns into critical self-reflection. It is followed by externalization, which at first is a violation of cultural norms. When the activity reaches its apex, new solutions are produced. Participants then switch back to internalization in their sustained processes of learning (Cole & Engestrom, 1993).

As time passes, however, what was once new becomes traditional. Csikszentmihalyi (1988) reinforces this point: A work is considered creative at a certain historical time when it is first recognized as a significant, domain-changing contribution. But it frequently loses its novel status as it is embraced by the domain and becomes conventional. Other researchers have come to similar conclusions. Gardner's (1993) notion of fruitful asynchrony as applied to Csikszentmihalyi's (1988) systems model parallels Engestrom's notion of violation. Feldman's (1994) continuum of domain development shows how a new idea or variation starts first as idiosyncratic and, as it becomes perceived as useful and significant, undergoes several reorganizations. At the end of this process, members of the next generation learn and internalize the assimilated ideas. In the creative domain of poetry, Martindale (1975) showed how writers work within culturally defined aesthetic traditions. At the same time, however, they can only gain prestige by breaking from that tradition. This continued pressure toward greater originality eventually destroys existing styles and requires the construction of new conventions. In summary, people and artifacts are conferred creative status socially: They are creative because others, at a certain time, think they are creative. That creative status changes over historical time.

The Relationship of Individual and Historical Creativity

Turning our attention to the collective creativity, which unites all these insignificant fragments, comes the realization of what a great part belongs to the collective creative work or unknown inventors.

    LEV VYGOTSKY, "Imagination and Creativity in Childhood"

Contemporary researchers have separated creativity into variations that a person adds to socially standardized practices or procedures ("little *c*") and breakthroughs that are accepted by the field, which transform the domain ("big *C*") (Csikszentmihalyi, 1988; Gardner, 1993). Most creativity researchers have focused on big *C* creators—such as Einstein, Picasso, and other high-level performers—to determine what makes these individuals different from others who have not made a domain-transforming contribution (Gardner, 1993; Gruber, 1989). Other researchers, especially those following the cultural-historical tradition, have focused more on little *c* introductions of variations (Engestrom, 1987; Rogoff, 1990). Vygotsky's ideas would suggest that he considered little *c*, or individual inventiveness, and big *C*, or historical creativity, as dialectically connected.

Most people who engage in creative activities do not make a major impact on cultural domains; they go unrecognized. For Vygotsky (1965/1971), there is no basic difference in the creative process between a storyteller and a famous creator. According to his theory, both appropriate the results of big *C* Creativity from the historical past through social interaction and cultural artifacts, then adapt that information and expand it on the basis of their own experiences. These variations are shared with others, which may lead to the variation's being conventionalized by the domain and passed on to the next generation.

Although artists, scientists, and inventors have many tools and symbols at their disposal, when they are being potentially big *C* creative, they are operating at the edge of their domains, in the fuzzy boundary between the field's meaning and the individual's sense (John-Steiner, 1995). There are no socially agreed-on terms or definitions for what they are working on. They are walking an ideational tightrope without a cultural web of meaning to support them. There are no reliable reference points, at the time the creator engages in a particular new process, for others to know that the work is creative. As Gardner (1993) described this experience: "These are the times that try the mettle of the creator. No longer do the conventional symbol systems suffice; the creator must begin, at first largely in isolation, to work out a new, more adequate form of symbolic expression" (p. 34). In Vygotskian terms, potential big *C* creators have internalized what the domain has to offer at a particular historical moment and must now try to make socially acceptable new meaning. They have met the future before the rest of their field and are traveling on a journey without any landmarks.

CREATIVITY AND COLLABORATION

Every symbolic activity . . . was at one time a social form of cooperation.
      LEV VYGOTSKY, "Tool and Sign in the Development of the Child"

Collaboration is a particularly fruitful social venue for people on the edge of transforming their domains because it provides scaffolding in expanding social meaning. Although Vygotsky did not study groups, his concept of the zone of proximal development provides an important basis of exploration. Collaboration is shared creation and discovery of "two or more individuals with complementary skills interacting to create a shared understanding that none had previously possessed or could have known on their own" (Schrage, 1990, p. 40). It is not just an intellectual endeavor; rather, it is like an affair of the mind in which emotions can transform the participants and the work itself is interesting and supportive. Because the emotional intensity of collaboration is quite high, the process can also be painful at times. In Vygotskian terms, as collaborators form new functional relationships, they create varied social expressions of their joint commitment. The zone of proximal development is not solely dyadic; it can also apply to thought communities and communities of practice.

Creativity often thrives in a collaborative environment. Although some studies by organizational theorists (Abra & Abra, 1999; Paulus, Brown, & Ortega, 1999) claim to study collaboration, they are not addressing the same phenomenon as we are here. In some of their studies, collaboration helps spur creativity, whereas in others, creativity is hindered. These contradictory findings reflect an experimental design that throws strangers together and does not allow time for trust and complementarity to emerge. These researchers do not take the developmental perspective that Vygotsky asserted is crucial to creative development and production. Brainstorming and other similar group processes do not represent the characteristics of collaboration, which are long-term engagement, voluntary connection, trust, negotiation, and jointly chosen projects. These are the features we have found essential to successful collaboration (John-Steiner, 2000).

A particularly well documented case of creative collaboration is the invention of cubist painting at the turn of the 20th century (John-Steiner, 2000). Sometimes, this creative breakthrough is attributed solely to Pablo Picasso. However, this domain-transforming process was the result of an intense collaboration between Picasso and Georges Braque. Each painter played off the other's techniques and visions when dealing with the same subject matter, such as harbor landscapes. Their interaction formed a mutual zone of proximal development in which the two painters negotiated their shared meanings. By working together so closely, they expanded the possibilities of their talents. Each grew as an artist by being exposed to and appropriating the perspective offered by the other. In addition, they scaffolded each other professionally and emotionally by sharing the risks of rejection and self-doubt that arise in creative endeavors. As their techniques and subject matter became interrelated, so, too, did their personalities. Picasso remembered, "At that time our work was a kind of laboratory research from which every pretension of individual vanity was excluded" (as quoted in Richardson, 1991, p. 245–246). The simultaneous juxtaposition and intertwining of the temperaments, skills, interests, and processes of these two painters led to a painting method that not only changed the way artists viewed art, but how the general public saw the world.

Methodologically, studying creative collaborations follows Vygotsky's call to research the creative process as it happens; the study of collaborative activity aids in discovering covert processes, because they are expressed and verbalized. Engestrom (1987) concurs: "One of the most persistent methodological difficulties of studying thinking has to do with access to online data from thought processes. When thinking is defined as a private, individual phenomenon only indirect data is accessible. Thinking embedded in collaborative practical activity must to a significant degree take the form of talk, gesture, use of artifacts, or some other publicly accessible mediational instrumentality; otherwise mutual formation of ideas would be rendered impossible. Collaborative thinking opens up access to direct data on thought processes" (p. 45).

Another interesting tie between Vygotskian theory and collaboration is that many tensions within creativity and development are present within these long-term partnerships: the dialectics of personality and culture, meaning and sense, emotion and cognition. Collaborations provide a microcosm for the study of creativity and development. In certain learning dyads, a novice's problem or solution at the edge of social meaning may be labeled as error and possibly corrected. But among equal collaborators who encourage each other to take risks, new solutions are more likely to be socially presented and found useful in the larger society. Through collaboration, individuals can form thought communities and mutual zones of proximal development in which to continue their own and each other's creative development. Most of these collaborations are domain-specific, following the lines of Vygotsky's cognitive pluralism perspective.

BUILDING ON VYGOTSKY'S IDEAS TODAY

Psychology has for a long time ascribed too great a significance to just such established stereotypic forms of development that were themselves the result of already developed and fixed processes of development, that is, processes that are concluded and are only repeated and reproduced.

LEV VYGOTSKY, "The History of the Development
of Higher Mental Functions"

Vygotsky left much work to be done; he primarily mapped the terrain and left to others the task of empirical exploration. As we have shown, his work is not separate from, but supports and is supported by, much creativity research completed after his death. Contemporary creativity researchers have done an admirable job of understanding the cognitive and personality traits associated with creativity; now it is time to study how those traits come to be, how they develop in specific contexts. The main challenge is to capture creativity *in the making*, to focus on where turning points are most likely to occur, and to focus on the social transformation of emotional and cognitive experience.

The promise of Vygotsky's approach contrasts with creativity research that has focused on persons, products, and short-term events. Researchers using a psychodynamic or cognitive approach have begun to take a more developmental and life-span perspective. In fact, one of the great contributions of creativity research to the developmental literature has been to show that development continues beyond physical maturation. In addition, *systems* and *dynamics* have become key terms in the study of creative people and processes (Csikszentmihalyi, 1988; Gruber, 1989; Sawyer, this volume). However, these methods often still fall short of Vygotsky's more comprehensive developmental perspective, because they do not take into account all three timescales of creative activity, individual life span, and historical time. History is usually the timescale left out.

Another way to look at creativity research is on a temporal-methodological continuum. At one end are psychometric testing and laboratory experiments, which focus on the isolated individual at one time; at the other end are cultural-historical theorists and, more recently, systems and dynamics theorists, who present a complex picture of the interaction of individual creators, other people, tools, artifacts, socioeconomic forces, and historical time, all in motion. Vygotsky's approach supports the latter. However, it used to be believed that such a high number of variables in motion simultaneously could only be studied qualitatively or narratively; as a result, case studies were often used.

The case-study approach tries to re-create the process of creation over time through the close examination of highly creative people's lives, works, works in progress, and journals (Gardner, 1993; Gruber, 1989; John-Steiner, 1997). For example, John Steinbeck's daily letters to his editor provide detailed data of the microgenesis of his novels (John-Steiner, 1997, p. 130). These case studies place the individual's motivations, thoughts, and actions within his or her specific cultural-historical milieu and often examine the influences of others, artifacts, symbols and tools on the creative person's developing ideas. These approaches have led to the realization, as Vygotsky suggested, that creativity is not an individual phenomenon, but rather relies on the interaction and judgment of people, socially and historically.

Newer complex systems methods are providing possible avenues to capture and explain the complexity quantitatively. Complex systems theory has barely acknowledged creativity as a topic for research. This theory—which parallels many of Vygotsky's ideas of transformation, interacting systems and multiple timescales—argues that the whole is more than the sum of its parts and is irreducible. It is a mathematical approach that emphasizes *becoming* over *being*, interaction with the environment, and emergence or self-organization (Sawyer, this volume). As a result, a complex system is difficult to study retrospectively, as Vygotsky suggested about both development and creativity. Researchers are just beginning to use the new mathematical methods that have become accessible with increasing computing power. For example, Van Geert (1994) has presented a mathematical model that shows how Vygotsky's zone of proximal development might operate to form different developmental trajectories based on the interaction of different actual and potential growth rates, equilibrium levels, and goals. However, this methodology is relatively untapped in both developmental and creativity research.

In addition to tying in with these new complex systems concepts and tools, Vygotsky's ideas provide a foundation for a synthesize-and-build approach, as opposed to the Cartesian-inspired approach of positivist science. It welcomes and makes use of the contradictions so characteristic of creativity, rather than trying to explain them away. In fact, Vygotsky's own work is full of contradiction; in the process of his own creativity, he picks up and occasionally discards different ideas (e.g., his move from studying signs to studying meaning). In addition, although his theory focuses on the importance of social interaction, he often falls back on describing the interaction's impact on personal experience, not the interaction itself. He understood the methodological and conceptual difficulties of researching creativity formatively, and it may be because of these challenges that many contemporary cultural-historical researchers did not follow in his footsteps in studying creativity.

Because of its focus more on stable elements than dynamic relationships, conceptual and methodological progress has been slow in mainstream Western research. Many contemporary theorists have said that no one element is sufficient to explain creativity. Vygotsky's approach concurs with this belief. With theoretical systems frameworks (including Vygotsky's) and the new dynamic tools available, now is the time to study creativity in relationship, not in isolation. Such an approach will be demanding and complex, and it will require scholars to collaborate in new ways. But as Csikszentmihalyi (1993) observed: "The desire to achieve complexity will have limited value as long as it is held by separate individuals, each nursing it in the privacy of his or her own consciousness. It must be shared to become effective" (p. 281). From the new possibilities that arise in developmental and creativity research as a synthesized domain, we need to cultivate, not reduce, contradictions. Vygotsky's work has inspired us to bring to light and synthesize tensions, to hold and move among different perspectives, and to build on the dynamics of the individual and the social in the construction of the new.

REFERENCES

Abra, J., & Abra, G. (1999). Collaboration and competition. In M. A. Runco & S. R. Pritker (Eds.), *Encyclopedia of creativity* (pp. 283–293). San Diego: Academic Press.

Ayman-Nolley, S. (1999). A Piagetian perspective on the dialectic process of creativity. *Creativity Research Journal, 12*(4), 267–275.

Cole, M. (1996). *Cultural psychology: A once and future discipline*. Cambridge, MA: Harvard University Press.

Cole, M., & Engestrom, Y. (1993). A cultural-historical approach to distributed cognition. In G. Salomon (Ed.), *Distributed cognitions: Psychological and educational considerations* (pp. 1–46). New York: Cambridge University Press.

Csikszentmihalyi, M. (1988). Society, culture, and person: A systems view of creativity. In R. J. Sternberg (Ed.), *The nature of creativity* (pp. 325–339). Cambridge, UK: Cambridge University Press.

Csikszentmihalyi, M. (1993). *The evolving self*. New York: HarperCollins.

Csikszentmihalyi, M. (1996). *Creativity: Flow and the psychology of discovery and invention*. New York: HarperCollins.

Diderot, D. (1936). Paradoxe sur le comédien. In F. C. Green (Ed.), *Diderot's writings on the theatre* (pp. 249–317). New York: Cambridge University Press. (Original work published in 1773)

Engestrom, Y. (1987). *Learning by expanding. An activity-theoretical approach to developmental research*. Helsinki, Finland: Orienta-Konsultit Oy.

Engestrom, Y. (1996). Development as breaking away and opening up: A challenge to Vygotsky and Piaget. *Swiss Journal of Psychology 55,* 126–132.

Engestrom, Y., Miettinen, R., & Punamaki, R.-L. (1999). *Perspectives on activity theory*. Cambridge, UK: Cambridge University Press.

Feldman, D. (1994). *Beyond the universals of cognitive development* (2nd ed.). Norwood, NJ: Ablex.

Gardner, H. (1983). *Frames of mind*. New York: Basic Books.

Gardner, H. (1993). *Creating minds*. New York: Basic Books.

Gardner, H. (1994). *The arts and human development*. New York: Basic Books.

Getzels, J. W., & Csikszentmihalyi, M. (1976). *The creative vision*. New York: Wiley.

Greenfield, P. (in press). *Weaving generations together: Evolving creativity in the Maya of Chiapas*. Santa Fe, NM: School of Americas Research Press.

Gruber, H. (1989). The evolving systems approach to creative work. In D. B. Wallace & H. E. Gruber (Eds.), *Creative people at work* (pp. 3–24). New York: Oxford University Press.

Guilford, J. P. (1970). Traits of creativity. In P. E. Vernon (Ed.), *Creativity: Selected readings* (pp. 126–136). Baltimore: Penguin Books.

John-Steiner, V. (1995). Cognitive pluralism: A sociocultural approach. *Mind, Culture, & Activity, 2*(1), 2–11.

John-Steiner, V. (1997). *Notebooks of the mind: Explorations in thinking* (Rev. ed.). New York: Oxford University Press.

John-Steiner, V. (2000). *Creative collaboration*. New York: Oxford University Press.

John-Steiner, V., & Mahn, H. (1996). Sociocultural approaches to learning and development: A Vygotskian framework. *Educational Psychologist, 31*(4), pp. 191–206.

Leontiev, D. A. (1990). Personal meaning and the transformation of a mental image. *Soviet Psychology, 28*(2), 5–24.

Luria, A. R. (1976). *Cognitive development: Its cultural and social foundations*. Cambridge, MA: Harvard University Press.

Martindale, C. (1975). *Romantic progression: The psychology of literary history*. Washington: Hemisphere.

Paulus, P. B., Brown, V., & Ortega, A.H. (1999). Group creativity. In R. E. Purser & A. Montuori (Eds.), *Social creativity* (Vol. 2, pp. 151–176). Cresskill, NJ: Hampton Press.

Piaget, J. (1962). *Play, dreams and imitation in childhood*. New York: W. W. Norton.

Piaget, J., & Inhelder, B. (1969). *The psychology of the child*. New York: Basic Books.

Prawat, R. S. (1999). Social constructivism and the process-content distinction as viewed by Vygotsky and the pragmatists. *Mind, Culture, and Activity, 6*(4), 255–273.

Richardson, J. (1991). *The life of Picasso*. New York: Random House.

Rogoff, B. (1990). *Apprenticeship in thinking*. New York: Oxford University Press.

Russ, S. W., Robins, D., & Christiano, B. (1999). Pretend play: Longitudinal prediction of creativity and affect and fantasy in children. *Creativity Research Journal, 12*, 129–139.

Sawyer, R. K. (1997). *Pretend play as improvisation: Conversation in the preschool classroom*. Mahwah, NJ: Erlbaum.

Sawyer, R. K. (in press). Acting. To appear in J. C. Kaufman and J. Baer (Eds.), *Faces of the muse: How people think, work, and act creatively in diverse domains*. Mahwah, NJ: Erlbaum.

Schrage, M. (1990). *Shared minds: The new technologies of collaboration*. New York: Random House.

Scribner, S. (1977). Modes of thinking and ways of speaking: Culture and logic reconsidered. In P. N. Johnson-Laird and P. C. Wason (Eds.), *Thinking: Readings in cognitive science*. Cambridge, UK: Cambridge University Press.

Scribner, S. (1985). Vygotsky's uses of history. In J. M. Wertsch (Ed.), *Culture, communication and cognition: Vygotskian perspectives* (pp. 119–145). Cambridge, UK: Cambridge University Press.

Simonton, D. K. (1997). Historiometric studies of creative genius. In M. A. Runco (Ed.), *The creativity research handbook* (Vol. 1, pp. 3–28). Cresskill, NJ: Hampton Press.

Singer, D., & Singer, J. L. (1990). *The house of make-believe*. Cambridge, MA: Harvard University Press.

Smolucha, F. (1992). A reconstruction of Vygotsky's theory of creativity. *Creativity Research Journal, 5*(1), 49–67.

Smolucha, L. W., & Smolucha, F. C. (1986). L. S. Vygotsky's theory of creative imagination. *SPIEL, 5*(2), 299–308. Frankfurt, Germany: Verlag Peter Lang.

Van Geert, P. (1994). Vygotskian dynamics of development. *Human Development, 37,* 346–365.

Vygotsky, L. S. (1962). *Thought and language* (E. Hanfmann & G. Vakar, Trans.). Cambridge: MIT Press. (Original work published as *Myshlenie I Rech'*, Moscow-Leningrad: Sotsekgiz, 1934).

Vygotsky, L. S. (1971). *The psychology of art* (Scripta Technica, Inc., Trans.). Cambridge: MIT Press. (Original work published as *Psikhologiia iskusstva,* 1965)

Vygotsky, L. S. (1978). *Mind in society: The development of higher psychological processes* (M. Cole, V. John-Steiner, S. Scribner, & E. Souberman, Eds.). Cambridge, MA: Harvard University Press.

Vygotsky, L. S. (1987). Emotions and their development in childhood. In R. W. Rieber & A. S. Carton (Eds.), *The collected works of L. S. Vygotsky* (Vol. 1, N. Minick, Trans., pp. 325–338). New York: Plenum Press. (Original work published in *Voprosy Psikhologii, 3,* 1959)

Vygotsky, L. S. (1987). Imagination and its development in childhood. In R. W. Rieber & A. S. Carton (Eds.), *The collected works of L. S. Vygotsky* (Vol. 1, N. Minick, Trans., pp. 339–350). New York: Plenum Press. (Original work published in *Razvitie vysshikh psikhicheskikh funktsii,* Moscow: Izd-vo APN RSFSR, 1960)

Vygotsky, L. S. (1993). The dynamics of child character. In R. W. Rieber & A. S. Carton (Eds.), *The collected works of L. S. Vygotsky* (Vol. 2, J. Knox & C. B. Stevens, Trans., pp. 153–163). New York: Plenum Press. (Original work published in *Pedologija I Vospitanie [Pedology and Education],* pp. 99–119, Moscow: Rabotnik Prosveshchenija, 1928)

Vygotsky, L. S. (1994a). The problem of the cultural development of the child. In R. Van der Veer & J. Valsiner (Eds.), *The Vygotsky reader* (pp. 57–72). Malden, MA: Blackwell Publishers. (Original work published in *Journal of Genetic Psychology, 36,* 415–432, 1929)

Vygotsky, L. S. (1994b). The problem of the environment. In R. Van der Veer & J. Valsiner (Eds.), *The Vygotsky reader* (T. Prout, Trans., pp. 338–354). Malden, MA: Blackwell. (Original work published in *Osnovy Pedologii,* pp. 58–78, Leningrad: Izdanie Instituta, 1935)

Vygotsky, L. S. (1997a). Conclusion; further research; development of personality and world view in the child. In R. W. Rieber (Ed.), *The collected works of L. S. Vygotsky* (Vol. 4, M. J. Hall, Trans., pp. 241–251). New York: Plenum Press. (Original work published in *Sobr. Soch. V 6-ti t, Vol. 3,* pp. 5–228, Moscow: Pedagogika, 1983)

Vygotsky, L. S. (1997b). The history of the development of higher mental functions. In R. W. Rieber (Ed.), *The collected works of L. S. Vygotsky* (Vol. 4, M. J. Hall, Trans., pp. 1–251). New York: Plenum Press. (Original work published as *Razvitie vysshikh psikhicheskikh funktsii,* Moscow, 1960)

Vygotsky, L. S. (1997c). The instrumental method in psychology. In R. W. Rieber & J. Wollock (Eds.), *The collected works of L. S. Vygotsky* (Vol. 3, R. Van der Veer, Trans., pp. 85–89). New York: Plenum Press. (From Vygotsky's private archives)

Vygotsky, L. S. (1997d). Mind, consciousness, the unconscious. In R. W. Rieber & J. Wollock (Eds.), *The collected works of L. S. Vygotsky (*Vol. 3, R. Van der Veer, Trans., pp. 109–122). New York: Plenum Press. (Original work published in *Elementy obshchej psikhologii,* pp. 48–61, Moscow: Isdatelstvo BZO pri Pedfake 2-go MGU, 1930)

Vygotsky, L. S. (1997e). On psychological systems. In R. W. Rieber & J. Wollock (Eds.), *The collected works of L. S. Vygotsky* (Vol. 3, R. Van der Veer, Trans., pp. 91–108). New York: Plenum Press. (Original work published in *Sobr. Soch. V 6-ti t,* pp. 109–131, Moscow: Pedagogika, 1982)

Vygotsky, L. S. (1997f). The problem of consciousness. In R. W. Rieber & J. Wollock (Eds.), *The collected works of L. S. Vygotsky* (Vol. 3, R. Van der Veer, Trans., pp. 129–138). New York: Plenum Press. (Original work published in *Psikhologija Grammatiki,* pp. 178–196, Moscow: Izd-vo Moscow University, 1968)

Vygotsky, L. S. (1997g). Self control. In R. W. Rieber (Ed.), *The collected works of L. S. Vygotsky* (Vol. 4, M. J. Hall, Trans., pp. 207–219). New York: Plenum Press. (Original work published in *Sobr. Soch. v 6-ti t, Vol. 3,* pp. 5–228, Moscow: Pedagogika, 1983)

Vygotsky, L. S. (1998a). Development of interests at the transitional age. In R. W. Rieber (Ed.), *The collected works of L. S. Vygotsky* (Vol. 5, M. J. Hall, Trans., pp. 3–28). New York: Plenum Press. (Original work published in *Pedologija podrostka,* Moscow: Izd-vo BZO pri Pedfake 2-go MGU, 1931)

Vygotsky, L. S. (1998b). Development of thinking and formation of concepts in adolescence. In R. W. Rieber (Ed.), *The collected works of L. S. Vygotsky* (Vol. 5, M. J. Hall, Trans., pp. 29–82). New York: Plenum Press. (Original work published in *Pedologija podrostka,* Moscow: Izd-vo BZO pri Pedfake 2-go MGU, 1931)

Vygotsky, L. S. (1998c). Imagination and creativity in childhood. *Soviet psychology, 28* (10), 84–96. (Original work published as *Voobrazhenie i tvorchestvo v shkol'nom voraste,* Moscow-Leningrade: GIZ, 1930)

Vygotsky, L. S. (1998d). Imagination and creativity in the adolescent. In R. W. Rieber (Ed.), *The collected works of L. S. Vygotsky* (Vol. 5, M. J. Hall, Trans., pp. 151–166). New York: Plenum Press. (Original work published in *Pedologija podrostka,* Moscow: Izd-vo BZO pri Pedfake 2-go MGU, 1931)

Vygotsky, L. S. (1998e). The problem of age. In R. W. Rieber (Ed.), *The collected works of L. S. Vygotsky* (Vol. 5, M. J. Hall, Trans., pp. 187–205). New York: Plenum Press. (From Vygotsky's private archives)

Vygotsky, L. S. (1999a). On the problem of the psychology of the actor's creative work. In R. W. Rieber (Ed.), *The collected works of L. S. Vygotsky* (Vol. 6, M. J. Hall, Trans., pp. 237–244). New York: Kluwer Academic/Plenum Publishers. (Original work published in P. M. Yakobson, *Psikhologiya stsenicheskikh chuvstv aktera,* pp. 197–211, Moscow, 1936)

Vygotsky, L. S. (1999b). Tool and sign in the development of the child. In R. W. Rieber (Ed.), *The collected works of L. S. Vygotsky* (Vol. 6, M. J. Hall, Trans., pp. 1–68). New York: Kluwer Academic/Plenum Press. (Original work published in *Sobr. Soch. V 6-ti-t, Vol. 6,* pp. 5–90, Moscow: Pedagogika, 1984)

Wallas, G. (1926). *The art of thought.* New York: Harcourt, Brace, & World.

Wertsch, J. V. (1991). *Voices of the mind: A sociocultural approach to mediated action.* Cambridge, MA: Harvard University Press.

Winner, E. (1982). *Invented worlds.* Cambridge, MA: Harvard University Press.

CHAPTER THREE

The Development of Creativity as a Decision-Making Process

Robert J. Sternberg

What is creativity and how does it develop? Underlying the chapter is a single central notion—that, to a large extent, creativity is a decision. The chapter is divided into three parts: the decision to be creative, the decision of how to be creative, and implementation of these decisions.

In the first part of this chapter, I briefly review one of the kinds of approaches that have been taken to address this question, namely, the confluence approach. After describing some alternative views, I then describe my own particular variant of this approach. My theory, called the investment theory, concerns the *decision to be creative.* It is based on the notion that creative people *decide* to buy low and sell high in the world of ideas—that is, they generate ideas that tend to defy the crowd (buy low), and then, when they have persuaded many people of the value of the ideas, they move on. First I describe the proposed theory. Then I describe empirical work supporting at least some aspects of the theory.

In the second part of the chapter, I discuss the *decision of how to be creative.* According to the proposed *propulsion* theory, a person having made the decision to be creative can be creative in a variety of (eight different) ways.

In the third part of the chapter, I discuss the implications of the investment theory for enhancing creativity in oneself and others. This discussion concerns *how to implement the decision to be creative* and *the decision of how to be creative.*

In discussing creativity, I talk about creativity both in a minor ("little *c*") sense and in a major ("big *C*") sense. Often, the difference between the two is whether a contribution is creative only with respect to oneself or with respect to a field as well. Psychologically, however, the processes may be quite similar. From the point of view of the field, of course, the contributions are quite different.

CONFLUENCE APPROACHES TO THE STUDY OF CREATIVITY

A Review of Confluence Approaches

Many recent works on creativity hypothesize that multiple components must converge in a confluence for creativity to occur (Amabile, 1983, 1996; Csikszentmihalyi, 1988, 1999; Gardner, 1993; Gruber, 1989; Gruber & Wallace, 1999; John-Steiner, 1997; Lubart, 1994; Mumford & Gustafson, 1988; Nakamura & Csikszentmihalyi, 2001; Perkins, 1981; Simonton, 1988, 1999; Sternberg, 1985a; Sternberg & Lubart, 1991, 1995, 1996; Weisberg, 1993; Woodman & Schoenfeldt, 1989). One study (Sternberg, 1985b), for example, examined laypersons' and experts' conceptions of the creative person. These conceptions contain a combination of cognitive and personality elements, such as "connects ideas," "sees similarities and differences," "has flexibility," "has aesthetic taste," "is unorthodox," "is motivated," "is inquisitive," and "questions societal norms."

At the level of explicit theories, Amabile (1983, 1996, 2001; Collins & Amabile, 1999) describes creativity as the confluence of intrinsic motivation, domain-relevant knowledge and abilities, and creativity-relevant skills. The creativity-relevant skills include (a) a cognitive style that involves coping with complexities and breaking one's mental set during problem solving; (b) knowledge of heuristics for generating novel ideas, such as trying a counterintuitive approach; and (c) a work style characterized by concentrated effort, an ability to set aside problems, and high energy.

Gruber (1981, 1989) and his colleagues (Gruber & Davis, 1988; Gruber & Wallace, 2001) proposed a developmental *evolving-systems model* for understanding creativity. A person's knowledge, purpose, and affect grow over time, amplify deviations that an individual encounters, and lead to creative products. Developmental changes in *knowledge* have been documented in cases such as Charles Darwin's thoughts on evolution. *Purpose* refers to a set of interrelated goals, which also develop and guide an individual's behavior. Finally, the *affect* or mood system includes the influence of joy or frustration on the projects undertaken.

Csikszentmihalyi (1988, 1996, 1999; Nakamura & Csikszentmihalyi, 2001) has taken a different systems approach and highlights the interaction of the individual, domain, and field. An individual draws upon information in a domain and transforms or extends it via cognitive processes, personality traits, and motivation. The field, consisting of people who control or influence a domain (e.g., art critics and gallery owners), evaluates and selects new ideas. The domain, a culturally defined symbol system, preserves and transmits creative products to other individuals and future generations. Gardner (1993; see also Policastro & Gardner, 1999) has conducted case studies that suggest that the development of creative projects may stem from an anomaly within such a system (e.g., tension between competing critics in a field) or moderate asynchronies between the individual, domain, and field (e.g., unusual individual talent for a domain). In particular, Gardner (1993) has analyzed the lives of seven individuals who made highly creative contributions in the twentieth century, with each specializing in one of the multiple intelligences (Gardner, 1983, 1999): Sigmund Freud (intrapersonal intelligence), Albert Einstein (logical-mathematical intelligence), Pablo Picasso (spatial intelligence), Igor Stravinsky (musical intelligence), T. S. Eliot (linguistic intelligence), Martha Graham (bodily-kinesthetic intelligence), Mohandas Gandhi (interpersonal intelligence), and Charles Darwin (naturalist intelligence). Gardner points out, however, that most of these individuals actually had strengths in more than one intelligence, and that they had notable weaknesses in others (e.g., Freud's weaknesses may have been in spatial and musical intelligences). In more recent work, Gardner and his colleagues have asked the question of how creativity can be used in a way that contributes to the societal good (Gardner, Csikszentmihalyi, & Damon, 2002).

Although creativity can be understood in terms of uses of multiple intelligences to generate new and even revolutionary ideas, Gardner's (1993) analysis goes well beyond the intellectual. For example, Gardner pointed out two major themes in the behavior of these creative giants. First, they tended to have had a matrix of support at the time of their creative breakthroughs. Second, they tended to drive Faustian bargains, whereby they gave up many of the pleasures people typically enjoy in life to attain extraordinary success in their careers. It is not clear that these attributes are intrinsic to creativity per se, however; rather, they seem to be associated with those who have been driven to exploit their creative gifts in a way that leads them to attain eminence.

Gardner followed Csikszentmihalyi (1988, 1996) in distinguishing between the domain (the body of knowledge about a particular subject area) and the field (the context in which this body of knowledge is studied and elaborated, including the persons working with the domain, such as critics, publishers, and other gatekeepers). Both are important to the development and, ultimately, the recognition of creativity.

Although Csikszentmihalyi distinguishes three levels—the person, domain, and field—John-Steiner (2000) makes the important point that many creative works have been produced in collaborations. Often, the result of two people or a larger team of people working together is greater than the sum of its parts. In this case, one might wish to distinguish a fourth level—namely, the team of collaborators.

The investment theory described in the following section has in common with the theories previously described the emphasis upon a confluence of factors underlying creativity. It thus builds on past confluence theories in this respect. It differs, perhaps, in placing more of an emphasis on the decision to be creative than do some of the other theories.

The Investment Theory of Creativity

A final confluence theory considered here is Sternberg and Lubart's (1991, 1995a *investment theory of creativity*. According to this theory, creative people are the ones who are willing and able to buy low and sell high in the realm of ideas (see also Rubenson & Runco, 1992, for use of concepts from economic theory). Buying low means pursuing ideas that are unknown or out of favor but have growth potential. Often, when these ideas are first presented, they encounter resistance. The creative individual persists in the face of this resistance and eventually sells high, moving on to the next new or unpopular idea.

Research within the investment framework has yielded support for this model (Lubart & Sternberg, 1995). This research has used tasks such as (a) writing short stories using unusual titles (e.g., the octopus's sneakers), (b) drawing pictures with unusual themes (e.g., the earth from an insect's point of view), (c) devising creative advertisements for boring products (e.g., cufflinks), and (d) solving unusual scientific problems (e.g., how we could tell if someone had been on the moon within the past month). This research showed creative performance to be moderately domain-specific, and to be predicted by a combination of certain resources, as described subsequently.

According to the investment theory, creativity requires a confluence of six distinct but interrelated resources: intellectual abilities, knowledge, styles of thinking, personality, motivation, and environment. Although levels of these resources are sources of individual differences, often the decision to use a resource is a more important source of individual differences. Next, I discuss the resources and the role of decision making in each.

Intellectual skills. Three intellectual skills are particularly important: (a) the synthetic skill to see problems in new ways and to escape the bounds of conventional thinking, (b) the analytic skill to recognize which of one's ideas are worth pursuing and which are not, and (c) the practical-contextual skill to know how to persuade others of—to sell other people on—the value of one's ideas (Sternberg, 1985a). The confluence of these three skills is also important. Analytic skills used in the absence of the other two skills results in powerful critical (but not creative) thinking. Synthetic skill used in the absence of the other two skills results in new ideas that are not subjected to the scrutiny required to improve them and make them work. And practical-contextual skill in the absence of the other two skills may result in societal acceptance of ideas not because the ideas are good, but rather, because the ideas have been well and powerfully presented.

To be creative, one must first decide to generate new ideas, analyze these ideas, and sell the ideas to others. In other words, a person may have synthetic, analytical, or practical skills but may not apply them to problems that potentially involve creativity. For example, one may decide to follow other people's ideas rather than synthesize one's own; one may decide not to subject one's ideas to a careful evaluation; or one may decide to expect other people to accept one's ideas (and therefore decide not to try to persuade other people of the value of these ideas). The skill is not enough: One first needs to make the decision to use the skill.

We have sought to test the role of intelligence in creativity through a variety of studies. My colleagues and I presented 80 individuals with novel kinds of reasoning problems that each had a single best answer. For example, they might be told that some objects are green and others blue, but that still other objects might be *grue*, meaning green until the year 2000 and blue thereafter, or *bleen*, meaning blue until the year 2000 and green thereafter (based on Goodman's [1955] new riddle of induction). Or they might be told of four kinds of people on the planet Kyron: *blens*, who are born young and die young; *kwefs*, who are born old and die old; *balts*, who are born young and die old; and *prosses*, who are born old and die young (Sternberg, 1982; Tetewsky & Sternberg, 1986). Their task was to predict future states from past states, given incomplete information. In another set of studies, 60 people were given more conventional kinds of inductive reasoning problems, such as analogies, series completions, and classifications, and were told to solve them. The problems had premises that were either conventional (dancers wear shoes) or novel (dancers eat shoes). The participants had to solve the problems as though the counterfactuals were true (Sternberg & Gastel, 1989a, 1989b).

These studies (Sternberg, 1982; Sternberg & Gastel, 1989a, 1989b; Tetewsky & Sternberg, 1986) found that correlations with conventional kinds of tests depended on how novel or nonentrenched the conventional tests were. The more novel the items, the higher the correlations of our tests with scores on successively more novel conventional tests. Thus, the components isolated for relatively novel items would tend to correlate more highly with more unusual tests of fluid abilities, which are skills involved in coping with novelty in a flexible and effective manner (e.g., the tests of Cattell & Cattell, 1973) than with tests of crystallized abilities, which form the accumulated knowledge base we use in accessing vocabulary and general information. My colleagues and I also found that when response times on the relatively novel problems were componentially analyzed, some components better measured the creative aspect of intelligence than did others. For example, in the grue-bleen task mentioned previously, the information-processing component requiring people to switch from conventional green-blue thinking to grue-bleen thinking and then back to green-blue thinking again was a particularly good measure of the ability to cope with novelty.

One aspect of switching between conventional and unconventional thinking is the decision that one is willing and able to think in unconventional ways—that one is willing to accept thinking in terms different from those to which one is accustomed and with which one feels comfortable. People show reliable individual differences in willingness to do so (Dweck, 1999). Some (whom Dweck calls "entity theorists") prefer to operate primarily or even exclusively in domains that are relatively familiar to them. Others (whom Dweck calls "incremental theorists") seek new challenges and new conceptual domains within which to work.

Knowledge.   Concerning knowledge: On one hand, one needs to know enough about a field to move it forward. One can't move beyond where a field is if one doesn't know where it is. On the other hand, knowledge about a field can result in a closed and entrenched perspective, resulting in a person's not moving beyond the way in which he or she has seen problems in the past (Frensch & Sternberg, 1989). Thus, one must decide to use one's past knowledge but must also decide not to let the knowledge become a hindrance rather than a help. Everyone has a knowledge base. How each person chooses to use it is a decision each must make.

Thinking styles.   Thinking styles are preferred ways of using one's skills. In essence, they are decisions about how to deploy one's skills. With regard to thinking styles, a "legislative" style is particularly important for creativity (Sternberg, 1988, 1997a), that is, a preference for thinking in new ways and a decision to think in new ways. This preference needs to be distinguished from the ability to think creatively: Someone may like to think along new lines but not do it well, or vice versa. It also helps, in becoming a major creative thinker, if one is able to think globally as well as locally, distinguishing the forest from the trees and thereby recognizing which questions are important and which ones are not.

Personality.   Numerous research investigations (summarized in Lubart, 1994, and Sternberg & Lubart, 1991, 1995) have supported the importance of certain personality attributes for creative functioning. These attributes include, but are not limited to, willingness to overcome obstacles, willingness to take sensible risks, willingness to tolerate ambiguity, and self-efficacy. In particular, buying low and selling high typically means defying the crowd, so one must be willing to stand up to conventions if one wants to think and act in creative ways. Often, creative people seek opposition, in that they decide to think in ways that countervail how others think. Note that none of the attributes of creative thinking is fixed. One can *decide* to overcome obstacles, take sensible risks, and so forth.

Motivation.   Intrinsic, task-focused motivation is also essential to creativity. The research of Amabile (1983) and others has shown the importance of such motivation for creative work and has suggested that people rarely do truly creative work in an area unless they really love what they are doing and focus on the work rather than the potential rewards. Motivation is not something inherent in a person: One *decides* to be motivated by one thing or another. Often, people who need to work in a certain area that does not particularly interest them will decide that, given the need to work in that area, they had better find a way to make it interest them. They will then look for some angle on the work they need to do that makes this work appeal to rather than bore them.

Environment.   Finally, one needs an environment that is supportive and rewarding of creative ideas. One could have all of the internal resources needed in order to think creatively, but without some environmental support (such as a forum for proposing those ideas), the creativity that a person has within him or her might never be displayed.

Environments typically are not fully supportive of the use of creativity. The obstacles in a given environment may be minor (as when an individual receives negative feedback on creative thinking) or major (as when one's well-being or even life is threatened if one thinks in a manner that defies convention). The individual therefore must decide how to respond in the face of the almost omnipresent environmental challenges. Some people let unfavorable forces in the environment block their creative output; others do not.

Confluence.   Concerning the confluence of these six components: Creativity is hypothesized to involve more than a simple sum of a person's level on each component. First, there may be thresholds for some components (e.g., knowledge) below which creativity is not possible, regardless of the levels on other components. Second, partial compensation may occur in which a strength on one component (e.g., motivation) counteracts a weakness on another component (e.g., environment). Third, interactions may also occur between components, such as intelligence and motivation, in which high levels on both components could multiplicatively enhance creativity.

Creative ideas are both novel and valuable. But they are often rejected when the creative innovator stands up to vested interests and defies the crowd (cf.

Csikszentmihalyi, 1988). The crowd does not maliciously or willfully reject creative notions. Rather, it does not realize, and often does not want to realize, that the proposed idea represents a valid and advanced way of thinking. Society often perceives opposition to the status quo as annoying, offensive, and reason enough to ignore innovative ideas.

Evidence abounds that creative ideas are often rejected (Sternberg & Lubart 1995). Initial reviews of major works of literature and art are often negative. Toni Morrison's *Tar Baby* received negative reviews when it was first published, as did Sylvia Plath's *The Bell Jar*. The first exhibition in Munich of the work of Norwegian painter Edvard Munch opened and closed the same day because of the strong negative response from the critics. Some of the greatest scientific papers have been rejected not just by one, but by several journals before being published. For example, John Garcia, a distinguished biopsychologist, was immediately denounced when he first proposed that a form of learning called classical conditioning could be produced in a single trial of learning (Garcia & Koelling, 1966).

From the investment view, then, the creative person buys low by presenting an idea that initially is not valued and by then attempting to convince other people of its value. After convincing others that the idea is valuable, which increases the perceived value of the investment, the creative person sells high by leaving the idea to others and moving on to another undervalued idea. People typically want others to love their ideas, but immediate universal applause for an idea often indicates that it is already valued by the market and thus cannot be radically creative.

Creativity is as much a decision about and an attitude toward life as it is a matter of ability. Creativity is often obvious in young children, but it may be harder to find in older children and adults because their creative potential has been suppressed by a society that encourages intellectual conformity (see chapter 6, this volume).

Up to now, I have discussed the investment theory view of creativity as, in part, a decision to buy low and sell high. But, in fact, there are different kinds of decisions one can make as to how to be creative. These kinds of decisions are considered in the next section.

A PROPULSION THEORY OF TYPES OF CREATIVE CONTRIBUTIONS

There are tens of thousands of artists, musicians, writers, scientists, and inventors today.[1] What makes some of them stand out from the rest? Why will some of them become distinguished contributors in the annals of their fields and others be forgotten? Although many variables may contribute to determining who stands out from the crowd, certainly creativity is one of them. The standouts are often those who are doing particularly creative work in their lines of professional pursuit. Are these highly creative individuals simply doing a greater quantity of highly creative work than their less visible counterparts, or does the creativity of their work also differ in quality? One possibility is that creative contributors make different decisions regarding *how* to express their creativity. This section describes a propulsion theory of creative contributions (Sternberg, 1999b; Sternberg, Kaufman, & Pretz, 2002) that addresses this issue of how people decide to invest their creative resources. The basic idea is that creativity can be of different kinds, depending on how it propels existing ideas forward. When developing creativity in children, we can develop different kinds of creativity, ranging from minor replications to major redirections in their thinking.

Creative contributions differ not only in their amounts but also in the types of creativity they represent. For example, both Sigmund Freud and Anna Freud were highly creative psychologists, but the nature of their contributions was different. Sigmund Freud proposed a radically new theory of human thought and motivation, and Anna Freud largely elaborated on and modified Sigmund Freud's theory. How do creative contributions differ in quality and not just in quantity of creativity?

The type of creativity exhibited in a creator's works can have at least as much of an effect on judgments about that person and his or her work as does the amount of creativity exhibited. In many instances, it may have more of an effect on these judgments. For example, a contemporary artist might have thought processes, personality, motivation, and even background variables similar to those of Monet, but that artist, painting today in the style of Monet, probably would not be judged to be creative in the way Monet was. He or she was born too late. Artists, including Monet, have already experimented with impressionism, and unless the contemporary artist introduced some new twist, he or she might be viewed as imitative rather than creative.

The importance of context is illustrated by the difference, in general, between creative discovery and rediscovery. For example, BACON and related computer programs of Langley, Simon, Bradshaw, and Zytkow (1987) rediscover important scientific theorems that were judged to be creative discoveries in their time. The processes by which these discoveries are made via computer simulation are presumably not identical to those by which the original discoverers made them. One difference derives from the fact that contemporary programmers can provide, in their input of information into computer simulations, representations and particular organizations of data that may not have been available to the original creators. Moreover, the programs solve problems but do not define them. But putting aside the question of whether the processes are the same, a rediscovery might be judged to be creative with respect to the rediscoverer but would not be judged to be creative with respect to the field at the time the rediscovery is made.

Given the importance of purpose, creative contributions must always be defined in some context. If the creativity of an individual is always judged in a context, then it will help to understand how the context interacts with how people are judged. In particular, what are the types of creative contributions a person can make within a given context? Most theories of creativity concentrate on attributes of the individual (see Sternberg, 1988, 1999a). But to the extent that creativity is in the interaction of person with context, we would need as well to concentrate on the attributes of the individual and the individual's work relative to the environmental context.

A taxonomy of creative contributions needs to deal with the question not only of in what domain a contribution is creative, but of what the type of creative contribution is. What makes one work in biology more creative or creative in a different way from another work in biology, or what makes its creative contribution different from that of a work in art? Thus, a taxonomy of domains of work is insufficient to elucidate the nature of creative contributions. A field needs a basis for scaling how creative contributions differ quantitatively and, possibly, qualitatively.

EIGHT TYPES OF CREATIVE CONTRIBUTIONS

A creative contribution represents an attempt to propel a field from wherever it is to wherever the creator believes the field should go. Thus, creativity is by its nature *propulsion*. It moves a field from some point to another. It also always represents a decision to exercise leadership. The creator tries to bring others to a particular point in the multidimensional creative space. The attempt may or may not succeed. There are different kinds of creative leadership that the creator may attempt to exercise, depending on how he or she decides to be creative.

The propulsion model suggests eight types of contributions that can be made to a field at a given time. Although the eight types of contributions may differ in the extent of creative contribution they make, the scale of eight types presented here is intended as more of a nominal than an ordinal one. There is no fixed a priori way of evaluating *amount* of creativity on the basis of *type* of creativity. Certain types of creative contributions probably tend, on average, to be greater in amounts of novelty than are others. But creativity also involves quality of work, and the type of creativity does not make any predictions regarding quality of work.

The panels of Figure 3.1 summarize the eight types of contributions and are referred to in the following discussion. To foreshadow the following discussion, the eight types of creative contributions are divided into three major categories:

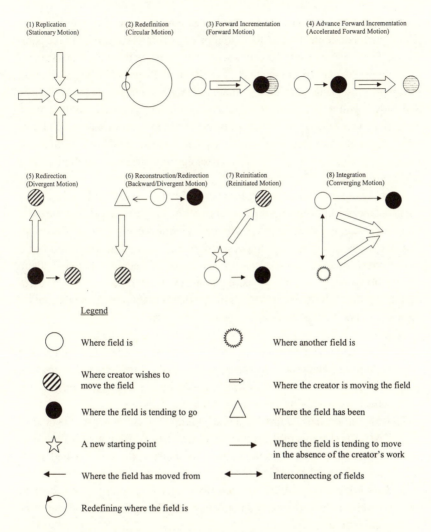

FIGURE 3.1. Types of creativity: (1) Replication helps solidify the current state of a field. (2) Redefinition involves a change in perception as to where the field is. (3) Incrementation occurs when a piece of work takes the field where it is and moves it forward from that point in the space of contributions in the direction work is already going. (4) Advance incrementation occurs when an idea is ahead of its time. (5) Redirection involves taking the field where it is at a given time but attempting to move it in a new direction. (6) Reconstruction/redirection involves moving the field backward to a point where it previously was but then moving in a direction different from that it has moved in. (7) Reinitiation occurs when a contributor suggests that a field or subfield has reached an undesirable point or has exhausted itself moving in the direction that it is moving. The contributor suggests moving in a different direction from a different point in the multidimensional space of contributions. (8) Integration occurs when a contributor suggests putting together ideas or kinds of ideas that formerly were seen as distinct and unrelated or even as opposed.

contributions that accept current paradigms, contributions that reject current paradigms, and contributions that attempt to integrate multiple current paradigms. There are also subcategories within each of the three categories: paradigm-preserving contributions that leave the field where it is (Types 1 and 2), paradigm-preserving contributions that move the field forward in the direction it already is going (Types 3 and 4), paradigm-rejecting contributions that move the field in a new direction from an existing or preexisting starting point (Types 5 and 6), paradigm-rejecting contributions that move the field in a new direction from a new starting point (Type 7), and paradigm-integrating contributions that combine approaches (Type 8).

Thus, Type 1, the limiting case, is not crowd-defying at all (unless the results come out the wrong way). Type 2 may or may not be crowd-defying, if the redefinition goes against the field. Type 3 typically leads the crowd. Type 4 goes beyond where the crowd is ready to go, so may well be crowd-defying. And Types 5 to 8 typically are crowd-defying in at least some degree. Obviously, there often is no crowd out there just waiting to attack. Rather, there is a field representing people with shared views regarding what is and is not acceptable, and if those views are shaken, the people may not react well.

1. *Replication.* The contribution is an attempt to show that the field is in the right place. The propulsion keeps the field where it is rather than moving it. This type of creativity is represented by stationary motion, as of a wheel that is moving but staying in place.
2. *Redefinition.* The contribution is an attempt to redefine where the field is. The current status of the field thus is seen from different points of view. The propulsion leads to circular motion, such that the creative work leads back to where the field is, but as viewed in a different way.
3. *Forward Incrementation.* The contribution is an attempt to move the field forward in the direction it already is going. The propulsion leads to forward motion.
4. *Advance Forward Incrementation.* The contribution is an attempt to move the field forward in the direction it is already going, but by moving beyond where others are ready for it to go. The propulsion leads to forward motion that is accelerated beyond the expected rate of forward progression.
5. *Redirection.* The contribution is an attempt to redirect the field from where it is toward a different direction. The propulsion thus leads to motion in a direction that diverges from the way the field is currently moving.
6. *Reconstruction/Redirection.* The contribution is an attempt to move the field back to where it once was (a reconstruction of the past) so that it may move onward from that point, but in a direction different from the one it

took from that point onward. The propulsion thus leads to motion that is backward and then redirective.

7. *Reinitiation*. The contribution is an attempt to move the field to a different, as-yet-unreached starting point and then to move from that point. The propulsion is thus from a new starting point in a direction that is different from that the field previously has pursued.

8. *Integration.* The contribution is an attempt to integrate two formerly diverse ways of thinking about phenomena into a single way of thinking about a phenomenon. The propulsion thus is a combination of two different approaches that are linked together.

The eight types of creative contributions just described are largely qualitatively distinct. Within each type, however, there can be quantitative differences. For example, a forward incrementation can represent a fairly small step forward or a substantial leap. A reinitiation can restart a subfield (e.g., the work of Leon Festinger on cognitive dissonance) or an entire field (e.g., the work of Einstein on relativity theory). Thus, the theory distinguishes contributions both qualitatively and quantitatively.

In the discussion that follows, I demonstrate each type of creative contribution with exemplars from a variety of fields, including especially one of my own fields of research, the field of intelligence. The examples are from Sternberg (1999b) and from Sternberg, Kaufman, and Pretz (2002).

Paradigm-Preserving Contributions That Leave the Field Where It Is

The first two types of contribution are paradigm preserving: replication and redefinition.

Type 1: Replication.   Replication is illustrated in Panel 1 of Figure 3.1. Replications help to solidify the current state of a field. The goal is not to move a field forward so much as to establish that it really is where it is supposed to be. Thus, in science, if a finding is surprising, then a replication can help establish that the finding is a serious one. If the replication fails, contributors in the field need to question whether they are where they have supposed themselves or perhaps have hoped themselves to be. In art or literature, replications essentially show that a style of work can be applied not just to a single artwork or literary work, but to other works as well.

Replications are limiting cases in that they, in some sense, seem (at face value) to offer the least that is new in terms of the types of creative contributions that are considered in this taxonomy of types of contributions. Yet replications are important because they can help to establish either the validity (or invalidity) of contributions or the utility (or lack of utility) of approaches that have been offered.

For example, consider the choice reaction-time paradigm and its implications. As background, Jensen (1982) and others argued that correlations between scores on choice reaction-time tests and scores on intelligence tests suggest that individual differences in human intelligence could be traced to individual differences in velocity of neural conduction. Because tests of choice reaction time in no way measure neural conduction velocity, such interpretations of results were wholly speculative.

Vernon and Mori (1992) tested and seemingly confirmed Jensen's hypothesis. They developed a paradigm whereby they could measure speed of neural conduction in the arm. They found that neural-conduction velocity did indeed predict scores on conventional tests of intelligence. This was a startling finding, because it suggested that what previously had been a speculative claim that at best was very loosely tied to data was instead a serious empirically-supported claim. However, Wickett and Vernon (1994) later reported a failure to replicate this result, so its empirical status was cast into doubt. The Wickett and Vernon study was a replication study, and the failure to replicate arguably was as important to the field as would have been a replication. Failures to replicate can prevent a field from pursuing red herrings.

Although work designed to yield exact replications and conceptual replications (where the generality of a finding or kind of product is assessed by trying to replicate it under circumstances somewhat different from those that originally gave rise to it) is about as unglamorous as any kind of work can be, it is necessary for the development of a field. Without replications, the field would be (and probably often is) very susceptible to Type I errors (false alarms). In science, replications help to ensure the solidity of the base of empirical findings on which future researchers build.

In the arts and letters, replications help to ensure that an approach is robust and can generate a number and variety of works. For example, many artists imitated Monet's impressionistic techniques, and although they added nothing new to his techniques, they showed the robustness of the techniques for producing varied artworks. Perhaps the limiting case in the art world is the work of forgers, who attempt to reproduce exactly the work of a (usually well-known) creator. However, replications are not limited to forgers. Many visitors to museums have encountered individuals studiously copying great works of art and proudly displaying their work for what it is.

Perhaps the crucial insight for the contributor is to know when there is a need for replication in the first place. In science, this need is associated with findings that are surprising or that seem at face value to be sufficiently dubious that either their existence or their generality needs to be demonstrated. In the arts and letters, this need is associated with techniques that may seem to be limited only to a single artwork or artist, or literary work or writer, but that could be used more widely.

Type 2: Redefinition.   Redefinition is illustrated in Panel 2 of Figure 3.1. Redefinition, like replication, involves little or even no change of where a field is. What redefinition involves is a change in perception as to where that is. It is analogous to the realization of a navigator that a vehicle the navigator had thought to be in one place is really in another place. The place does not change, but the definition of where that place is does change. Similarly, a redefinition in a conceptual space leads people to realize that the field is not where they had thought. Work of this type is judged to be creative to the extent that the redefinition of the field is different from the earlier definition (novelty) and to the extent that the redefinition is judged to be plausible or correct (quality).

An example of a redefinition is provided by the work of Thomson (1939), who reinterpreted the work of Spearman (1904, 1927). Spearman was the English psychologist who invented factor analysis and who used this technique to argue that underlying all tests of mental abilities is a general factor, which he labeled g. Spearman's analysis had a powerful effect on the field and even continues to have such an effect today, with many theorists still believing in the existence and importance of the general factor (e.g., Brand, 1996; Carroll, 1993; Horn, 1994; Jensen, 1998).

Spearman believed his work to show that a single mental entity was responsible for interesting and consequential individual differences in performance on mental tests. Spearman (1927) suggested that this entity was mental energy. Thomson (1939) proposed that although Spearman was correct in asserting a general factor underlying mental tests, he was incorrect in his interpretation of it. According to Thomson, the general factor actually represents the workings of multitudinous "bonds." These bonds are all alleged to be those mental processes that are common to performance on all mental tests. Thus, because all such tests require people to understand the instructions, read the terms of the problems, provide a response, and so forth, there might be many different sources of individual differences shared across these tests. They might appear via factor analysis to be a single entity, but in fact they are multifarious. Thus, Thomson proposed to change not the empirical status of work on intelligence, but how its empirical status was conceptualized. He argued that the field was not where Spearman and others thought it to be.

Similarly, Minkowski r-metrics represent a redefinition of the notion of spatial metaphors (see Kruskal, 1964a, 1964b). In computing distances in a multidimensional space, people traditionally had assumed that distance is Euclidean— that in the formula for computing distances, one should square differences between coordinates and then take the square root of the sum of the squared differences in order to compute distances. Minkowski's generalization shows that there is nothing privileged about the r-value of 2. One can use any number at all as the basis for exponentiation. For example, an r-value of 1 yields a city-block metric, where distances are computed as they would be in a city where it is impossible to construct a hypotenuse through buildings that block one's attempt to shortcut the city blocks. An r-value of infinity yields a max metric, where only the longest within-dimensional distance contributes to the total distance. Thus, the Minkowski r-metric shows that the way distances were computed was not unique but rather one of many possible cases: The r-metric redefines through a generalization the already existing distance construct.

An interesting example of redefinition in the arts is the work of the late Roy Lichtenstein. Lichtenstein took a form of art—the comic—that was viewed as a debased form of art and turned it into a serious art form. Lichtenstein's work originally met with tremendous opposition, and this opposition never really ended, at least from some quarters. Yet in his later career, his comic works of art brought extremely large sums of money as well as the kind of serious study that showed that what had been perceived as a base art form had come to be taken seriously, at least by many. Andy Warhol is a second example of an artist in this tradition, turning, for example, studies of soda bottles into pieces of art valued by many collectors.

Paradigm-Preserving Contributions That Move the Field Forward in the Direction It Already Is Going

The third and fourth types of contribution are paradigm preserving, yet move the field forward: forward incrementation and advance forward incrementation.

Type 3: Forward incrementation.   This type of creative contribution is illustrated in Panel 3 of Figure 3.1. It probably represents the most common type of creative contribution. It occurs when a piece of work takes the field at the point where it is and moves it forward from that point in the space of contributions in the direction work is already going. There is no change in the trajectory of the field. Work of this type is judged to be creative to the extent that it seems to move the field forward from where it is and to the extent that the movement appears to be correct or desirable.

Hunt, Frost, and Lunneborg (1973) proposed that intelligence could be studied by investigators' examining individual differences in cognitive performance on the kinds of tasks cognitive psychologists study in their laboratories. A few years later, Hunt, Lunneborg, and Lewis (1975) published an incrementation study that extended the range of tasks that could be studied using this paradigm, and that suggested that certain ones of these tasks were particularly useful for studying individual differences in verbal ability. The second study was an incrementation study, building on a paradigm that Hunt and his colleagues had already established. The second study provided a fairly substantial increment in both increasing the range of tasks and in focusing on verbal ability.

Most studies published in scientific journals can be characterized as forward incrementations. For example, after the initial groundbreaking study of Festinger and Carlsmith (1959) on cognitive dissonance, huge numbers of follow-up studies were done on phenomena of cognitive dissonance and cognitive consistency (Abelson et al., 1968). These studies helped to elucidate the phenomenon and its limiting circumstances. As these forward incrementations made more clear the limits of the cognitive-dissonance phenomenon, other theories came to be proposed that provided alternative (Bem, 1967) or more refined explanations of when people exhibit cognitive dissonance and when they exhibit other kinds of reactions—such as self-perception reactions—in the face of cognitive inconsistencies (Fazio, Zanna, & Cooper, 1977).

Forward incrementations can also be found in genre fiction that pushes the envelope. The hard-boiled detective story pioneered by Dashiell Hammett and Raymond Chandler has been elaborated upon by countless writers, some of them moving the genre forward in major ways, such as Ross MacDonald, who introduced identity confusions as a major theme in his work. But MacDonald's work and that of others has its roots in the paradigm introduced by Hammett and Chandler.

Jonathan Kellerman's psychological thrillers take the genre a step further by having as their hero Alex Delaware, a clinical psychologist. Patricia Cornwell's suspense novels have Kay Scarpetta, a medical examiner, as the protagonist. Using these nonstandard professions instead of the usual cops and detectives adds an extra layer of authenticity to the stories and allows for much more technical detail to be realistically added to the plots. Kellerman's plots, for example, often hinge on Delaware's identifying various psychological syndromes (for example, Munchausen Syndrome by Proxy), whereas Cornwell has Scarpetta discover essential clues in her autopsies. Forward incrementations can also be found in the plots of genre fiction—Agatha Christie's classic *The Murder of Roger Ackroyd* (1926) is a fairly standard murder mystery—until the then-startling ending of the narrator's winding up being the killer. These advances certainly move the field forward, but in an expected, nonstartling way. Kellerman and Cornwell still work within the preestablished conventions of the field, and Christie's famed novel still obeyed most of the "rules" of a murder mystery.

Type 4: Advance forward incrementation.   This type of creative contribution is illustrated in Panel 4 of Figure 3.1. Advance incrementation occurs when an idea is ahead of its time. The field is moving in a certain direction but is not yet ready to reach a given point ahead. Someone has an idea that leads to a point not yet ready to be reached; the person pursues the idea and produces a work. Often the value of the work is not recognized at the time because the field has not yet reached the point where the contribution of the new work can be adequately understood. The creator accelerates beyond where others in his or her field are ready to go—often skipping a step that others will need to take. The value of the work may be recognized later than otherwise would be the case, or some other creator who has the idea at a more opportune time may end up getting credit for the idea.

For example, Alfred Binet is best known for his work on intelligence, but as pointed out by Siegler (1992), Binet also did work on the nature of expertise in outstanding chess play and on the validity of eyewitness testimony. The work, which did not fit even remotely into existing paradigms of the time, was largely ignored. By the second half of the twentieth century, these and other topics that Binet had studied gained prominence. Binet, however, is virtually never cited in current work on these topics.

Royer (1971) published an article that was an information-processing analysis of the digit-symbol task on the Wechsler Adult Intelligence Scale (WAIS). In the article, Royer showed how information-processing analysis could be used to decompose performance on the task and understand the elementary information processes underlying performance on it. Royer's work foreshadowed the later work of Hunt (Hunt, Frost, & Lunneborg, 1973; Hunt, Lunneborg, & Lewis, 1975) and especially of Sternberg (1977, 1983), but his work went largely (although not completely) unnoticed. There could be any number of reasons for this, but one of the reasons is likely to have been that the field was not quite ready for Royer's contribution. The field and possibly even Royer himself did not recognize fully the value of the approach he was taking.

An advance forward incrementation is a work whose potential typically is not realized at first yet is later recognized as a step along the historical path of a genre and is often considered a work ahead of its time. For example, the ancient Greek philosopher Democritus was way ahead of his time in proposing ideas that later gave rise to the theory of atoms. In the nineteenth century, Ignaz Semmelweis, a Hungarian obstetrician, proposed the idea of microorganisms contaminating the hands of doctors and was so scoffed at that eventually he was driven crazy. Often it is only later that the value of such works is appreciated. Perhaps the most memorable premiere in music history was that of Igor Stravinsky's ballet *The Rite of Spring* in 1913. This performance so shocked its Parisian audience that the instrumentalists could not hear themselves play over the riotous crowd. At the time, French ballet music was very backward looking and accompanied a very stylized choreography. Of course, the usual ballet patrons were bound to be overwhelmed by the enactment of barbaric rituals accented by pulsating rhythms and dissonant harmonies featured in Stravinsky's new work.

Although the premiere of *The Rite of Spring* was vehemently rejected, Stravinsky's innovation was rooted in the past and proved to be an important step on the future course of music history. The pressing and irregular rhythms of ritual in this work continued the rhythmic experimentation begun by Stravinsky's teacher, Nikolai Rimsky-Korsakov. Its deemphasis of melody and harmony is also characteristic of works later in the century. Just as Stravinsky borrowed elements from folk music for this piece, many twentieth-century composers also made extensive use of non-art music sources in their compositions. Although *The Rite of Spring* was poorly received at its premiere, its contribution to the field of music was ahead of its time (Machlis, 1979).

Paradigm-Rejecting Contributions That Move the Field in a New Direction from an Existing or Preexisting Starting Point

Unlike the first four types of creative contribution—which preserve the existing paradigm—the fifth, sixth, and seventh types reject the existing paradigm. These three types are redirection, reconstruction/redirection, and reinitiation.

Type 5: Redirection.   Redirection is illustrated in Panel 5 of Figure 3.1. Redirection begins with the field where it is at a given time but attempts to move it in a new direction. Work of this type is creative to the extent that it moves a field in a new direction (novelty) and to the extent that this direction is seen as desirable for research (quality).

The pioneering Hunt, Frost, and Lunneborg (1973) article mentioned earlier suggested that researchers of intelligence use cognitive-psychological paradigms to study intelligence. The basic idea was to correlate scores on cognitive tasks with scores on psychometric tests. Sternberg (1977) used cognitive techniques as a starting point, but suggested that research move in a direction different from that suggested by Hunt. In particular, he suggested that complex cognitive tasks (such as analogies and classifications) be used instead of simple cognitive tasks (such as lexical access) and that the goal should be to decompose information processing on these tasks into its elementary information-processing components. Sternberg argued that Hunt was right in suggesting the use of cognitive tasks, but wrong in suggesting the use of very simple ones, which he believed involved only fairly low levels of intelligent thought. Sternberg was thus suggesting a redirection in the kind of cognitive work Hunt had initiated.

Edward Tolman (1932) made an effort to redirect the field of learning, an effort that today has earned him a place in virtually every serious textbook on learning or even on introductory psychology. Tolman accepted many of the conventions of the day—experiments with rats, use of mazes, and multitrial learning laboratory learning experiments. But he proposed to take all of these features of research in a new direction, one that would allow for purposiveness and latent learning on the part of the animals he was studying. Today, of course, these concepts are widely accepted, although at the time Tolman proposed them, the reaction was mixed, at best.

Beethoven's work can also be viewed as a redirection from the classical style of music that had been employed so successfully by Haydn, Mozart, and others. Beethoven used many of the same classical forms as had his predecessors. But he also showed that a greater level of emotionality could be introduced into the music without sacrificing the classical forms.

Kurt Vonnegut, in *Slaughterhouse Five,* questioned the very fabric of what constitutes a war novel, and in doing so pointed a path for the field to take. Re-creations and straightforward stories of the horrors of war (such as Stephen Crane's *The Red Badge of Courage* or MacKinlay Kantor's *Andersonville*) are powerful, Vonnegut might argue, but to truly convey the nature of war an author must go beyond this. In *The Things They Carried*, O'Brien (1991) picks up on Vonnegut's path and takes it in yet another direction: An author *cannot* convey the nature of war to someone who has not experienced it. All he or she can do is convey the feelings and thoughts one might have in these types of situations. O'Brien and Vonnegut are not reinitiators (Type 7), because they are accepting the same starting point for war novels that other novelists have used. Their work is also not merely a type of forward incrementation (Types 3 and 4), however, because they have taken a radically different view of the way in which a war novel should be written.

Type 6: Reconstruction/redirection.   This type of creative contribution is illustrated in Panel 6 of Figure 3.1. In using reconstruction, an individual suggests that the field should move *backward* to a point where it previously was but then should move in a direction divergent from that it has moved in. In other words, the individual suggests that at some time in the past, the field went off track. The individual suggests the point at which this occurred and how the field should have moved forward from that point. The work is judged as creative to the extent that the individual is judged as correctly recognizing that the field has gone off track and to the extent that the new direction suggested from the past is viewed as a useful direction for the field to pursue.

In the early part of the century, intelligence tests seemed to have potential for helping society understand why certain groups rose to the top of the society and other groups fell to the bottom of that society (see Carroll, 1982; Ceci, 1996; Gould, 1981). This often thinly disguised social Darwinism was based on the notion that those groups with more adaptive skills, on average, should and in fact did tend to have more success in adapting to the demands of the social structure of the society. In contrast, those groups with fewer adaptive skills, on average, did and should fall to the bottom. This kind of thinking became unpopular in the latter half of the century. Environment came to be seen as much more important than it had seemed before (Kamin, 1974; Lewontin, 1982). As a result, intelligence test scores were no longer looked at as a cause of group differences, but rather, as an effect.

This balance was upset when Herrnstein and Murray (1994) argued that the older views were most likely correct in many respects: It is plausible, they argued, to believe that group differences in IQ are in fact due to genetic factors, and that these group differences result in social mobility. Herrnstein and Murray further suggested that what they considered a humane social policy could be constructed on the basis of these alleged facts. Many people who were more comfortable with the older views or who were ready to be persuaded of these views found the Herrnstein-Murray arguments convincing. Others, especially those believing in multiple intelligences or the importance of environment, were not convinced.

My goal here is not to argue about the validity of the Herrnstein-Murray position, which I have discussed elsewhere (Sternberg, 1995a). Rather, it is to suggest that the work of Herrnstein and Murray served a reconstructive function. Herrnstein and Murray were suggesting that the field had gone off course in the desire of its members to accept certain beliefs that, however charitable they might be, were incorrect. These authors suggested that the field return to a point that many (although certainly not all) investigators thought had been left behind, and that the field then advance from that point.

B. F. Skinner's (1972) analysis of creativity represents another example of reconstruction/redirection. Skinner apparently was perturbed that the analysis of creativity had moved further and further away from the kinds of behavioristic principles that he and his colleagues believed they had shown as applicable to *all* behavior. The 1972 paper was, in large part, an argument that the field of creativity had lost its foundations and that it needed to return to the kind of behavioristic analyses that Skinner believed he and others had shown could account for creative behavior.

Some literary scholars are now suggesting that literary criticism, too, has gone off track—that the kind of deconstructionism introduced by Derrida (1992) and others has produced a literary nihilism that has resulted in a degeneration of the field of literary criticism. These individuals (e.g, Bloom, 1994), suggest that literary scholars return to their earlier tradition of finding meaning in literary works rather than asserting that virtually any meaning can be read into any literary work.

Raymond G. Fox's musical *Take It Easy* (1996) is an exemplar of reconstruction/redirection. It takes place in the 1940s, and the music is a reconstruction of the swing sound. The characters are intentionally stereotypes, such as the Bookworm and the All-American Hero. The ultimate goal of the show is to re-create the feel of a 1940s college musical, with young, good-looking, and patriotic characters. Several other recent Broadway shows, such as *Triumph of Love* (book by James Magruder, music by Jeffrey Stock, and lyrics by Susan Birkenhead) and *Big* (book by John Weidman, music by David Shire, and lyrics by Richard Maltby, Jr.) have been throwback musicals that reflect the more simplistic plot, characters, and musical tone of musicals of the 1950s. Unlike more modern shows, which tend to be entirely sung and have either an operatic or rock musical style, these shows take the structure and values of more classic musicals (such as *Oklahoma!* or *My Fair Lady*) and update the topics and sensibilities to the 1990s (e.g., in *Big,* characters refer to rap music).

Type 7: Reinitiation. This type of creative contribution is illustrated in Panel 7 of Figure 3.1. In reinitiation, a contributor suggests that a field or subfield has reached an undesirable point or has exhausted itself moving in the direction that it is moving. But rather than suggesting that the field or subfield move in a different direction from where it is (as in redirection), the contributor suggests moving in a different direction from a different point in the multidimensional space of contributions. In effect, the contributor is suggesting that people question their assumptions and start over from a point that most likely makes different assumptions. This form of creative contribution represents a major paradigm shift.

Two notable examples of this type of creativity can be found in the contributions to the field of intelligence made by Spearman (1904) and by Binet and Simon (1905/1916). Spearman reinvented the field of intelligence theory and research by his invention of factor analysis and by his proposal of the two-factor theory (general ability and specific abilities) based on his factor-analytic results. Spearman's contribution was to put theorizing about intelligence on a firm quantitative footing, a contribution that lives on today, whether or not one agrees with either Spearman's theory or his methodology. Binet and Simon (1905/1916) reinvented the field of intelligence measurement. Whereas Galton (1883) had proposed that intelligence should be understood in terms of simple psychophysical processes, Binet and Simon proposed that intelligence should be understood instead in terms of higher order processes of judgment. For the most part, the measurements of intelligence today are still based on this notion of Binet and Simon.

Spearman's (1904, 1927) reinitiating emphasis on general ability was not shared by all investigators. For example, Thurstone (1938), Guilford (1967), and many other theorists suggested that intelligence comprises multiple abilities and that any general factor obtained in factor analyses was likely to be unimportant, at best, and epiphenomenal, at worst. In all cases, however, intelligence was accepted as a unitary construct; what differed were investigators' views on how, if at all, the unitary construct should be divided up.

Festinger and Carlsmith's (1959) initial paper on cognitive dissonance, mentioned earlier, represents a reinitiation, an attempt to make a new start in the field of social psychology. A more recent example of a reinitiation is Bem's (1996) theory of homosexuality, according to which what initially is exotic for an individual becomes erotic later in life. Bem's is a theory arguing for environmental causes of homosexuality, at a time when biological theories largely have gained acceptance.

Revolutionary works tend to be major reinitiations. In the field of linguistics, Chomsky's (1957) transformational grammar changed the way many linguists looked at language. Linguists following Chomsky began analyzing deep syntactic structures, not just surface structures. And of course, Einstein revolutionized physics, showing that Newtonian physics represented only a limiting case of physics, in general, and further showing the relativity of notions about space and time. Reinitiations can apply to entire fields, as in the case of Einstein, or to smaller subfields; in each case, however, the creators are arguing for a fresh approach to creative work.

Reinitiative contributions are often bold and daring gestures. One prime example can be found in sculpture, with Marcel Duchamp's 1917 *Fountain*. Duchamp's Dada piece is simply a urinal turned on its back. The very act of entering such a piece in an art show is a statement about art—Duchamp's sculpture initiated a new focus on the definition of exactly what art is and what art can be. Duchamp's urinal became a piece of art, and he and his fellow Dada creators set the stage for other modern art that exists, in part, to challenge our ideas of what art encompasses (Hartt, 1993).

Another radical reinitiator was one of Duchamp's friends, the composer John Cage. He often employed unconventional sound materials and spent a period in which his compositional process (and often performance) was determined entirely by chance. The philosophy that led Cage to compose in this unorthodox manner can be considered essentially a rejection of some basic tenets of the Western musical tradition, including the definition of music itself. Cage declared all sound to be music, including the whispers and heartbeats we perceive only when we are silent. Cage's affinity for Eastern philosophy caused him to focus on the importance of awareness in the human experience, and he used his music to foster awareness in his listeners.

An illustration of this point is his piece *4'33"*. The performance of this piece consists of 4 minutes and 33 seconds of "silence," or rather, in Cage's terminology, "unintentional sound." In performance, the instrumentalist approaches her instrument, prepares to play, and proceeds to sit, motionless and without sound, for 4 minutes and 33 seconds. The only pauses are those indicated by Cage that signal the change of movement. The music, therefore, is that sound that exists in the environment during that period of time. Cage's statement was that there is music being played around us all the time; we must reject the notion of music as organized melody, harmony, and rhythm and embrace a new concept of music that includes all intentional sound, even the rush of traffic beyond the door and the buzzing of the fluorescent lights above our heads (Cage, 1961; Hamm, 1980).

The Final Type of Contribution: Integration

The eighth and final type of contribution is integration, illustrated in panel 8 of figure 3.1. This type of contribution belongs in its own category because it does not exactly accept or reject an existing paradigm; rather, it merges together two paradigms that previously were seen as unrelated or even as opposed.

What formerly were viewed as distinct ideas now are viewed as related and capable of being unified. Integration is a key means by which progress is attained in the sciences and the arts.

One example of an integration is *Fatherland*, Robert Harris's (1992) best-selling novel of historical speculation. The genre of historical speculation is one in which the author imagines a world different from the one we live in because of a fundamental change in history. One possibility is a world in which a famous event in the past did not occur (e.g., if John F. Kennedy had not been assassinated). Another possibility is a world in which some event occurred that did not, in fact, happen (e.g., a world in which Adolf Hitler was assassinated before gaining power). In *Fatherland*, Harris conceptualizes a world in which Germany defeated the Allies in World War II. But rather than spending the majority of the book setting up the world and describing the new history, Harris plunges right in and begins a suspense thriller. Harris took the two genres—historical speculation and suspense thrillers—and fused them together into a well-received novel.

Another example of integration is the innovative artwork of Rob Silvers. Silvers (1997) takes Georges Seurat's pointillist technique of using many small dots to form a larger work and combines it with the field of photography. Silvers uses thousands of tiny photographs and puts them together to form a larger image. His type of work, called photo mosaics, has become well-known; Silvers designed the movie poster for *The Truman Show* and has done portraits of such disparate individuals as Princess Diana, Abraham Lincoln, and Darth Vader.

General Issues

In considering the eight types of creative contributions, one must realize that certain types of creative contributions may be, in practice, more highly creative than other types, but that there can be no claim in principle that contributions of one type are more creative than contributions of another type (with the possible exception that replications are generally less creative). The reason is that any type of contribution can vary in its novelty and quality vis-à-vis a given mission. Consider, as an example, a reinitiation versus a forward incrementation. A reinitiation is, on average, more defiant of existing paradigms than is a forward incrementation. But a reinitiation is not necessarily more creative than a forward incrementation. The reinitiation may differ only trivially from existing paradigms, or it may differ in a way that moves the field in a fruitless direction. The forward incrementation, on the other hand, may be one that has eluded all or almost all other investigators and thus is highly novel; moreover, it may be a contribution that takes just the step that makes a great difference to a field, such as the step that yields a vaccine against a serious illness. Thus, types of creative contributions do not immediately translate into levels of creative contributions. The relative levels of creativity of two contributions have to be determined on other grounds.

Nevertheless, individual investigators or institutions may have preferences for one type of creative contribution over another. The management of one institution may feel threatened by redefinitions or reinitiations, whereas the management of another institution welcomes them. One graduate adviser may encourage his or her students to strike out on their own in crowd-defying directions, whereas another graduate adviser insists that students work only within existing paradigms or perhaps even only the adviser's own paradigm. Undoubtedly, graduate training plays an important role not only in socializing students with respect to doing worthwhile research but also with respect to the kinds of research that are considered to be worthwhile. As always, what is viewed as creative will depend on the match between what an individual has to offer and what the context is willing to value. We also need to keep in mind that contributions are judged on the basis of many attributes, not just their creativity. A contribution that is creative may be valued or devalued in a society for any number of reasons, for example, its political correctness or the gender, ethnic group, or status of its creator.

Understanding Creativity-Related Phenomena via the Propulsion Model

The propulsion model may help explain several creativity-related phenomena, although of course it does not provide a unique explanation.

First, the propulsion model may help to reconcile the fact that creativity tends to generate negative reactions with the fact that most people seem to believe that they support creativity (Sternberg & Lubart, 1995). The present model suggests that the positivity or negativity of reactions to a given contribution are likely to vary with the type of creativity that is evinced in a given creative contribution. For example, the kind of paradigm-rejecting, crowd-defying creativity dealt with by the investment theory of creativity (Sternberg & Lubart, 1995) is probably largely of the paradigm-rejecting types: redirection (Type 5), reconstruction/redirection (Type 6), and especially reinitiation (Type 7). Paradigm-accepting creativity is more likely to generate a favorable response, at least initially. Forward incrementations, for example, are creative but occur within existing paradigms and hence are more likely to engender favorable reactions, whether from journal editors, grant reviewers, or critics of music and art. In the short run, artists, scientists, and others who provide forward incrementations may have the easiest time getting their work accepted; in the long run, however, their contributions may not be the longest lasting or the most important to where the field goes.

Second, the propulsion model helps psychologists to better understand the nature of the relation between creativity and leadership (see, e.g., Gardner, 1993, 1995). Leadership, like creativity, is propulsion. Hence, creativity always represents at least a weak attempt to lead. But in the case of replication, the attempt is rather trivial. In the case of redirection, reconstruction/redirection, or reinitiation, it may be quite dramatic. In each of these cases, the creative individual is trying to lead the field in a direction different from the one it already is going in. Even advance incrementation represents an impressive form of leadership, in that it attempts to lead a field rather far away from where it is in the multidimensional space, albeit in the same direction that the field already is going.

Examples of the application of the propulsion model to creative leadership can be inferred from an analysis of university presidents by Levine (1998). Levine provides examples of two failed presidents—Francis Wayland of Brown (president from 1827 to 1855) and Henry Tappan of the University of Michigan (1852 to 1863)—both of whom failed because their ideas were ahead of their time. Their ideas would later succeed in other institutions. Both presidents exemplified forward advance incrementations in the attempts at creative leadership of their institutions. Robert Hutchins, president of the University of Chicago from 1929 to 1951, was removed from his presidency because his ideas were behind the times. Hutchins wished to set off in a new direction from a set of ideas that had become passé in the minds of his constituents. Hutchins illustrated reconstruction/redirection. Clark Kerr, president of the University of California, Berkeley, from 1959 to 1967, ultimately failed because he became the wrong person at the wrong time when Ronald Reagan was elected governor of California. In essence, Reagan moved the multidimensional space to a new point, one that left Kerr outside the realm that was viewed as acceptable. The mantle of creative leadership thus was taken on by a governor, leaving the university president out of a job.

Third, the propulsion model helps to address the question of whether programs based on artificial intelligence are creative (see discussions in Boden, 1990, 1999; Csikszentmihalyi, 1988; Dreyfus, 1992). To the extent that computer programs *replicate* past discoveries, no matter how creative those discoveries were, they are nevertheless replications, which is creativity (Type 1), although perhaps of a more modest type. To the extent that computers actually are able to more a field forward or in a new direction, they may be creative in other senses. My reading of the present literature is that these programs are certainly creative in the sense of replication and that they also probably have been creative in the sense of forward incrementations. It is not clear that they have shown the more crowd-defying forms of creativity (Types 5 to 7: redirection, reconstruction/redirection, reinitiation).

Fourth, the propulsion model may be relevant to the long-standing issue (noted previously) of the extent to which creativity is domain-specific or domain-general. I would speculate that the ability to do reasonably successful forward incrementations may be largely domain-general and may even be highly correlated with scores on tests of conventional (analytical) abilities. A forward incrementation seems to require, for the most part, a high level of understanding of an extant knowledge base and an analysis of the trajectory of that field. The ability to acquire, understand, and analyze a knowledge base is largely what is measured by conventional standardized tests (Sternberg, 1997a). But the ability to perform a reinitiation may be quite a bit more domain-specific, requiring a sense or even feeling for a field that goes well beyond the kinds of more generalized analytical abilities measured by conventional tests. Indeed, people who engage in creativity of Types 5 (redirection), 6 (reconstruction/redirection), and 7 (reinitiation) may be people who are less susceptible than others to the entrenchment that can accompany expertise (Frensch & Sternberg, 1989; Sternberg & Lubart, 1995).

The propulsion model certainly has weaknesses and ambiguities. First, it is new and has yet to be quantitatively tested. Such tests are planned based on classifications of creative contributions and analyses of various measures of their impact. Second, contributions cannot be unequivocally classified into the different types. Bach, for example, was viewed in his time as, at best, making small forward incremental contributions or even as being a replicator. Today, he is perceived by many as having helped to redefine Baroque music. Moreover, because we are always making judgments from whatever perspective we may hold, it is impossible to ensure objective judgments of the type of creative contribution a particular work makes or has made. Third, the model proposed here is probably not exhaustive with respect to the types of creative contributions that can be made. There may well be others, and the ones proposed here almost certainly could be subdivided. Fourth, a given contribution may have elements of more than one type of contribution. Finally, the spatial metaphor used as a basis for the theory obviously is an oversimplification. There is no one point in a multidimensional space that adequately can represent a field or a subfield, nor is all research in the field or subfield moving in a single direction.

Ultimately, it is unlikely that there is any one "right" model of types of creative contributions. Rather, models such as this one can help people expand their thinking about the types of creative contributions that can be made in a field. Creative contributions differ not only in amounts but also in types, and the eight types represented here are ones that presumably occur in all fields at all times. We should be aware of them when they occur. We also may wish to steer our children and ourselves toward certain types of creative contributions: ideally, the types that are most compatible with what these children or we, respectively, ideally wish to offer. Do we wish our children to be replicators, to be forward incrementers, to be redirecters, to know when to be which? These are the decisions we must make in the way we socialize our children, and ultimately, the children will need to decide for themselves, as they grow older, how they wish to unlock and express their creative potential.

DEVELOPING CREATIVITY: 21 WAYS TO DECIDE FOR CREATIVITY

How can one encourage people to decide for creativity? According to the view of creativity as a decision, fomenting creativity is largely a matter of fomenting a certain attitude toward problem solving and even toward life. Creativity researchers may have a great deal of academic knowledge about creativity, but they do not necessarily interact with students in a way that maximizes the chances that students will decide for creativity.

In the following section, I consider 21 different ways to encourage students to decide for creativity. I consider some data that address the question of whether the use of such strategies can improve school achievement, if teachers encourage rather than discourage students in deciding for creativity.

Redefine the Problem

Redefining a problem means taking a problem and turning it on its head. Many times in life, an individual has a problem and just doesn't see how to solve it. That person is stuck in a box. Redefining a problem essentially means extricating oneself from the box. It is an aspect of problem finding, as opposed to merely problem solving. This process is the divergent part of creative thinking.

A good example of redefining a problem is summed up in the story of an executive at one of the biggest automobile companies in the Detroit area. The executive held a high-level position, and he loved his job and the money he made on the job. However, he despised the person he worked for, and because of this, he decided to find a new job. He went to a headhunter, who assured him that a new job could be easily arranged. After this meeting, the executive went home and talked to his wife, who was teaching a unit on redefining problems as part of a course she was teaching on Intelligence Applied (Sternberg & Grigorenko, in press). The executive realized that he could apply what his wife was teaching to his own problem. He returned to the headhunter and gave the headhunter his boss's name. The headhunter found a new job for the executive's boss, which the boss—having no idea what was going on—accepted. The executive then got his boss's job. The executive decided for creativity by redefining a problem.

There are many ways that teachers and parents can encourage children to define and redefine problems for themselves, rather than—as is so often the case—doing it for them. Teachers and parents can promote creative performance by encouraging their children to define and redefine *their own* problems and projects. Adults can encourage creative thinking by having children choose their own topics for papers or presentations, choose their own ways of solving problems, and sometimes having them choose again if they discover that their selection was a mistake. Teachers and parents should also allow their children to pick their own topics, subject to the adults' approval, on projects the children do. Approval ensures that the topic is relevant to the lesson and has a chance of leading to a successful project.

Adults cannot always offer children choices, but giving choices is the only way for children to learn how to choose. A real choice is not deciding between drawing a cat or a dog, nor is it picking one state in the United States to present at a project fair. Giving children latitude in making choices helps them to develop taste and good judgment, both of which are essential elements of creativity.

At some point, everyone makes a mistake in choosing a project or in the method he or she selects to complete it. Teachers and parents should remember that an important part of creativity is the analytic part—learning to recognize a mistake—and give children the chance and the opportunity to redefine their choices.

Question and Analyze Assumptions

Everyone has assumptions. Often one does not know he or she has these assumptions because they are widely shared. Creative people question assumptions and eventually lead others to do the same. Questioning assumptions is part of the analytical thinking involved in creativity. When Copernicus suggested that Earth revolves around the sun, the suggestion was viewed as preposterous, because everyone could see that the sun revolves around Earth. Galileo's ideas, including the relative rates of falling objects, caused him to be banned as a heretic. When an employee questions the way the boss manages the business, the boss does not smile. The employee is questioning assumptions that the boss and others simply accept—assumptions that they do not wish to open up to questions.

Sometimes it is not until many years later that society realizes the limitations or errors of their assumptions and the value of the creative person's thoughts. Those who question assumptions allow for cultural, technological, and other forms of advancement.

Teachers and parents can be role models for questioning assumptions by showing children that what they assume they know, they really do not know. Of course, children shouldn't question every assumption. There are times to question and try to reshape the environment, and there are times to adapt to it. Some creative people question so many things so often that others stop taking them seriously. Everyone must learn which assumptions are worth questioning and which battles are worth fighting. Sometimes it's better for individuals to leave the inconsequential assumptions alone so that they have an audience when they find something worth the effort.

Teachers and parents can help children develop this talent by making questioning a part of the daily exchange. It is more important for children to learn what questions to ask—and how to ask them—than to learn the answers. Adults can help children evaluate their questions by discouraging the idea that the adults ask questions and children simply answer them. Adults need to avoid perpetuating the belief that their role is to teach children the facts, and instead help children understand that what matters is the children' ability to use facts. This can help children learn how to formulate good questions and how to answer questions.

Society tends to make a pedagogical mistake by emphasizing the answering and not the asking of questions. The good student is perceived as the one who rapidly furnishes the right answers. The expert in a field thus becomes the extension of the expert student—the one who knows and can recite a lot of information. As John Dewey (1933) recognized, how one thinks is often more important than what one thinks. Schools need to teach children how to ask the right questions (questions that are good, thought provoking, and interesting) and lessen the emphasis on rote learning.

Do Not Assume That Creative Ideas Sell Themselves: Sell Them

Everyone would like to assume that their wonderful, creative ideas will sell themselves. But they do not. On the contrary, creative ideas are often viewed with suspicion and distrust, just as are stocks that sell at a low price/earnings (P/E) ratio. Moreover, those who propose such ideas may be viewed with suspicion and distrust as well. Because people are comfortable with the ways they already think, and because they probably have a vested interest in their existing ways of thinking, it can be extremely difficult to dislodge them from their current ways of thinking.

Thus, children need to learn how to persuade other people of the value of their ideas. This selling is part of the practical aspect of creative thinking. If children do science projects, it is a good idea for them present those and demonstrate why they make important contributions. If they create pieces of artwork, they should be prepared to describe why they think their works have value. If they develop plans for new forms of government, they should explain why these are better than the existing form of government. At times, teachers may find themselves having to justify their ideas about teaching to their principal. They should prepare their students for the same kind of experience.

Encourage Idea Generation

As mentioned earlier, creative people demonstrate a legislative style of thinking: They like to generate ideas (Sternberg, 1997b). The environment for generating ideas can be constructively critical, but it must not be harshly or destructively critical. Children need to realize that some ideas are better than others. Adults and children should collaborate to identify and encourage any creative aspects of ideas that are presented. When ideas are suggested that don't seem to have much value, teachers should not just criticize. Rather, they should suggest new approaches, preferably ones that incorporate at least some aspects of the previous ideas that seemed, in themselves, not to have much value. Children should be praised for generating ideas, regardless of whether some are silly or unrelated, while being encouraged to identify and develop their best ideas into high-quality projects.

Recognize That Knowledge Is a Double-Edged Sword and Act Accordingly

One cannot be creative without knowledge. Quite simply, one cannot go beyond the existing state of knowledge if one does not know what that state is. Many children have ideas that are creative with respect to themselves but not with respect to the field because others have had the same ideas before. Those with a greater knowledge base can be creative in ways that those who are still learning about the basics of the field cannot be.

At the same time, those who have an expert level of knowledge can experience tunnel vision, narrow thinking, and entrenchment. Experts can become so stuck in a way of thinking that they become unable to extricate themselves from it. In a study of expert and novice bridge players, for example (Frensch & Sternberg, 1989), we found that experts outperformed novices under regular circumstances. When a superficial change was made in the surface structure of the game, both the experts and novices were hurt slightly in their playing but quickly recovered. When a profound, deep-structural change was made in the game, the experts initially were hurt more than the novices, although the experts later recovered. The reason, presumably, is that experts make more and deeper use of the existing structure and hence have to reformulate their thinking more than do novices when there is a deep-structural change in the rules of the game.

Encourage Children to Identify and Surmount Obstacles

Buying low and selling high means defying the crowd. And people who defy the crowd—people who think creatively—almost inevitably encounter resistance. The question is not whether one will encounter obstacles; one will. When one buys low, one defies the crowd and generally engenders in others a reaction of, at best, puzzlement and, at worst, hostility. The question is whether the creative thinker has the fortitude to persevere. I have often wondered why so many people start off their careers doing creative work and then vanish from the radar screen. I think I know at least one reason why: Sooner or later, they decide that being creative is not worth the resistance and punishment. The truly creative thinkers pay the short-term price because they recognize that they can make a difference in the long term. But often it is a long while before the value of creative ideas is recognized and appreciated.

Parents and teachers can prepare children for these types of experiences by describing obstacles that they, their friends, and well-known figures in society have faced while trying to be creative; otherwise, children may think that they are the only ones confronted by obstacles. Teachers should include stories about people who weren't supportive, about bad grades for unwelcome ideas, and about frosty receptions to what they might have thought were their best ideas. To help children deal with obstacles, parents and teachers can remind them of the many creative people whose ideas were initially shunned and help them to develop an inner sense of awe of the creative act. Suggesting that children reduce their concern over what others think is also valuable. However, it is often difficult for children to lessen their dependence on the opinions of their peers.

When children attempt to surmount obstacles, they should be praised for the effort, whether or not they were entirely successful. Teachers and parents alike can point out aspects of the effort that were successful and why, and suggest other ways to confront similar obstacles. Having the class brainstorm about ways to confront a given obstacle can get the class thinking about the many strategies people can use to confront problems. Some obstacles are within oneself, such as performance anxiety. Other obstacles are external, such as others' bad opinions of one's actions. Whether internal or external, obstacles must be overcome.

Encourage Sensible Risk-Taking

When creative people defy the crowd by buying low and selling high, they take risks in much the same way as do people who make financial investments. Some such investments simply may not pan out. Similarly, the creative person may generate an idea that is unpopular when it first is generated and that stays unpopular over the long term. Moreover, defying the crowd means risking the crowd's disdain for buying into the wrong idea, or even its wrath for disagreeing with others. But there are levels of sensibility to keep in mind when defying the crowd. Creative people take sensible risks and produce ideas that others ultimately admire and respect as trendsetting. In taking these risks, creative people sometimes make mistakes, fail, and fall flat on their faces.

I emphasize the importance of sensible risk-taking because I am not talking about risking life and limb for creativity. To help children learn to take sensible risks, adults can encourage them to take some intellectual risks with courses, with activities, and with what they say to adults—to develop a sense of how to assess risks.

Nearly every major discovery or invention entails some risk. When a movie theater was the only place to see a movie, someone created the idea of the home video machine. Skeptics questioned whether anyone would want to see videos on a small screen. Another initially risky idea was the home computer. Many wondered if anyone would have enough use for a home computer to justify the cost. These ideas were once risks that are now ingrained in our society.

Few children are willing to take risks in school, because they learn that taking risks can be costly. Perfect test scores and papers receive praise and open up future possibilities. Failure to attain a certain academic standard is perceived as deriving from a lack of ability and motivation and may lead to scorn and lessened opportunities. Why risk taking hard courses or saying things that teachers may not like when that may lead to low grades or even failure? Teachers may inadvertently advocate children's only learning to play it safe when they give assignments without choices and allow only particular answers to questions. Thus, teachers need not only to encourage sensible risk-taking, but also to reward it.

Encourage Tolerance of Ambiguity

People often like things to be in black and white. People like to think that a country is good or bad (ally or enemy) or that a given idea in education works or does not work. The problem is that there are a lot of grays in creative work, just as there are when one invests in a stock whose value may or may not go up. Many stocks are low-valued. The ambiguities arise as to which will go up, when they will go up, and even, for some individuals, what they can do to make them go up. Artists working on new paintings and writers working on new books often report feeling scattered and unsure in their thoughts. They frequently need to figure out whether they are even on the right track. Scientists often are not sure whether the theories they have developed are exactly correct. These creative thinkers need to tolerate ambiguity and uncertainty until they get their ideas just right.

A creative idea tends to come in bits and pieces and to develop over time. However, the period in which the idea is developing tends to be uncomfortable. Without time or the ability to tolerate ambiguity, many may jump to a less than optimal solution. When a student has almost the right topic for a paper or almost the right science project, it's tempting for teachers to accept the near miss. To help children become creative, teachers need to encourage them to accept and extend the period during which their ideas do not quite converge. Children need to be taught that uncertainty and discomfort are a part of living a creative life. Ultimately, they will benefit from their tolerance of ambiguity by coming up with better ideas.

Help Children Build Self-Efficacy

Many people eventually reach a point at which they feel as if no one believes in them. I reach this point frequently, feeling that no one values or even appreciates what I am doing. Because creative work often doesn't get a warm reception, it is extremely important that creative people believe in the value of what they are doing. This is not to say that individuals should believe that every idea they have is a good idea. Rather, individuals need to believe that, ultimately, they have the ability to make a difference.

The main limitation on what children can do is what they think they can do. All children have the capacity to be creators and to experience the joy associated with making something new, but first they must be given a strong base for creativity. Sometimes teachers and parents unintentionally limit what children can do by sending messages that express or imply limits on children's potential accomplishments. Instead, these adults need to help children believe in their own ability to be creative.

I have found that probably the best predictor of success in my children is not their ability, but their belief in their ability to succeed. If children are encouraged to succeed and to believe in their own ability to succeed, they very likely will find the success that otherwise would elude them.

Help Children Find What They Love to Do

Teachers must help children find what excites them, to unleash their children's best creative performances. In the investment metaphor, one needs to find an area in which to invest about which one feels some excitement, so that one will do what one can to maximize the value of investments. Teachers need to remember that what they happen to teach may not be what really excites all of their students. People who truly excel creatively in a pursuit, whether vocational or avocational, almost always genuinely love what they do. Certainly, the most creative people are intrinsically motivated in their work (Amabile, 1996). Less creative people often pick a career for the money or prestige and are bored with or loathe their careers. Most often, these people do not do work that makes a difference in their fields.

Helping children find what they really love to do is often hard and frustrating work. Yet, sharing the frustration with them now is better than leaving them to face it alone later. To help children uncover their true interests, teachers can ask them to demonstrate special talents or abilities for the class and explain that it doesn't matter what they do (within reason), only that they love the activities they choose.

Teach Children the Importance of Delaying Gratification

Part of being creative means being able to work on a project or task for a long time without immediate or interim rewards, just as in financial investing one often must wait quite a while for the value of a stock to rise. Children must learn that rewards are not always immediate and that there are benefits to delaying gratification. The fact of the matter is that, in the short term, people are often ignored when they do creative work or even punished for doing it.

Many people believe that they should reward children immediately for good performance, and that children should expect rewards. This style of teaching and parenting emphasizes the here and now and often comes at the expense of what is best in the long term.

An important lesson in life—and one that is intimately related to developing the discipline to do creative work—is to learn to wait for rewards. The greatest rewards are often those that are delayed. Teachers can give their children examples of delayed gratification in their lives and in the lives of creative individuals and help them apply these examples to their own lives.

Hard work often does not bring immediate rewards. Children do not immediately become expert baseball players, dancers, musicians, or sculptors. And the reward of becoming an expert can seem very far away. Children often succumb to the temptations of the moment, such as watching television or playing video games. The people who make the most of their abilities are those who wait for rewards and recognize that very few serious challenges can be met in a moment. Ninth-grade children may not see the benefits of hard work, but the advantages of solid academic performance will be obvious when they apply to college.

The short-term focus of most school assignments does little to teach children the value of delaying gratification. Projects are clearly superior in meeting this goal, but it is difficult for teachers to assign home projects if they are not confident of parental involvement and support. By working on a task for many weeks or months, children learn the value of making incremental efforts for long-term gains.

Model Creativity

There are many ways teachers and parents can provide an environment that fosters creativity (Sternberg & Williams, 1996). The most powerful way for teachers to develop creativity in children is to *model creativity.* Children develop creativity not when they are told to, but when they are shown how.

The teachers most people probably remember from their school days are not those who crammed the most content into their lectures, but those whose thoughts and actions made them role models. Most likely, they balanced teaching content with teaching children how to think with and about that content. The Nobel laureates, before they received their prizes, made excellent role models, largely because they were outstanding examples of creativity in action whom students could emulate (Zuckerman, 1977, 1983).

Cross-Fertilize Ideas

Teachers also can stimulate creativity by helping children to cross-fertilize in their thinking to think across subjects and disciplines. The traditional school environment often has separate classrooms and classmates for different subjects and seems to influence children into thinking that learning occurs in discrete boxes—the math box, the social studies box, and the science box. However, creative ideas and insights often result from integrating material across subject areas, not from memorizing and reciting material.

Teaching children to cross-fertilize draws on their skills, interests, and abilities, regardless of the subject. If children are having trouble understanding math, teachers might ask them to draft test questions related to their special interests. For example, teachers might ask the baseball fan to devise geometry problems based on a game. The context may spur creative ideas because the student finds the topic (baseball) enjoyable, and it may counteract some of the anxiety caused by geometry. Cross-fertilization motivates children who aren't interested in subjects taught in the abstract.

One way teachers can enact cross-fertilization in the classroom is to ask children to identify their best and worst academic areas. Children can then be asked to come up with project ideas in their weak areas based on ideas borrowed from their strongest areas. For example, teachers can explain to children that they can apply their interest in science to social studies by analyzing the scientific aspects of trends in national politics.

Allow Time for Creative Thinking

Teachers also need to allow children the time to think creatively. Often, creativity requires time for incubation (Wallas, 1926). Many societies today are societies in a hurry. People eat fast food, rush from one place to another, and value quickness. Indeed, one way to say someone is smart is to say that the person is *quick* (Sternberg, 1985a), a clear indication of an emphasis on time. This is also indicated by the format of many of the standardized tests used—lots of multiple-choice problems squeezed into a brief time slot.

Most creative insights do not happen in a rush (Gruber & Davis, 1988). People need time to understand a problem and to toss it around. If children are asked to think creatively, they need time to do it well. If teachers stuff questions into their tests or give their children more homework than they can complete, they are not allowing them time to think creatively.

Instruct and Assess for Creativity

Teachers also should instruct and assess for creativity. If a teacher gives only multiple-choice tests, children quickly learn that the teacher values memorization and correct answers. If teachers want to encourage creativity, they need to include at least some opportunities for creative thought in assignments and tests. Questions that require factual recall, analytic thinking, *and* creative thinking should be asked. For example, children might be asked to learn about a law, analyze the law, and then think about how the law might be improved.

Reward Creativity

Teachers also need to reward creativity. They may choose differentially to reward the different kinds of creative contributions, depending on the circumstances and the students. For example, if teachers ask students to be bold in their thinking, the teachers may choose to provide a smaller reward for conceptual replications than for bolder redirections (at levels of innovation characteristic of students, of course). Thus, teachers may choose not to limit their rewards to crowd-defying creativity but may choose to allocate rewards depending on circumstances and expectations for particular students. It is not enough to talk about the value of creativity; children are used to authority figures who say one thing and do another. They are exquisitely sensitive to what teachers value when it comes to the bottom line—namely, the grade or evaluation.

Creative efforts also should be rewarded. For example, teachers can assign a project and remind children that they are looking for them to demonstrate their knowledge, analytical and writing skills, and creativity. Teachers should let children know that creativity does not depend on the teacher's agreement with what children write, but rather with ideas they express that represent a synthesis between existing ideas and their own thoughts. Teachers need to care only that the ideas are creative from the student's perspective, not necessarily creative with regard to the state-of-the-art findings in the field. Children may generate an idea that someone else has already had, but if the idea is an original to the student, the student has been creative.

Some teachers complain that they cannot apply as much objectivity to grading creative responses as they can to multiple-choice or short-answer responses. They are correct in that there is some sacrifice of objectivity. However, research shows that evaluators are remarkably consistent in their assessments of creativity (Amabile, 1996; Sternberg & Lubart, 1995). If the goal of assessment is to instruct children, then it is better to ask for creative work and evaluate it with somewhat less objectivity than to evaluate children exclusively on uncreative work. Teachers should let children know that there is no completely objective way to evaluate creativity.

Allow Mistakes

Teachers also need to allow mistakes. Buying low and selling high carries a risk. Many ideas are unpopular simply because they are not good. People often think in the established way because that way works better than other ways. But once in a while, a great thinker comes along—a Freud, a Piaget, a Chomsky, or an Einstein—and shows us a new way to think. These thinkers made contributions because they allowed themselves and their collaborators to take risks and make mistakes.

Many of Freud's and Piaget's ideas turned out to be wrong. Freud confused Victorian issues regarding sexuality with universal conflicts and Piaget misjudged the ages at which children could perform certain cognitive feats. Their ideas were great not because they lasted forever, but rather because they became the basis for other ideas. Freud's and Piaget's mistakes allowed others to profit from their ideas.

Although being successful often involves making mistakes along the way, schools are often unforgiving of mistakes. An error in schoolwork is often marked with a large and pronounced X. When a student responds to a question with an incorrect answer, some teachers pounce on the student for not having read or understood the material, which results in classmates' snickering. In hundreds of ways and in thousands of instances over the course of a school career, children learn that it is not all right to make mistakes. The result is that they become afraid to risk the independent and sometimes flawed thinking that leads to creativity.

When children make mistakes, teachers should ask them to analyze and discuss these mistakes. Often, mistakes or weak ideas contain the germ of correct answers or good ideas. In Japan, teachers spend entire class periods asking children to analyze the mistakes in their mathematical thinking. For the teacher who wants to make a difference, exploring mistakes can be an opportunity for learning and growing.

Teach Children to Take Responsibility for Both Successes and Failures

Another aspect of teaching children to be creative is teaching them to take responsibility for both successes and failures. Teaching children how to take responsibility means teaching children to (a) understand their creative process, (b) criticize themselves, and (c) take pride in their best creative work. Unfortunately, many teachers and parents look for—or allow children to look for—an outside enemy responsible for failures.

It sounds trite to say that teachers should teach children to take responsibility for themselves, but sometimes there is a gap between what people know and how they translate thought into action. In practice, people differ widely in the extent to which they take responsibility for the causes and consequences of their actions. Creative people need to take responsibility for themselves and for their ideas.

Encourage Creative Collaboration

Teachers also can work to encourage creative collaboration (Chadwick & Courtivron, 1996; John-Steiner, 2000; Sawyer, 2001). Creative performance often is viewed as a solitary occupation. We may picture the author writing alone in a studio, the artist painting in a solitary loft, or the musician practicing endlessly in a small music room. In reality, people often work in groups. Collaboration can spur creativity. Teachers can encourage children to learn by example by collaborating with creative people.

Teach Children to Imagine Things from Others' Points of View

Children also need to learn how to imagine things from other viewpoints. An essential aspect of working with other people and getting the most out of collaborative creative activity is to imagine oneself in other people's shoes. Individuals can broaden their perspective by learning to see the world from different points of view. Teachers and parents should encourage children to see the importance of understanding, respecting, and responding to other people's points of view. This is important, as many bright and potentially creative children never achieve success because they do not develop practical intelligence (Sternberg, 1985a, 1997a). They may do well in school and on tests, but they may never learn how to get along with others or to see things and themselves as others see them.

Maximize Person-Environment Fit

Teachers also need to help children recognize person-environment fit. What is judged as creative is an interaction between a person and the environment (Csikszentmihalyi, 1988, 1996; Gardner, 1993; Sternberg & Lubart, 1995). The very same product that is rewarded as creative in one time or place may be scorned in another.

In the movie *Dead Poets' Society,* a teacher whom the audience might well judge to be creative is viewed as incompetent by the school's administration. Similar experiences occur many times a day in many settings. There is no absolute standard for what constitutes creative work. The same product or idea may be valued or devalued in different environments. The lesson is that individuals need to find settings in which their creative talents and unique contributions are rewarded, or they need to modify their environments.

By building a constant appreciation of the importance of person-environment fit, teachers prepare their students to choose environments that are conducive to their creative success. Encourage children to examine environments to help them learn to select and match environments with their skills. (And while encouraging children to do it, do it yourself.)

DO THESE STRATEGIES WORK?

If students use strategies such as the ones just discussed, will they be able to enhance their creative performance, and particularly, will it make any difference to their academic achievement? We have done a series of studies testing the theory of successful intelligence (Sternberg, 1997a), of which creative thinking is a component. In each of the studies, one of the manipulations used was to teach school subject matter for creativity, encouraging students to use strategies such as the ones described earlier to break out of the box in their learning of new material. Teachers in some (experimental) conditions were taught these principles regarding how to teach for creativity, using as a reference the material that is now available in *Teaching for Successful Intelligence* (Sternberg and Grig-orenko, 2000).

In a first set of studies, researchers explored the question of whether conventional education in school systematically discriminates against children with creative and also practical strengths (Sternberg & Clinkenbeard, 1995; Sternberg, Ferrari, Clinkenbeard, & Grigorenko, 1996; Sternberg, Grigorenko, Ferrari, & Clinkenbeard, 1999). Motivating this work was the belief that the systems in most schools strongly tend to favor children with strengths in memory and analytical abilities. The investigators used the Sternberg Triarchic Abilities Test (Sternberg, 1993) to identify creative as well as analytical and practical abilities of students. The test was administered to 326 children (around the United States and in some other countries) who were identified by their schools as gifted by any standard whatsoever. Children were selected for a summer program in (college-level) psychology at Yale University if they fell into one of five ability groupings: high analytical, high creative, high practical, high balanced (high in all three abilities), or low balanced (low in all three abilities). Students were then divided into four instructional groups. Students in all four instructional groups used the same introductory psychology textbook (a preliminary version of Sternberg, 1995b) and listened to the same psychology lectures. What differed were the types of afternoon discussion sections to which they were assigned. Each was assigned to an instructional condition that emphasized either memory, analytical, creative, or practical instruction. For example, in the memory condition, participants might be asked to describe the main tenets of a major theory of depression. In the analytical condition, they might be asked to compare and contrast two theories of depression. In the creative condition, they might be asked to formulate their own theories of depression. In the practical condition, they might be asked how they could use what they had learned about depression to help a friend who was depressed.

Students in all four instructional conditions were evaluated in terms of their performance on homework, a midterm exam, a final exam, and an independent project. Each type of work was evaluated for memory, analytical, creative, and practical quality. Thus, all students were evaluated in exactly the same way.

Our results suggested the utility of our framework. This utility showed itself in several ways.

First, the investigators observed when the students arrived at Yale that the students in the high-creative and high-practical groups were much more diverse in terms of racial, ethnic, socioeconomic, and educational backgrounds than were the students in the high-analytical group, suggesting that correlations of measured intelligence with status variables such as these may be reduced by using a broader conception of intelligence. More important, just by expanding the range of abilities measured, the investigators discovered intellectual strengths that might not have been apparent through a conventional test.

Second, the investigators found that all three ability tests—analytical, creative, and practical—significantly predicted course performance. When multiple-regression analysis was used, at least two of these ability measures contributed significantly to the prediction of each of the measures of achievement. Perhaps as a reflection of the difficulty of deemphasizing the analytical way of teaching, one of the significant predictors was always the analytical score.

Third and most important, there was an aptitude-treatment interaction whereby students who were placed in instructional conditions that better matched their pattern of abilities outperformed students who were mismatched. In other words, when students are taught in a way that fits how they think, they do better in school. Children with creative and practical abilities who are almost never taught or assessed in a way that matches their patterns of abilities may be at a disadvantage in course after course, year after year.

In short, by encouraging students to think creatively—to create, imagine, suppose, discover, invent—teachers can help students improve their achievement. Some students already do these things and typically are not reinforced or even may be punished by their schools. Teachers can reconstruct classrooms, however, so that deciding for creativity is rewarded rather than punished, resulting in improved student achievement.

A follow-up study (Sternberg, Torff, & Grigorenko, 1998a, 1998b) examined the learning of social studies and science by third graders and eighth graders. The 225 third graders were students in a very low-income neighborhood in Raleigh, North Carolina. The 142 eighth graders were students who were largely middle- to upper-middle-class in Baltimore, Maryland, and Fresno, California. In this study, students were assigned to one of three instructional conditions. In the first condition, they were taught the course that they would have learned had there been no intervention. The emphasis in the course was on memory. In a second condition, students were taught in a way that emphasized critical (analytical) thinking. In the third condition, they were taught in a way that emphasized analytical, creative, and practical thinking. All students' performances were assessed for memory learning (through multiple-choice assessments) as well as for analytical, creative, and practical learning (through performance assessments).

As expected, students in the condition that encouraged a mix of analytical, creative, and practical thinking outperformed the other students. More important, however, was the result that children in the analytical-creative-practical condition outperformed the other children even on the multiple-choice memory tests. In other words, to the extent that one's goal is just to maximize children's memory for information, teaching for diverse modes of thinking is still superior. It enables children to capitalize on their strengths and to correct or to compensate for their weaknesses, and it allows children to encode material in a variety of interesting ways.

Grigorenko and her colleagues (Grigorenko, Jarvin, & Sternberg, 2002) have now extended these results to reading curricula at the middle school and high school levels. In a study of 871 middle school students and 432 high school students, researchers taught reading either analytically, creatively, and practically or through the regular curriculum. At the middle school level, reading was taught explicitly. At the high school level, reading was infused into instruction in mathematics, physical sciences, social sciences, English, history, foreign languages, and the arts. In all settings, students who were taught triarchially substantially outperformed students who were taught in standard ways (Grigorenko, Jarvin, & Sternberg, 2002).

Thus, it appears that teaching can encourage students to think creatively as well as for practical applications of their creative thinking. When students are taught in such a way, their achievement increases. Ultimately, then, our goal in schools should be to teach in a way that makes deciding for creativity normative rather than counternormative.

NOTES

Preparation of this chapter was supported by Grant REC-9979843 from the National Science Foundation and under the Javits Act Program (Grant No. R206R000001) as administered by the Office of Educational Research and Improvement, U.S. Department of Education. Grantees undertaking such projects are encouraged to express freely their professional judgment. This chapter, therefore, does not necessarily represent the position or policies of the Office of Educational Research and Improvement or the U.S. Department of Education, and no official endorsement should be inferred.

1. Portions of this section are based on a collaborative work with James Kaufman and Jean Pretz.

REFERENCES

Abelson, R. P., Aronson, E., McGuire, W. J., Newcomb, T. M., Rosenberg, M. J., & Tannenbaum, P. H. (Eds.). (1968). *Theories of cognitive consistency: A sourcebook.* Chicago: Rand McNally.

Amabile, T. M. (1983). *The social psychology of creativity.* New York: Springer-Verlag.

Amabile, T. M. (1996). *Creativity in context.* Boulder, CO: Westview.

Amabile, T. M. (2001). Beyond talent: John Irving and the passionate craft of creativity. *American Psychologist, 56,* 333–336.

Bem, D. J. (1967). Self-perception: An alternative interpretation of cognitive dissonance phenomena. *Psychological Review, 74,* 183–200.

Bem, D. J. (1996). Exotic becomes erotic: A developmental theory of sexual orientation. *Psychological Review, 103,* 320–335.

Binet, A., & Simon, T. (1916). *The development of intelligence in children.* Baltimore: Williams & Wilkins. (Original work published 1905)

Bloom, H. (1994). *The Western canon: The books and school of the ages.* New York: Harcourt Brace.

Boden, M. A. (1990). *The creative mind: Myths and mechanisms.* New York: Basic Books.

Boden, M. A. (1999). Computer models of creativity. In R. J. Sternberg (Ed.), *Handbook of creativity* (pp. 351–372). New York: Cambridge University Press.

Brand, C. (1996). *The g factor: General intelligence and its implications.* Chichester, UK: Wiley.

Cage, J. (1961). *Silence.* Middletown, CT: Wesleyan University Press.

Carroll, J. B. (1982). The measurement of intelligence. In R. J. Sternberg (Ed.), *Handbook of human intelligence* (pp. 29–120). New York: Cambridge University Press.

Carroll, J. B. (1993). *Human cognitive abilities: A survey of factor-analytic studies.* New York: Cambridge University Press.

Cattell, R. B., & Cattell, H. E. P. (1973). *Measuring intelligence with the Culture Fair Tests.* Champaign, IL: Institute for Personality and Ability Testing.

Ceci, S. J. (1996). *On intelligence: A bioecological treatise on intellectual development* (Exp. ed.). Cambridge, MA: Harvard University Press.

Chadwick, W., & Courtivron, I. D. (Eds.). (1996). *Significant others: Creativity and intimate partnership.* London: Thames & Hudson.

Chomsky, N. (1957). *Syntactic structures.* The Hague, Netherlands: Mouton.

Collins, M. A., & Amabile, T. M. (1999). Motivation and creativity. In R. J. Sternberg (Ed.), *Handbook of creativity* (pp. 297–312). New York: Cambridge University Press.

Csikszentmihalyi, M. (1988). Society, culture, and person: A systems view of creativity. In R. J. Sternberg (Ed.), *The nature of creativity* (pp. 325–339). New York: Cambridge University Press.

Csikszentmihalyi, M. (1996). *Creativity: Flow and the psychology of discovery and invention.* New York: HarperCollins.

Csikszentmihalyi, M. (1999). Implications of a systems perspective for the study of creativity. In R. J. Sternberg (Ed.), *Handbook of creativity* (pp. 313–335). New York: Cambridge University Press.

Derrida, J. (1992). *Acts of literature* (D. Attridge, Ed.). New York: Routledge.

Dewey, J. (1933). *How we think: A restatement of the relation of reflective thinking to the educative process.* Boston: Heath.

Dreyfus, H. L. (1992). *What computers still can't do.* Cambridge: MIT Press.

Dweck, C. S. (1999). *Self-theories: Their role in motivation, personality, and development.* Philadelphia: Psychology Press.

Fazio, R. H., Zanna, M. P., & Cooper, J. (1977). Dissonance and self-perception: An integrative view of each theory's proper domain of application. *Journal of Experimental Social Psychology, 13,* 464–479.

Festinger, L., & Carlsmith, J. M. (1959). Cognitive consequences of forced compliance. *Journal of Abnormal and Social Psychology, 58,* 203–210.

Frensch, P. A. & Sternberg, R. J. (1989). Expertise and intelligent thinking: When is it worse to know better? In R. J. Sternberg (Ed.), *Advances in the psychology of human intelligence* (Vol. 5, pp. 157–188). Hillsdale, NJ: Erlbaum.

Galton, F. (1883). *Inquiry into human faculty and its development*. London: Macmillan.

Garcia, J., and Koelling, R. A. (1966). The relation of cue to consequence in avoidance learning. *Psychonomic Science, 4,* 123–124.

Gardner, H. (1983). *Frames of mind: The theory of multiple intelligences*. New York: Basic Books.

Gardner, H. (1993). *Creating minds*. New York: Basic Books.

Gardner, H. (1995). *Leading minds*. New York: Basic Books.

Gardner, H. (1999). *Intelligence reframed: Multiple intelligences for the 21st century*. New York: Basic Books.

Gardner, H., Csikszentmihalyi, M., & Damon, W. (2002). *Good work*. New York: Basic Books.

Goodman, N. (1955). *Fact, fiction, and forecast*. Cambridge, MA: Harvard University Press.

Gould, S. J. (1981). *The mismeasure of man*. New York: Norton.

Grigorenko, E. L., Jarvin, L., & Sternberg, R. J. (2002). School-based tests of the triarchic theory of intelligence: Three settings, three samples, three syllabi. *Contemporary Educational Psychology, 27,* 167–208.

Gruber, H. (1981). *Darwin on man: A psychological study of scientific creativity* (2nd ed.). Chicago: University of Chicago Press.

Gruber, H. E. (1989). The evolving systems approach to creative work. In D. B. Wallace & H. E. Gruber (Eds.), *Creative people at work: Twelve cognitive case studies* (pp. 3–24). New York: Oxford University Press.

Gruber, H. E., and Davis, S. N. (1988). Inching our way up Mount Olympus: The evolving-systems approach to creative thinking. In R. J. Sternberg (Ed.), *The nature of creativity* (pp. 243–270). New York: Cambridge University Press.

Gruber, H. E., & Wallace, D. B. (1999). The case study method and evolving systems approach for understanding unique creative people at work. In R. J. Sternberg (Ed.), *Handbook of creativity* (pp. 93–115). New York: Cambridge University Press.

Gruber, H. E., & Wallace, D. B. (2001). Creative work: The case of Charles Darwin. *American Psychologist, 56,* 346–349.

Guilford, J. P. (1967). *The nature of human intelligence*. New York: McGraw-Hill.

Hamm, C. (1980). John Cage. In *The new Grove dictionary of music and musicians* (Vol. 3, pp. 597–603). London: Macmillan.

Hartt, F. (1993). *Art: A history of painting, sculpture, architecture* (4th Ed). Englewood Cliffs, NJ: Prentice Hall.

Herrnstein, R. J., & Murray, C. (1994). *The bell curve*. New York: Free Press.

Horn, J. L. (1994). Theory of fluid and crystallized intelligence. In R. J. Sternberg (Ed.), *The encyclopedia of human intelligence* (Vol. 1, pp. 443–451). New York: Macmillan.

Hunt, E., Frost, N., & Lunneborg, C. (1973). Individual differences in cognition: A new approach to intelligence. In G. Bower (Ed.), *The psychology of learning and motivation* (Vol. 7, pp. 87–122). San Diego, CA: Academic Press.

Hunt, E. B., Lunneborg, C., & Lewis, J. (1975). What does it mean to be high verbal? *Cognitive Psychology, 7*, 194–227.

Jensen, A. R. (1982). Reaction time and psychometric *g*. In H. J. Eysenck (Ed.), *A model for intelligence* (pp. 93–132). Heidelberg, Germany: Springer-Verlag.

Jensen, A. R. (1998). *The g factor: The science of mental ability*. Westport, CT: Praeger/Greenwoood.

John-Steiner, V. (1997). *Notebooks of the mind: Explorations of thinking* (2nd ed.). New York: Oxford University Press.

John-Steiner, V. (2000). *Creative collaboration*. New York: Oxford University Press.

Kamin, L. (1974). *The science and politics of IQ*. Hillsdale, NJ: Erlbaum.

Kruskal, J. B. (1964a). Multidimensional scaling by optimizing goodness of fit to a nonmetric hypothesis. *Psychometrika, 20*, 1–27.

Kruskal, J. B. (1964b). Nonmetric multidimensional scaling: A numerical method. *Psychometrika, 20*, 115–129.

Langley, P., Simon, H. A., Bradshaw, G. L., & Zytkow, J. M. (1987). *Scientific discovery: Computational explorations of the creative process*. Cambridge: MIT Press.

Levine, A. (1998). Succeeding as a leader; failing as a president. *Change*, January/February, 43–45.

Lewontin, R. (1982). *Human diversity*. New York: Freeman.

Lubart, T. I. (1994). Creativity. In R. J. Sternberg (Ed.), *Thinking and problem solving* (pp. 290–332). San Diego, CA: Academic Press.

Lubart, T. I., & Sternberg, R. J. (1995). An investment approach to creativity: Theory and data. In S. M. Smith, T. B. Ward, & R. A. Finke (Eds.), *The creative cognition approach* (pp. 269–302). Cambridge: MIT Press.

Machlis, J. (1979). *Introduction to contemporary music*. (2nd ed.). New York: Norton.

Mumford, M. D., & Gustafson, S. B. (1988). Creativity syndrome: Integration, application, and innovation. *Psychological Bulletin, 103*, 27–43.

Nakamura, J., & Csikszentmihalyi, M. (2001). Catalytic creativity: The case of Linus Pauling. *American Psychologist, 56*, 337–341.

Perkins, D. N. (1981). *The mind's best work*. Cambridge, MA: Harvard University Press.

Policastro, E., & Gardner, H. (1999). From case studies to robust generalizations: An approach to the study of creativity. In R. J. Sternberg (Ed.), *Handbook of creativity* (pp. 213–225). New York: Cambridge University Press.

Royer, F. L. (1971). Information processing of visual figures in the digit symbol substitution task. *Journal of Experimental Psychology, 87*, 335–42.

Rubenson, D. L., & Runco, M. A. (1992). The psychoeconomic approach to creativity. *New Ideas in Psychology, 10*, 131–147.

Sawyer, R. K. (2001). *Creating conversations: Improvisation in everyday discourse*. Cresskill, NJ: Hampton.

Siegler, R. S. (1992). The other Alfred Binet. *Developmental Psychology, 28*, 179–190.

Simonton, D. K. (1988). *Scientific genius*. New York: Cambridge University Press.

Simonton, D. K. (1999). Talent and its development: An emergenic and epigenetic mode. *Psychological Review, 106*, 435–457.

Skinner, B. F. (1972). A lecture on "having" a poem. In B. F. Skinner, *Cumulative record: A selection of papers* (3rd ed., pp. 345–355). New York: Appleton-Century-Crofts.

Spearman, C. E. (1904). 'General intelligence' objectively determined and measured. *American Journal of Psychology, 15*, 201–293.

Spearman, C. E. (1927). *The abilities of man.* London: Macmillan.

Sternberg, R. J. (1977). *Intelligence, information processing, and analogical reasoning: The componential analysis of human abilities.* Hillsdale, NJ: Erlbaum.

Sternberg, R. J. (1982). Natural, unnatural, and supernatural concepts. *Cognitive Psychology, 14*, 451–488.

Sternberg, R. J. (1983). Components of human intelligence. *Cognition, 15*, 1–48.

Sternberg, R. J. (1985a). *Beyond IQ: A triarchic theory of human intelligence.* New York: Cambridge University Press.

Sternberg, R. J. (1985b). Implicit theories of intelligence, creativity, and wisdom. *Journal of Personality and Social Psychology, 49*(3), 607–627.

Sternberg, R. J. (Ed.). (1988). *The nature of creativity: Contemporary psychological perspectives.* New York: Cambridge University Press.

Sternberg, R. J. (1993). *Triarchic abilities test.* Unpublished test. New Haven, CT: Yale University.

Sternberg, R. J. (1995a). For whom the bell curve tolls [Review of *The bell curve*]. *Psychological Science, 6*, 257–261.

Sternberg, R. J. (1995b). *In search of the human mind.* Ft. Worth, TX: Harcourt College Publishers.

Sternberg, R. J. (1997a). *Successful intelligence.* New York: Plume.

Sternberg, R. J. (1997b). *Thinking styles.* New York: Cambridge University Press.

Sternberg, R. J. (Ed.). (1999a). *Handbook of creativity.* New York: Cambridge University Press.

Sternberg, R. J. (1999b). A propulsion model of types of creative contributions. *Review of General Psychology, 3*, 83–100.

Sternberg, R. J., & Clinkenbeard, P. R. (1995). The triarchic model applied to identifying, teaching, and assessing gifted children. *Roeper Review, 17*(4), 255–260.

Sternberg, R. J., Ferrari, M., Clinkenbeard, P. R., & Grigorenko, E. L. (1996). Identification, instruction, and assessment of gifted children: A construct validation of a triarchic model. *Gifted Child Quarterly, 40*(3), 129–137.

Sternberg, R. J., & Gastel, J. (1989a). Coping with novelty in human intelligence: An empirical investigation. *Intelligence, 13,* 187–197.

Sternberg, R. J., & Gastel, J. (1989b). If dancers ate their shoes: Inductive reasoning with factual and counterfactual premises. *Memory and Cognition, 17,* 1–10.

Sternberg, R. J., & Grigorenko, E. L. (2000). *Teaching for successful intelligence.* Arlington Heights, IL: Skylight.

Sternberg, R. J., & Grigorenko, E. L. (in press). *Intelligence applied* (2nd ed.). New York: Oxford University Press.

Sternberg, R. J., Grigorenko, E. L., Ferrari, M., & Clinkenbeard, P. (1999). A triarchic analysis of an aptitude-treatment interaction. *European Journal of Psychological Assessment, 15*, 1–11.

Sternberg, R. J., Kaufman, J. C., & Pretz, J. (2002). *The creativity conundrum.* Philadelphia: Psychology Press.

Sternberg, R. J., & Lubart, T. I. (1991). An investment theory of creativity and its development. *Human Development, 34,* 1–31.

Sternberg, R. J., & Lubart, T. I. (1995a). *Defying the crowd: Cultivating creativity in a culture of conformity.* New York: Free Press.

Sternberg, R. J., & Lubart, T. I. (1996). Investing in creativity. *American Psychologist, 51,* 677–688.

Sternberg, R. J., Torff, B., & Grigorenko, E. L. (1998a). Teaching for successful intelligence raises school achievement. *Phi Delta Kappan, 79,* 667–669.

Sternberg, R. J., Torff, B., & Grigorenko, E. L. (1998b). Teaching triarchically improves school achievement. *Journal of Educational Psychology, 90,* 374–384.

Sternberg, R. J., & Williams, W. M. (1996). *How to develop student creativity.* Alexandria, VA: Association for Supervision and Curriculum Development.

Tetewsky, S. J., & Sternberg, R. J. (1986). Conceptual and lexical determinants of nonentrenched thinking. *Journal of Memory and Language, 25,* 202–225.

Thomson, G. H. (1939). *The factorial analysis of human ability.* London: University of London Press.

Thurstone, L. L. (1938). *Primary mental abilities.* Chicago: University of Chicago Press.

Tolman, E. C. (1932). *Purposive behavior in animals and men.* New York: Appleton-Century-Crofts.

Vernon, P. A., & Mori, M. (1992). Intelligence, reaction times, and peripheral nerve conduction velocity. *Intelligence, 8,* 273–288.

Wallas, G. (1926). *The act of thought.* London: Watts.

Weisberg, R. W. (1993). *Creativity: Beyond the myth of genius.* New York: Freeman.

Wickett, J. C., & Vernon, P. A. (1994). Peripheral nerve conduction velocity, reaction time, and intelligence: An attempt to replicate Vernon and Mori. *Intelligence, 18,* 127–132.

Woodman, R. W., & Schoenfeldt, L. F. (1989). Individual differences in creativity: An interactionist perspective. In J. A. Glover, R. R. Ronning, & C. R. Reynolds (Eds.), *Handbook of creativity.* New York: Plenum.

Zuckerman, H. (1977). *Scientific elite: Nobel laureates in the United States.* New York: Free Press.

Zuckerman, H. (1983). The scientific elite: Nobel laureates' mutual influences. In R. S. Albert (Ed.), *Genius and eminence* (pp. 241–252). Oxford, UK: Pergamon.

CHAPTER FOUR

The Creation of Multiple Intelligences Theory

A Study in High-Level Thinking

**David Henry Feldman, with the
collaboration of Howard Gardner**

As the field of creativity studies has grown and prospered to its current highly active and productive level of work, it has nonetheless remained relatively silent when it comes to precisely how significant creative works are accomplished. The present chapter is intended to add to the relatively small amount of information available to the field that deals with how works of recognized significance are created (see Gruber, 1974, 1981; Gruber & Wallace, 1989). Its special feature is that it is perhaps the first study to be done in which the two participants are longtime colleagues, occasional collaborators on research relevant to the topic under scrutiny, and have both been involved in the field of creativity studies for many years. Although the focus of this study—the theory of multiple intelligences—is not about creativity per se, it was constructed during the period when its author (Howard Gardner) and the present author were close collaborators and heavily involved in work on creativity (see Feldman, 1982; Feldman, Csikszentmihalyi, & Gardner, 1994).

Additionally, the creation of the theory was itself a creative endeavor worthy of examination. It would be difficult to overestimate the impact that the theory of multiple intelligences has had in the field of education. From its introduction in 1983, the impact of Howard Gardner's *Frames of Mind: The Theory of Multiple Intelligences* has seemed to increase with each passing year. By this point in its history, there are thousands of schools that claim to use multiple intelligences

(MI) theory in planning their curricula, evaluation, and/or instructional approach, and hundreds of books and guides about how to implement the theory. In a limited Internet search in 2002, more than 100,000 sites were identified as MI-theory relevant. Clearly, MI theory has established a major beachhead in the fields of educational theory, policy, and practice. Not without its critics (see Traub, 1998), MI has nonetheless emerged as a force to be reckoned with in educational circles. It therefore meets the major criterion of high-strength creativity, namely, that it is a contribution recognized to be of great importance within an established domain of knowledge (Morelock & Feldman, 1999).

After a brief review of the major trends in the field of creativity studies during the past two decades, the data for the present chapter are presented. These data consist formally of a series of interviews about the creation of MI theory carried out by the author with Howard Gardner during the spring of 2001 and informally include the distillation of many years' association between author and subject. Our aim in the chapter is to describe how, over a period of years, the work known as MI theory was created.

CONTEMPORARY CREATIVITY RESEARCH

Thanks to the efforts of a cadre of contemporary researchers and theorists, we are now more informed about the historical circumstances that impact creative work (see, for example, Csikszentmihalyi, 1988, 1994, 1996; Simonton, 1999), the life stories of some of the most historically significant creative figures (see, for example, Gardner, 1993) and elder scientists (Csikszentmihalyi, 1996; Nakamura & Csikszentmihalyi, this volume), the circumstances under which promising children become eminent adults (Albert & Runco, 1990), and the motives that drive people to greater creative accomplishment (Amabile, 1983, 1996). We also have important new data on the problem-solving processes involved in creative solutions to challenging problems posed in the laboratory (see, for example, Sternberg, 1988; Ward, Smith, & Finke, 1999; Weisberg, 1999) and in computer simulation exercises (Boden, 1999; Simon, 1995). An important new study of collaboration in creative accomplishment has added a great deal to what is known about the vital role that other people play in achieving high levels of creative achievement (John-Steiner, 2000).

Other work done in recent years, although not about creativity per se, has added to our understanding of some of the constituent issues that are part of the creativity matrix. The study of expertise and its development have raised important questions about the importance of talent versus training in achieving high levels of performance in various domains (see, for example, Bloom, 1985; Chi, Glaser, & Farr, 1988; Ericcson, 1996; Howe, Davidson, & Sloboda, 1998). Other studies have focused on extreme cases, such as prodigies and savants, helping to establish distinctions between various specific forms of ability as well as some constraints on them that might limit their creative use (Howe, 1989; Feldman, 1986; Kanigel, 1991; Miller, 1989; Morelock & Feldman, 1999, 2000; Treffert, 1989).

Efforts within the related field of giftedness studies have had complex and sometimes ambivalent relationships to the study of creativity (see, for example, Feldman & Benjamin, 1998; Guilford, 1950, 1970; Ross, 1993). Researchers in the field of giftedness studies have struggled to establish an appropriate role for creativity as part of giftedness (see, for example, Feldhusen, 1997; Heller, Monks, & Passow, 1993; Torrance, 1988). For the most part, creativity has been conceptualized as an aspect or contributing component of giftedness, enhancing or extending giftedness into new areas of challenge but not eclipsing IQ. Efforts to assess or measure creativity have been major themes in this field (see, for example, Guilford, 1950, 1970; Torrance, 1966; Sternberg, 1999; Wallach & Kogan, 1965; Wallach & Wing, 1969). Although new knowledge about creative thinking and problem solving continues to emerge from this research tradition, the broader field has moved in different directions, diminishing the overall impact of work in this tradition.

Definitions of Creativity and Development

As do the other contributors to this volume, I describe here my own perspective on the two main themes of the book: creativity and development. I began thinking about the two topics at about the same time, during a year of study at the Harvard Graduate School of Education in 1965 to 1966. I wrote my first paper on creativity for a course in human development that year. Whereas development was to become the center of my studies and my career, creativity always remained an active sideline, a topic to which I found myself turning almost in spite of myself. For when I began studying creativity, the topic was not related to development in the research literature; it was part of the fields of clinical psychology (see Sanford, 1966) and psychometrics (see Guilford, 1950, 1970). It took several years for me to bring the two topics together, which I began to do in the early 1970s, publishing my first developmental treatment of creative thinking in 1974 (Feldman, 1974).

The main insight that brought creativity and development together for me was the realization that creativity was another form of cognitive developmental transition, sharing qualities with stage-to-stage transitions described by (especially) Piaget (1975). In retrospect, I now see that the kind of creativity I was thinking about was "high *C*" (also referred to as "big *C*"; see Morelock & Feldman, 1999, for our rationale in using the terms we have chosen), whereas the research field of creativity studies had been mostly dealing with "low *C*" creative thinking (e.g., Getzels & Jackson, 1962; Torrance, 1966; Wallach & Kogan,

1965; Wallach & Wing, 1969). At the time, I was amazed that the insights of the great thinkers might have been achieved using mental processes not unlike those of the preschooler trying to understand how liquids are conserved in quantity even as they are transformed in appearance (e.g., poured from a wide, low container into a high, narrow one). Although not without its problems, as Howard Gruber (1980) was to point out later, the idea that creativity can be seen as a kind of developmental transition, a move from one level of understanding to another, has animated my work ever since. All of my work on cognitive developmental transitions has been aimed at further illuminating the processes of thought that bring about major advances in understanding (see, for example, Feldman, 1980, 1994; Snyder & Feldman, 1977, 1984).

The main distinction between cognitive developmental transitions of different sorts, from my theoretical perspective, is the degree of universality or commonness that characterizes the shift. For the most common such shifts, it is reasonable to think of them as universal creative insights, whereas for the rarest shifts, we have moved into the realm of unique creative insights, of which the most powerful may be labeled works of genius (Feldman, 1980, 1986).

A universal cognitive developmental transition might be the initial realization that the actual amount of liquid does not alter in spite of the change in its appearance when moved from one container to another. A work of genius might be the theory of evolution by variation and natural selection as proposed by Charles Darwin in 1859, or Einstein's theory of relativity published during the first decade of the past century (Gruber, 1981; Gruber & Barrett, 1974). All three are creative in the sense that they represent major advances in the individual's understanding of a challenging problem, with profound implications for how that person thinks. The advance represented by recognition of the conservation of liquid (as it was labeled by Piaget) is one that is virtually guaranteed to occur in all children as they move from early to middle childhood. Darwin's advance in understanding, although similarly profound for his individual development as a thinker, was (when communicated several years later) to have great influence on (indeed to fundamentally transform) a highly challenging domain of knowledge. The experience of advancing in one's thinking in such a profound way may be similar across instances, but the domain within which the achievement takes place is vastly different (Feldman, 1974, 1989b). The participation in ever more unique domains is centrally what separates the Darwin advance from that of the child solving the conservation of liquids problem.

Granted that the analogy to developmental transitions may only apply to the more extreme forms of creative advances, the connection between the two, even at the extremes, has led to a number of changes in how creativity is conceptualized. I am not the only (nor the first) to have pursued the connection between creativity and cognitive development; Piaget continually used examples from the fields of mathematics, logic, and biology to describe cognitive developmental transitions (Piaget, 1971). Howard Gruber was the first to try to systematically explore the connection between common and exceptional creative advances, and the subject of the present chapter, Howard Gardner, is another scholar whose work has explored relationships between creativity and development (see Gardner, 1993; Gruber, 1981; Gruber & Barrett, 1974; Gruber & Wallace, 1989).

Much of my work since 1974, both theoretical and empirical, has been toward further illuminating the developmental transitions in domains between the universal and the unique regions that were juxtaposed in the previous few paragraphs. Theoretically, I have proposed a continuum of forms of cognitive development that can be placed between the extremes (see Figure 4.1). Each of the regions described on the continuum is assumed to contain a number of domains (organized bodies of knowledge and skill). Every time someone moves from one level or stage to another in any domain in any region of the universal to unique continuum, high-level creative thinking is involved. In other words, if development exists at all in a domain, then creative thinking appropriate to the domain is one of its markers (see Feldman, 1989b).

As with a number of my colleagues (including the subject in the current chapter and very likely the authors of other chapters in this volume), certain qualities are now central to my way of thinking about creativity. First, I believe that creative thinking is involved in all developmental transitions, whether of a mundane and common sort as can be expected to occur in virtually all human beings during their normal lives, or the more exalted sort that fundamentally reorganizes a body of knowledge (or even causes a new one to spring into existence). Second, I believe that creativity occurs within specific domains; there is no general trait of creativity (although there may well be, as the psychometricians have shown, a general ability to produce novel and innovative ideas). Third, I believe that creativity is best understood from several perspectives at the same time, including the individual or individuals involved in achieving the transition in understanding (and their collaborators; see John-Steiner, 2000), the distinct qualities of the domain in which the contribution might be important, and the wider field that judges which contributions will be recognized as significant and to what degree (see Csikszentmihalyi, 1988, 1994, 1996; also see Nakamura & Csikszentmihalyi, this volume). Broader contextual issues such as the historical record preceding a given event and the social and cultural realities

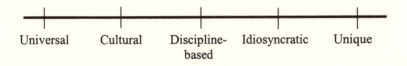

FIGURE 4.1. Developmental regions, from universal to unique

that provide constraints and opportunities for involvement in certain fields and not others must also be taken into account (see Simonton, 1984, 1988, 1999). Sternberg and Lubart (1996, 1999; Sternberg, this volume) have called this approach a confluence model, which seems an appropriate label for the perspective that I bring to the task of better understanding creativity and development.

Developmental transitions and creativity are inextricably intertwined; it is impossible to understand one without understanding the other. The challenge of creativity studies, then, is to specify the distinctive qualities as well as the shared markers that characterize each domain, including clear descriptions of the developmental stages or levels that represent the core knowledge and skill of the domain. This work is propaedeutic to the possibility of understanding the shared and distinctive kinds of thinking involved in movement from level to level. Creative thinking pervades the continuum, but what we tend to label creative typically appears at the unique end of the universal to unique continuum. For a transition to be labeled creative in the unique region of the continuum, an existing domain with an existing set of developmental levels must be transformed irreversibly through the efforts of an individual or individuals to solve a problem or contribute something of value to that domain. These potentially transforming events range in strength from minor changes (e.g., the better mousetrap) to substantial reorganizations of the body of knowledge and skill of the domain (e.g., laser surgery) (see Feldman, Csikszentmihalyi, & Gardner, 1994).

Howard Gruber's Study of Charles Darwin's Thinking

Although much of the research and theory carried out during the past two decades is of potential relevance to the work presented here, most of it is of only indirect relevance. The work that is most relevant is Howard Gruber's (1974) masterful study of the thinking of Charles Darwin during the period when he first created the theory (of evolution by natural selection) that changed the world after it was published in 1859. Along with his colleague Paul Barrett, a biologist, Gruber was able to shed dramatic new light on the processes through which Darwin constructed and reconstructed his revolutionary new theory. Gruber and Barrett uncovered theretofore-ignored materials (Darwin's *M* and *N* notebooks) in the Cambridge University Library that revealed details in the development of Darwin's thought (Gruber, 1974, 1981). By examining primary documents, Gruber and Barrett were able to reconstruct the form and substance of Darwin's reasoning as he unknowingly approached his epochal synthesis.

The process through which Darwin constructed his theory turned out to be a much more deductive one than previously believed. Apparently, Darwin had put together the formal features of his theory in the 2 years following the naturalist excursion he took around the world on the *Beagle*, when he was between the ages of 26 and 29. He spent the next 20 years gathering data in support of his theory, putting it to empirical test with studies of barnacles, earthworms, and other creatures, as well as reading the research literature to see how studies not designed to test the theory stood in relation to its claims.

Gruber's new interpretation stood in contrast to the prior belief that Darwin was a careful empirical scientist who only reluctantly and after many years of research built an inductive account that captured the features of the observed data. The notebooks revealed that Darwin employed discipline by ensuring that his claims of evolution by variation and natural selection were sufficiently supported by empirical evidence prior to publishing his theory. Had Alfred Wallace not proposed a similar theory, Darwin might not have published in 1859 (Gruber, 1974, 1981).

The technique used in the present study differs in certain respects from that of Gruber. Archival materials were used, but these were created by a living person, Howard Gardner. There were also opportunities for Gardner to interpret or add context to the written record, and for me to discuss with him the meaning and significance of certain documents. The effort to reconstruct the process through which MI theory was created, then, was in some ways similar to and in some ways different from Gruber's effort to reconstruct the creation of the theory of evolution by Charles Darwin.

Another difference is that both participants in this study had the advantage of Gruber's work as a guide. The influence of that existing work on the present one has been substantial, but the two projects differ in important ways as well. An advantage of the present study is that both participants are in the same field of scholarship, have a long history of association, and were able to jointly guide the effort to reconstruct the developmental process that led to the theory of MI (John-Steiner, 2000). In this respect, the present work is collaborative in ways that were not possible as Gruber pursued the progression of ideas that guided Darwin to his goal.

Having briefly summarized the work on creativity that is most relevant to this study, it is now appropriate to introduce the theory of MI itself and to interpret its place as a creative contribution of substantial significance.

MI THEORY

Though the intended audience was the field of intellectual development, MI theory is indisputably one of the most influential contributions to education in the last century. In order to appreciate the unique qualities of the theory that help explain its great influence, it is necessary to briefly describe the theories of intelligence that preceded MI theory and provided the context and backdrop for the appearance of MI theory in 1983 (for more extended accounts, see Ferrari &

Sternberg, 1998; Gardner, Kornhaber, & Wake, 1996; Gould, 1981; Resnick, 1976; Sternberg, 1982).

From its earliest manifestations, the study of intelligence has been a contentious and fractious affair (see Gould, 1981). Perhaps the most persistent issue within the field has been the one-versus-many-intelligences question. As early as the beginning of the last century, disputes erupted about whether there was a single, general (*g*) intelligence that governed all mental abilities or whether intelligence was more accurately described as a set of related abilities, each specialized to certain forms of content or certain kinds of mental processes (Gardner, Kornhaber, & Wake, 1996). Throughout its history, the question of one versus many intelligences has been a source of heated debate and sometimes acrimonious rhetoric.

In this respect, then, the theory of MI represents a contemporary manifestation of a venerable tradition. MI theory proposes eight relatively independent intelligences (seven in the original version), each with special competence to deal with relatively specific kinds of domains (bodily/kinesthetic, interpersonal, intrapersonal, natural qualities of the world, mathematical/logical, musical, spatial, and verbal or linguistic; Gardner, 1983).

The number and types of intelligences proposed, especially in the original 1983 version, closely resembles Thurstone and Thurstone's primary mental abilities theory (e.g., Thurstone & Thurstone, 1941) from nearly a half century earlier. Many other proposals for *g* (general) versus *s* (specific) intelligences have been made over the decades since Binet and Simon constructed the first viable intelligence test in Paris in about 1905; some of these have included both *g* and *s* components in their architecture, usually with *g* having the highest and most influential place in the system (see Gardner, Kornhaber, & Wake, 1996; Sternberg, 1982). One particularly influential *s*-oriented theory proposed by J. P. Guilford in the 1960s included 120 theoretically independent abilities in its original version and 180 in a later version (Guilford, 1967).

There seem to be a number of reasons why MI theory has been more influential than its predecessors, reasons distinctive to the theory itself as well as reasons having to do with the historical/cultural context within which the theory was proposed (Csikszentmihalyi, 1988; Feldman, Csikszentmihalyi, & Gardner, 1994). Internally, the theory departed from traditional psychometrics in building its case only marginally on testing and test score data, depending much more heavily on data and anecdotes from a variety of interdisciplinary sources (Gardner, 1983, 1993). Gardner examined archeological and paleontological records, psychological studies, and anecdotes of high-level achievement from various fields. Additionally, he analyzed existing symbol systems and extrapolated from theories of cognitive development. Perhaps most powerfully, Gardner relied heavily upon clinical research on brain-damaged individuals in the creation of his theory. Examples of the effects of brain damage on cognitive functioning are particularly compelling in that they are easily comprehended by non-technically trained readers. Examples from the ballet, from mime, from sports and poetry serve to bring the theory to life in ways that were not the case with the work of Gardner's predecessors, even those with similar commitments to sets of specific abilities at the core of intelligence. Most people can find a place for themselves within the broad and commodious tent of the theory's superstructure. MI theory seems to give everyone an opportunity to shine, to show distinctive and strong talents and abilities in realms of activity valued and valuable in most cultures (Chen, Krechevsky, & Viens, 1998).

Previous theories of intelligence (both g and s theories) were almost exclusively built from psychometric test data. The most sophisticated theories of multiple abilities used the arcane methods of factor analysis to support their central claims (Gould, 1981; Guilford, 1950, 1967). Even social scientists trained in the technique have difficulty understanding its inner workings, whereas those with little training have to essentially take the experts' word for the validity of the procedures used. Factor analysts have argued for decades over how many factors (or intelligences, in the terms of MI theory) there are, what specific factor-analytic techniques should be used to establish them, and what analytic tools should be applied in interpreting them, leaving most of the social science community looking in from the outside and the rest of society in total mystery about how it all is really done. These qualities of psychometric research have served to limit the appeal of its findings, as well as to give those findings an aura of powerful science.

In spite of their continued use in the public schools of this country, IQ and other standardized tests have not been an altogether comfortable medium for most educators; they rarely understand them technically (in common with most people outside the psychometric fraternity), nor are they necessarily drawn to the central claim that one overarching ability explains all forms of academic achievement (Gardner, 1999).

In these qualities lies the kernel of MI theory's success: It produced claims that were similar superficially to those of its predecessors, but its claims were built on a foundation that any interested person could readily comprehend. Thus, MI theory became a candidate for a revolution in education even as it was seen as lacking in scientific rigor by traditional psychometric scholars (Lubinski & Benbow, 1995). As Howard Gardner has acknowledged (personal communication, April 2001), the theory's impact has been much greater in education than in psychology.

The theory that Gardner proposed in 1983 was therefore constructed in a new way, a way that gave it much greater appeal than prior theories that appeared to be similar. But the theory also was composed of some elements that had never appeared in connection with the term *intelligence*, and these elements were also to contribute to its success and appeal. I am referring to two of the seven intelligences in the original theory, those that deal with personal, social, and emotional matters as a kind of intelligence. As we shall see in a later section, Gardner was uniquely prepared to take this bold step with his theory, but however prepared he might have been, the inclusion of interpersonal and intrapersonal intelligence was the most dramatic and most controversial of the theory's claims. Gardner argued that knowing oneself and one's inner life or knowing and understanding others' motives, ideas, wishes, and desires were distinctive, independent, specific kinds of intelligences. Indeed, the theory proposed that someone could be gifted at one of these (a future psychoanalyst perhaps) but not the other (a future political leader or military strategist, among other possibilities).

By juxtaposing some of the more traditional areas of intellectual functioning (verbal, visual, spatial, logical) with some areas of functioning that seem on first glance to be far removed from what we mean by intelligence (bodily, inter-, and intrapersonal), Gardner mixed a heady brew that, for many, was intoxicating and encouraging. Teachers and other educators in particular found refuge in the theory, often reporting that they at last found a theory that helped them express their own views of children and their learning capabilities (Albert, 1988; Olson, 1988).

Historical and Contextual Contributions to the Theory's Success

As just noted, the theory of MI is a distinctively accessible theory, built with different elements and using different data than previous theories. These without doubt contributed to its remarkable influence. Beyond the internal features of the theory, though, there were factors concerning when and under what conditions the new theory was introduced in 1983 that also help explain its success. These historical and cultural factors included the push for civil rights and the appreciation of diversity in education, the feminist movement, the waning of Piaget as the central theoretical figure in education, and a number of more local events that gave Howard Gardner's work support and recognition within and beyond his home base of Cambridge, Massachusetts.

When Louis and Thelma Thurstone (1941) introduced their factor-based theory of primary mental abilities in the 1940s, they did so to a very different professional community than that on the scene in the 1980s. Although Piaget was working productively in Geneva, his influence on this continent was minimal, and would be for another 20 years (Flavell, 1963). Testing in the psychometric tradition was the method of choice in the field of differential psychology. The influence of testing was also evident in the civil service, college admissions, education at the elementary and secondary levels, and in the military's use of it to establish hegemony over other approaches.

Given the centrality of testing then and arguably now (Lemann, 2000), it made sense that any viable challenge to the reign of *g* intelligence would be built on the same foundation as its adversary, psychometric testing. In this respect, factor theories were basically in-house arguments about how to conceptualize and interpret the same sorts of data, namely, test scores. There were no viable alternatives from which to mount an offensive against IQ.

When Howard Gardner entered the scene in the early 1980s, testing had been under fire for several years, most notably in the recurring controversies over race and intelligence (see, for example, Jensen, 1969), and over the value of using IQ gains as a measure of the success of early-intervention efforts with children of poverty (Bornstein & Krasnegor, 1989; Ramey, Lee, & Burchinal, 1989).

Differential psychology was a marginal specialty within the larger field of psychology by that point, having yielded center stage to the surging specialties of cognitive, developmental, clinical, neuropsychology and brain studies, among others. All of these fields offered alternative theoretical, methodological, and conceptual approaches to the question of one versus many capabilities, and Howard Gardner took an ecumenical stance when he embraced the whole set (including psychometrics itself).

In field terms (see Csikszentmihalyi, 1988; Feldman, Gardner, & Csikszentmihalyi, 1994), Howard Gardner had a wide set of influential alternative approaches from which to craft his new theory. The response of psychometrics to the theory after 1983 was, to be sure, frosty and dismissive (see Lubinski & Benbow, 1995), but the impact of such a reaction was by that point substantially diluted (see Hunt, 1997). Even as its political influence in the wider community increased, psychometrics as a subfield of psychology was increasingly marginal and peripheral. Although there were then and still are important advances in psychometrics, the mainstream action had largely moved to cognition and development, giving Howard Gardner more elbow room for his theory of MI to make its way.

The receptivity of the nonscholarly community to Gardner's proposal was intensified by the upheavals and preoccupations that preceded its appearance. Most notable, perhaps, were the many political efforts to increase the recognition of groups of individuals who had been marginalized in U.S. society. The civil rights movement, feminism, the struggle for gay rights and the rights of handicapped individuals were among the more successful of such movements. An increasingly diverse population was becoming visible, as projections of a *minority majority* (i.e., more people from cultures other than European origin than from those sources) were made. *Diversity* had become a watchword within higher education, with affirmative action toward greater diversity a major theme of the 1970s and 1980s. Gardner's ideas found ready acceptance as part of the broader social/cultural focus of these decades on greater recognition of diversity, including diversity in intellectual strengths and weaknesses (Chen, Krechevsky, & Viens, 1998). By the end of the twentieth century, affirmative action was under attack and losing ground, but in the 1980s and 1990s, it was a central tenet of policy in education. Similarly, immigration policies and practices, legal and extralegal, led to a changing demographic mosaic in the schools, forcing those in charge to reflect upon and modify long-standing ways of doing things. The idea of a minority majority moved toward becoming a demographic reality.

The van Leer Project

We have seen how the domain of psychology had evolved to the point at which psychometrics was no longer as central to its knowledge structures as it had been for more than 50 years. Cognitive, developmental, clinical, and brain research were increasingly central to the field, and the emerging interdisciplinary field of cognitive science was growing in importance as well. And we have seen how broader political and cultural events in U.S. society helped prepare it for a diversity-based perspective on intelligence. It is necessary to now turn to the more immediate context that surrounded Howard Gardner as he began to carry out the synthesis that would lead to the publication of *Frames of Mind* in 1983. Although (as we will see), the roots of MI theory can be found much earlier in Gardner's experience and training, the research project that was known as the van Leer project (named for its benefactor, Oscar van Leer) was pivotal (Howard Gardner, personal communication, April 2001).

In the introduction to *Frames of Mind,* Gardner (1983) described the purposes of the project in this way: "In 1979, the Bernard van Leer Foundation, concerned with supporting appropriate innovations in education to benefit the disadvantaged, asked the Harvard Graduate School of Education to assess the scientific knowledge concerning human potential and its realization and to summarize the findings in a form that would assist educational policy and practice throughout the world" (p. xiii). The explicit aims of the project included communication to policymakers around the world about the state of current knowledge of immediate use in designing programs and constructing policy initiatives. These directives were the key shifts in context that emboldened Gardner and enervated his efforts. He was no longer a relatively isolated researcher seeking grants and publishing results in scholarly journals and books. To be sure, his compass was always wider than that of the traditional scholar, but the catalytic effects of the van Leer project were enormous (Howard Gardner, personal communication, February 2001).

When the van Leer project was launched in 1979 and early 1980, Howard Gardner was a research associate at the Harvard Graduate School of Education, one of several contract researchers on a kind of shadow faculty that had grown up around Harvard as its eminence increased well beyond its ability to absorb the many talented scholars who wanted to work there. Basically, a scholar in this kind of role is an independent entrepreneur whose continued employment at the institution depends upon bringing in grants to cover salary, costs, and overhead to the university. For a decade, this is the way that Howard Gardner was able to stay at Harvard, by bringing in grants to Project Zero, a research center founded by one of Gardner's mentors, the philosopher of aesthetics and symbol systems, Nelson Goodman.

According to Gardner (personal communication, April 2001), the van Leer project was launched at least in part to provide the financial support that it would take to keep him at Harvard. The university had suspended granting tenure at its school of education, and there was little prospect of a permanent place at the school. Then-dean Paul Ylvisaker, valuing Gardner's contributions as a scholar and grant recipient, negotiated a grant from the Bernard van Leer Foundation of more than a million dollars (a very large sum indeed at the time) to give Gardner and a few others the financial cover they needed to wait out the tenure freeze Harvard had imposed on the school.

It is difficult to imagine the now-world-famous scholar (who holds the Hobbs Chair in Cognition and Education and is a MacArthur Fellowship winner) as a contract researcher, holding onto a fragile position that could have disappeared the moment a grant was refused. That is, however, the position that Howard Gardner was in when he began the research that would lead to *Frames of Mind*. As Gardner describes it, the van Leer project changed everything for him; the way that the theory of MI came out was a direct consequence of the impact that the van Leer project had on the young scholar (Howard Gardner, personal communication, April 2001).

Although always comfortable in the presence of great thinkers, and with an uncanny ability to engender paternalistic interest in his development and career (see Gardner, 1989), Howard Gardner was constrained in his work by the funding that was available and the priorities of those who gave it. Dean Paul Ylvisaker took a special interest in the young man, as had a number of other powerful mentors, including Erik Erikson as an undergraduate tutor; Jerome Bruner as a mentor after Gardner's graduation from Harvard in 1965; and Nelson Goodman, who sponsored Gardner's research at Project Zero. Along the way, Rudolf Arnheim and Norman Geschwind also took a special interest in the young scholar. As Dean Ylvisaker intended, the van Leer project, in effect, gave Gardner the prospect of several years of salary guaranteed, along with almost unimaginable resources with which to pursue his research interests, including enough money to put together a team of assistants and associates to help with the task. As one of those long-ago associates (from January to August 1980), I can attest to the extraordinary nature of the opportunity. What was less apparent to me at the time is how crucial the *security* of the van Leer project was to Gardner's work.

As Gardner tells it (personal communication, April 2001), the van Leer project had the paradoxical effect of both freeing and constraining his work on intelligence. The foundation sponsoring the work had certain goals in mind, and—Howard Gardner being basically the dutiful and responsible German-Jewish refugee's son that he is—Gardner felt obliged to try to do what Oscar van Leer and the others at the foundation expected him to do (see Gardner, 1989). These constraints would turn out to be crucial to the outcome. On the other side, with his release from the weight of constantly worrying about his immediate future and that of his young family of three children, Gardner felt a sense of greater freedom to move beyond the cautious confines of established boundaries: "We learned in 1979 that our project had, in fact, been funded for 4 years (and would eventually be extended to half a decade). This unexpected windfall—ultimately about $1.5 million—could not have come at a better time for me. While my own projects were funded for the next year, there was clearly trouble ahead. On the eve of the Reagan administration, funds for research were already being cut back drastically" (Gardner, 1989, p. 108).

As Gardner portrayed it in his autobiographical book *To Open Minds* (1989), his character is a mix of conservative and cautious (owing, he says, to his immigrant parents and his background), balanced by an American's insouciance and willingness to challenge authority. The balance between these two tendencies has always been the central tension in Gardner's life, but at crucial moments he has been willing to throw all his weight on the side of challenge and revolution, willing to challenge authority without reservation. One of the determinants of such a decision is how secure he feels and how confident he is in carrying out his obligations and responsibilities to his family (including his parents, who expected him to lead the family to prominence in the United States). The support of his mentors and the van Leer money gave him the necessary security and confidence to venture well beyond the synthetic works typical of his earlier career (see, for example, Gardner, 1972, 1974, 1978, 1980).

Perhaps the most important burden that Howard Gardner accepted dutifully, if not enthusiastically, was to aim his van Leer work toward policymakers and educational practitioners. Although blessed with an accessible writing style and always in touch with trends and issues in society, Gardner never saw his role as someone whose job was primarily to communicate with constituencies beyond his scholarly colleagues, although he has done so on a number of occasions. Other than an occasional foray into journalistic writing (for the *New York Times*, for example), Gardner saw his main purpose as doing innovative research on the development of artistic abilities and performing studies of breakdowns after brain damage. Reporting research results in professional journals and writing books about the work were the limits of his professional aspirations, although, as he reminded me, he has always had wider interests than psychology or neurology, including history, music, and especially the visual arts (Howard Gardner, personal communication, February 2001). Gardner reflected on this new dimension of his life in *To Open Minds* (1989):

> First of all, I had entered the International Arena. I was now going to Europe regularly—often in response to some real or imagined crisis in our dealings with the van Leer Foundation. Second, in traveling to parts of the world I had never dreamed I would visit, and gaining entrée to people I never thought I would meet, I was becoming interested in cross-cultural issues. . . .
>
>   Third, in spite of myself, I was learning diplomatic skills. . . . Till then I had really known only three relatively narrow circles: my German-Jewish extended family; middle-class American life; and Ivy League academics and researchers. Now, however, I was mixing with international civil servants, foundation officers, expatriate scholars, and middle-level political leaders. (pp. 120, 121)

New vistas were opening for Howard Gardner, and new responsibilities were being placed on his shoulders. As he began his work at the foundation, the context within which he proceeded had shifted markedly—and as time would tell, irreversibly—from parochial scholar to world citizen. The heady atmosphere of international power brokers and challenging new cultural variations, as well as the mandate to tackle the challenge of determining "the nature and modifiability of human potential" (as the van Leer Foundation described the project's purpose), lifted and widened Gardner's vision of his task.

As to how Gardner would carry out his mandate, he decided early in the history of the project what his message would be (Gardner, 1989). He recounted a meeting with Kenneth Keniston, a senior scholar and colleague who had been involved with projects of similar scope and scale for the Carnegie Corporation, in which Keniston gave this advice: "Decide in the first 6 months what it is that you want to say, and spend the next 3 1/2 years finding the supporting evidence so that you can say it as persuasively as possible" (quoted in Gardner, 1989, p. 109).

As a member of the research team during its first year, I must say that I did not have a clue about what Gardner was going to say 3 1/2 years later. I attended meetings with the research group and the group of 7 to 10 senior colleagues who served as a kind of board of directors for the project, I participated in sessions with visiting scholars reporting their work, and I drafted material based on my own work. I did all of this but had little sense of where the work was going. I thought, in retrospect, that Gardner was keeping his cards close to the vest and that he knew exactly where he was going but did not share it with the rest of us. But in my recent discussions with him (Gardner, personal communication, March 2001), he said that, at that time, he was not sure what he would do with the mountain of data that was being accumulated as we worked together in the spring and summer of 1980.

As I now interpret what Gardner meant in both the autobiographical account and in our one-on-one discussions, he was saying that he had set a general direction consistent with his background and previous work, but he did not have in mind that a theory of MI was going to be the outcome of the group's efforts. The general direction was to focus on cognitive, intellectual potentials (as contrasted with personal, emotional, social, spiritual, or cultural/historical potentials), using his experience as a clinician and researcher in neurology at the Veterans Administration (VA) Hospital in Jamaica Plain, Massachusetts, in addition to his training and background in cognitive developmental psychology. Having worked with severely brain-damaged patients at the VA Hospital, Gardner was able to draw upon a set of experiences that were highly unusual for someone with his background as a research-trained developmental psychologist. He was determined to give full voice to the diversity of his own experience and the variety of phenomena he had investigated as he approached the monumental task of surveying the entire literature on human (cognitive) potential.

The MacArthur Effect

On the basis of a successful text that Gardner wrote for an introductory course in developmental psychology (Gardner, 1978) and possibly for his other books such as *The Quest for Mind* (1972), *Artful Scribbles* (1980), and *Art, Mind, and Brain* (1982a), the MacArthur Foundation awarded Gardner one of its first "genius" grants. The effect of the MacArthur award was to provide both financial security that extended beyond the van Leer project and to make a powerful statement to the world that his work was important. For a scholar with impeccable credentials, Gardner had taken great professional risks in choosing the contract research route; beyond that, he had charted an unusual path by selecting seemingly marginal topics to pursue. His work in symbol systems and the development of artistry seemed unlikely to lead to a regular academic position at a good university. Gardner was thus given an enormous boost by the MacArthur grant (personal communication, February 2001). It may have been this happy event that provided the critical catalyst in transforming his approach at van Leer from magisterial synthesis to a more direct confrontation with the "intelligence mafia," as Gardner (1989) labeled it. (After reading a draft of this passage, both Gardner and his wife, Ellen Winner, suggested that, as a result of the MacArthur award, there may have been an emotional shift that was irreversible and represented a developmental change that affected all of his work subsequently. If so, the shift may bear on a later section of this chapter in which I suggest that no developmental shift occurred in Gardner's creation of MI theory.)

The recognition and prestige of the MacArthur award gave Gardner the emotional boost that he needed to move the work into a wider and more controversial arena. The recognition no doubt also helped to pave the way for Gardner's eventual appointment to a tenured professorship at the Harvard School of Education in 1986, but its timing in 1981 was crucial to his confidence and security just as he was about to write *Frames of Mind* (1983).

By Gardner's own account, the work done for *Frames of Mind* was in most respects similar to work he had been doing since his undergraduate days at Harvard. His natural bent is toward amassing enormous amounts of material from widely disparate sources, organizing and reorganizing the material into broad categories, then trying to figure out how to best represent the material in some appropriate organizational scheme within an overall theoretical framework. Looked at in this way, all of his earlier books represent instances of these synthesizing tendencies. There is a certain Aristotelian quality to the enterprise; find order and impose it on a body of knowledge, hoping that the categories "cut nature at its joints" (Plato, 2002, 265d–266a; a favorite phrase of Gardner's).

However, *Frames of Mind* was also different. Yes, it was based on a review of the literature probably unprecedented in scope and scale in our field. Never before had so much time and effort been put into gathering, recording, and organizing the evidence bearing on cognitive potential. Never before had the lens been widened to include research on extreme cases, on brain damage, on the fossil record, and on cross-cultural data, among other counterintuitive topics. Recall also that Gardner sensed that he had moved into a new and wider arena when the project sent him to various destinations around the world, connected him with new strata of the power elite, and empowered him to aim his report directly at those who make decisions and have the wherewithal to get things done. Still, without the confidence-reinforcing effect of the MacArthur grant, it is unlikely that *Frames of Mind* would have taken the form and the tone that it did.

Most of what is true about the preparation of *Frames of Mind* is also true about Gardner's earlier works. There was the voracious gathering of materials, the ceaseless categorizing and recategorizing of these materials into conceptually satisfying matrices or tables, the rapid-fire writing ability that allowed Gardner to produce drafts in days that would have taken others weeks or months, and the freshness of interpretation that shed new light on several domains. Gardner's preoccupation with artistic development as a valid and valuable area of cognitive development, a theme of several of his earlier works, was extended in *Frames of Mind* to embrace music, dance and athletics, and inter- and intrapersonal capabilities. However, without the well-timed MacArthur grant to augment Gardner's credibility and confidence, it is unlikely that the seven different areas that emerged from the analysis would have been called "intelligences." It is probable that this terminology impacted the success of the work. As James Traub wrote in the *New Republic* in 1998,

If Gardner hadn't used 'intelligence' he wouldn't be the colossal figure he is today. Gardner does not shy away from the 'political' dimension of his argument. "My claim that there are seven or eight X's is not a value judgment," he told me. "It's my best reading of the biological and cultural data. But my decision to call them 'intelligences' is clearly picking a fight with a group that thought it, and it alone, could decide what intelligence was." (Traub, 1998, p. 21)

Criteria for the Intelligences

When I teach MI theory, I try to emphasize the importance of the various criteria through which Gardner screened his candidate intelligences. In some respects, the criteria are the most creative feature of the theory; Gardner agrees with this (personal communication, March 2001). The intelligences themselves were found in earlier theories; or, at least, abilities similar to them had appeared before, especially in the Thurstones' version of almost a half century earlier (see Table 4.1). Perhaps an argument could be made that the personal intelligences represented a significant departure from previous theories, but otherwise they were a fairly standard set.

The two things that most distinguished the seven intelligences (and the eighth as well, although it was added later) were the criteria by which they were proposed and the use of the label *intelligences* for the proposed separate areas of cognitive functioning. The decision to call the eight areas of intellectual functioning intelligences was a strategic one that Gardner chose after he had been provided security, recognition, and encouragement to make bold claims. The criteria were another matter, however, being based on more than a decade's experience with symbol systems (Gardner & Wolf, 1983), brain damage (Gardner, 1974), artistic development (Gardner, 1980), and creativity (Gardner, 1982b).

In preparation for our discussions, Gardner was able to uncover several letters, grant proposal drafts, and a crucial book proposal called "Kinds of Minds"

TABLE 4.1. Comparison of Multiple Intelligences with Primary Mental Abilities

Multiple Intelligences	Primary Mental Abilities
Verbal	Verbal fluency
Logical-mathematical	Number
Spatial	Spatial visualization
Bodily-kinesthetic	Perceptual speed
Musical	Memory
Interpersonal	Inductive reasoning
Intrapersonal	Verbal comprehension
Naturalist (added in 1998)	

from the early to mid-1970s. These materials suggest that the sifting and sorting process, the efforts to find a satisfying set of categories based on a rigorous set of criteria, were ongoing preoccupations over a number of years (Howard Gardner, personal communication, February 2001). The basic form of the theory may well have been in place by the mid-1970s, even as its specific categories were being refined and reorganized.

When considering the eight criteria, we can see that they are largely based on Gardner's personal and professional experiences. As a young boy Gardner studied piano seriously (and accordion, flute, and organ less seriously), learning that musical ability is not necessarily the same as academic ability; his academic talents far exceeded his musical ones (Gardner, 1989). His work at the VA Hospital in Jamaica Plain, Massachusetts, with Norman Geschwind, had taught him that cognitive functioning very likely is differentiated by brain location, via his witnessing selective breakdown and recovery of various kinds of functioning based on the site of brain damage.

Research on symbol systems with Dennie Wolf also underscored his belief that abilities are more diverse than was generally believed when the work that led to MI theory was launched through the van Leer project. Much of the basic thinking that was later to appear in *Frames of Mind* was worked out in collaboration with Dennie Wolf. Participation in the Social Science Research Council's Committee on Giftedness, Creativity, and the Learning Process had introduced Gardner to extreme cases of specific giftedness, child prodigies, and others with remarkable gifts in a single area (e.g., chess) isolated from other areas of intellectual functioning (Feldman, 1982). These and other experiences were all actively brought into Gardner's efforts to erect a series of hoops through which candidate intelligences were made to jump successfully if they were to earn the label. Table 4.2 summarizes the criteria used to screen intelligence candidates described in chapter 4 of *Frames of Mind* (1983).

The order in which the criteria are presented in chapter 4 of *Frames of Mind* (1983) is, I believe, revealing. As indicated above, the main departure of MI theory from previous versions is methodological. Where previous claims for

TABLE 4.2. The Eight Criteria Used to Screen
Intelligences in *Frames of Mind*

Isolation by brain damage
Prodigies and savants
Identifiable end states and developmental sequences
Core abilities
Symbol systems
Primate and evolutionary evidence
Evidence from the psychometric laboratory
Evidence from the experimental laboratory

---

multiple intelligence theories were based on statistical procedures such as factor analysis and paper-and-pencil tests, Gardner's is based on evidence from a wide variety of scientific sources. Among these sources, the most powerful and persuasive comes from work with brain-damaged individuals. It is this criterion which leads the list of criteria in his chapter 4, followed by research done with prodigies and so-called idiots-savants, another compelling source of data and one not found in other theories.

Leading with his strengths, Gardner drew in the skeptical reader with a claim that MI theory is supported by information about the brain. Although this approach was apparently not as effective with scholarly audiences as a persuasive device, it helps to account, I believe, for the overwhelming acceptance of the theory among educational and other professional groups. MI theory helped to pave the way for what is now called brain-based education, an approach that is animated by the belief that the child's brain can be enriched and improved through early education (see, for example, Breuer, 1999; Shaw, 2000). Educators, including some in specialty areas such as music, have found inspiration in the possibility that their efforts might yield improvements in the brains of their charges. This is very heady stuff (as it were) for educators who are not used to having their work taken seriously by the community at large.

If one did not know Gardner's background and experience, some of the criteria for establishing a candidate area of ability as an intelligence would seem quite far afield from the topic. Brain damage and the study of prodigies had rarely been part of the conversation about intelligence before *Frames of Mind* was published in 1983 but are now very much in the mix. Issues of culture have been raised in arguments about the limitations of IQ for many years (e.g., Cole, Gay, Glick, & Sharp, 1971; Jensen, 1969, 1980), but Gardner's review questioned the existence of a general IQ-based intelligence, a much deeper criticism of prevailing views on the nature of intelligence. As part of a research team that included cross-cultural child development experts, Gardner was consistently exposed to powerful arguments about the Eurocentrism and ethnocentrism of traditional psychometric views.

Gardner's decision to place no greater emphasis on data from psychometric assessments than on data from his other sources generated displeasure on the part of psychometricians who had dominated the field of intelligence for nearly a century. Gardner did not see himself primarily as a crusader against psychometrics before, during, or even after the publication of *Frames of Mind.* The psychometric tradition was not part of the body of knowledge that Gardner was acquiring (however idiosyncratically) as part of his training. The attitude that he held toward differential psychology (mirroring that of his mentors) was distant and a bit condescending, but not hostile. In this respect, his stance with respect to his eventual adversaries was detached and professional. He intended no personal or destructive professional attack on IQ or the psychometric community. On the other hand, if his views were perceived as threats and were attacked, he was fully prepared to defend them, and of course has done so (Howard Gardner, personal communication, March 2001).

On a related note, it is probably relevant to MI theory and its place in the field to note that Gardner was not trained in psychometrics. Other than learning how to administer certain tests as part of his work at the VA Hospital (after he finished his Ph.D.), Gardner's training was as a developmental psychologist, a very different sort of preparation. In the Harvard psychology department, testing was not given much credibility as serious science or scholarship, whereas experiments and laboratory studies of basic processes of learning and development were the coin of the realm. Although Gardner did not fit altogether comfortably into the mold of the aspiring developmental psychology researcher (always feeling that the arts were unfairly neglected), he nonetheless took on many of the values, the beliefs, and possibly the prejudices that tend to be part of the socialization process into a field. Things might have been different had he been trained in the Harvard School of Education, where Gerald Lesser and others were doing work on patterns of abilities using psychometrics.

Psychology is probably no more extreme in its requirements for conforming to a set of values and beliefs as the price of admission than are other fields, but it is also probably no less extreme. Gardner (1989) described his experience as being limited to a small set of powerful professors, none of whom took psychometric studies seriously as science. Psychometrics was perceived as a different subfield of psychology, a less worthy one than developmental psychology. There were few interesting questions being asked in the testing community, and its purposes seemed to be more practical and its methods more technical than developmental psychology, which was asking deeper questions and looking for answers using innovative methods.

In short, the domain of knowledge and skill in which MI theory was to have its greatest impact was not the domain of knowledge and skill that Gardner most valued, aspired to contribute to, or intended to become an important participant in. This helps to explain why Gardner was somewhat bewildered by the response from psychometrics to his theory, why he tended to not take it as seriously as might have been expected, and why he was sometimes accused of being condescending and dismissive of his critics. As his wife, Ellen Winner, pointed out (personal communication, August 2001), Gardner tends to be very confident about his ideas and sees himself as someone who is trying to change things, accepting the consequences with relative equanimity. My interpretation is that the criticisms did not threaten Gardner's identity as a good researcher or scholar because they were coming from a different field from his, a field that he had not taken very seriously in the sense that his professional identity did not depend on acceptance in this community. He was able to confront an adversary whom he neither feared nor felt was superior.

In trying to understand how MI theory was developed and presented, the importance of the field or fields that responded to it is vital to the story. Although Gardner had for several years been crossing borders and going outside boundaries in his professional writing, this was the first time that he was stirring up a hornet's nest in a neighboring field. He did so at least in part with the intention of causing controversy in the wider social/cultural/political arena, but not because he held a longstanding animosity toward psychometrics. Even so, the amount of controversy and the degree of animus in reactions to *Frames of Mind* surprised Gardner, a man used to vigorous debates and arguments, but all within the refined and rarified seminar rooms of Harvard (Howard Gardner, personal communication, March 2001).

He said of the blurb I wrote for the original edition of *Frames of Mind* (1983) that he was surprised that I would see the book as a direct fusillade at IQ. Here is what I wrote in 1983: "It has taken more than 60 years, but with Howard Gardner's *Frames of Mind,* we at last have a book that should put IQ to rest." In his own mind, Gardner saw the book as an effort to make a contribution to the field of cognitive development, to help push the field to consider symbol systems and areas of development that had tended to be ignored, to make a contribution to the growing interest in modularity of mind and possibly of brain (although see the James Traub quote given previously). Gardner did not see his work as a crusade against IQ or testing, although his having chosen to use the word *intelligences* increased the likelihood that just such an interpretation of the work would be the result. Confronting the psychometric community was more a byproduct of the work than its main purpose (Howard Gardner, personal communication, March 2001). To be sure, he did share the concerns that many of us had about the excesses of testing and the reification of IQ in the culture at large (see Gould, 1981).

The fact that MI theory has had its major impact in two fields outside Gardner's own has given him a certain separation and distance from his own achievements. He understands and appreciates the enormous impact that his work has had in education, and he recognizes that the field of psychometrics will probably never be the same as a consequence of the impact of MI theory. He seems to appreciate his near-celebrity status but, at the same time, does not take it very seriously, particularly because the source of his visibility, fame, and fortune is not the source of his identity as a scholar, researcher, and theorist. I can honestly say that the Howard Gardner I sat with for several hours in the spring of 2001 is the same Howard Gardner I first knew and worked with in 1975. The changes in his career and life have not changed his character in any significant way, as far as I can tell.

CHANGE AND CONTINUITY: HOW
THE THEORY WAS CREATED

Recall an earlier section where I summarized my own perspective on creativity and development as particular forms of cognitive developmental transition. I tend to think of high-level creative work as having dramatic leaps forward, prepared for by a long set of efforts and followed by a long set of implications made possible by the new, reorganized understandings. Although I have been instructed by the writings of creativity scholars who argue for the importance of context (see, for example, the chapters by Nakamura & Csikszentmihalyi; Sawyer; and Moran & John-Steiner, this volume), I still see an internal process of reorganization of a domain to be central to the enterprise. A domain must exist and must resist being changed or at least set the conditions under which change can occur. And a field comprised of stakeholders and caretakers, institutions, traditions, practices, and pedagogies must surely control how much of an impact any given effort to change a domain will have (Csikszentmihalyi, 1988; 1996).

Even at the individual level, our colleague Howard Gruber (1981; Gruber & Wallace, 1989) has argued against the importance of flashes of insight or sudden shifts in understanding, primarily on the basis of his work on Charles Darwin. My own experience, as well as my reading of the case literature, nonetheless points in the direction of occasional major reorganizations of knowledge (Feldman, 1988). However, sudden and dramatic flashes of insight announcing the arrival of such a reorganization are not always necessary. According to the private notebooks of Darwin, written during the period when he worked out the essential components of his theory of evolution by variation and natural selection, there was no Malthusian insight. Nor, for that matter, were there any reports elsewhere of a eureka experience as Darwin pursued his ambitious goal.

Darwin, of course, wrote in his notebooks whenever and under whatever conditions he chose or was able, so we can not be certain that his emotions in reaction to various thoughts and possibilities were always recorded in a timely fashion. He was trained, after all, as a natural scientist, and he was a disciplined journal writer. Although not likely, it is possible that Darwin was giddy with delight at some of his novel ideas but chose not to record his feelings in scientific notebooks. The advantage of the present study over Gruber's study of Darwin's notebooks is that its subject is still alive and active. Like Darwin, Gardner is also an inveterate pack rat; virtually everything he has ever written is available, often including several drafts and revisions. On the other hand, Gardner is not a journal writer, so there is no day-to-day record of the ups and down, the false starts and bizarre reflections, that can be found in the notebooks that Gruber and Barrett discovered in the Cambridge University Library (Gruber & Barrett,

1974). Our unique situation is that works written may be revisited through conversations with Gardner. This situation has its limitations, too, but it offers a rare opportunity to gather information, even if only in retrospect.

We have an additional advantage in the present study: As noted earlier, I was a member of the research team and participated in many of its activities, in a period during which the work on MI was most active. On the other hand, it is more than 20 years since the project did its work, and the tendency to reconstruct and selectively remember events and activities is a real limitation on our methodology. At times during our discussions, Gardner and I were jointly trying to remember what happened during the time that we spent together working on the van Leer project. Of course, Gardner's time there started earlier and extended for more than 3 years beyond mine. Even though I stayed in close touch with the project, and even though Gardner and I started Project Spectrum (a close collaboration that went from 1982 until about 1988 and brought me to Cambridge weekly), I worked directly on the van Leer project for only 9 months, from January to August 1980.

Given the limitations as well as the advantages of the method, Gardner and I tried to reconstruct his thought processes and his techniques for doing the work as he moved toward the synthesis that was to become MI theory. We found that, for the most part, we agreed when it came to describing events during the period that we both were active at the van Leer project, but for Gardner (understandably), that 9 months tended to blend into the longer stretch of time of his own involvement in the project.

When I teach the theory, I tell my students that I had no clue about what was to come, even though I was right there when it was being created. Partly this was because I was involved in my own work and was pursuing my own goals, but I remember distinctly saying to myself that being at the van Leer project gave me an opportunity to learn how to work as a member of a team with someone else as the leader. This had not been something I was used to doing or felt that I was very good at it. So a personal challenge (of which I do not believe Gardner was aware), one that would have made me more attentive to direction from our leader, was to try to be of use to the research group Gardner directed. Yet, when I read *Frames of Mind* in manuscript form in 1982, I remember being stunned by it. I had no idea that *this* was what Gardner had been up to while I worked with his team.

In 2001, I asked him if he had intentionally not revealed his plan and simply directed us to gather the information he needed to put flesh on the skeleton of the theory. Gardner made clear that he did not have a well-worked-out plan in mind and that he was not keeping things to himself, or at least he did not remember it that way. It was only when we began to look for evidence to mark the beginnings of his efforts to synthesize the evidence on human intellectual potential that it became obvious that a form of his theory was guiding the work from the outset.

The Book Proposal: "Kinds of Minds"

Recall that Gardner was influenced by the advice of Kenneth Keniston, who urged him to figure out what he was going to say in the first year of the project, then spend the next 3 years buttressing his claims with the best evidence that could be mustered (Gardner, 1989). What seems likely is that he did have a general idea of the direction in which he would go, but he did not have a specific set of claims. Gardner strongly related to theorists' (such as Spearman's) advocating for specific abilities, but precise delineations of such capacities were not yet clear to him. Whatever they were, Gardner did not intend to place them subordinate to general intelligence, as most previous theories had done. And so the seeming contradiction between Gardner's claim, confirmed by my own experience, that he was not sure where the project's work would take him and his acknowledgment that Keniston's advice was seriously taken, is resolved. He did indeed have a general plan based on his sense that human intellectual potential is more varied and diverse than traditional approaches, whether Piagetian or psychometric. This was enough to give him a firm sense of direction, even as it left open the specific form that the synthesis was to take.

I took notes on a number of meetings and events during the 9 months that I was in residence with the van Leer project. Looking back over those notes, I found some possible hints about what was to come. At the time, however, the sense of where the work was going was not clear to me. A number of scholars visited the project and presented their perspectives on human potential and how to think about it: Jerome Bruner, Noam Chomsky, Michael Cole, Gavriel Salomon, and Peter Wolff gave seminars that spring and summer of 1980. Members of the van Leer team also were involved in discussions and occasionally led them. For example, Harry Lasker, the other young scholar central to the project, gave an important seminar on stage development, ego development, and the idea of constraints on development (Feldman's van Leer project notes, July 11, 1980). Lasker also was concerned about the intended audience of the project's reports and pushed for it to include "policymakers, decision makers: those who make decisions about using potential in countries around the world." In 1980, Gardner's formal role shifted from codirector of the project to director of his own research group only, giving him a greater opportunity to focus more completely on his own agenda.

Gardner gave a seminar himself on February 5, 1980, in which he described a meeting with Erik Erikson in San Francisco at which Erikson stressed a favorite term of Einstein's: *begrifflichkeit*, or *graspable*. Relativity was an exercise in *begrifflichkeit* par excellence because its essence could be grasped by a nonscientist. Erikson's way of describing the goal of the van Leer project was to provide Oscar van Leer with a "theory of relativity for human potential" and his opinion was that it was a reasonable goal.

As was true of Gardner since his undergraduate days at Harvard (and to some degree even before), he had privileged access to many of the great minds of the day as he proceeded with the task of building a theory of relativity for human potential. He seems to have a special gift that makes great people feel a special affinity for him and take him under their wings. Erik Erikson, at the height of his fame and power in the mid-1960s, became Gardner's tutor and mentor; many were to follow in this role. If there is one thing that stands out in Gardner's life and career (in addition to his prodigious gifts themselves), it is his tendency to develop close relationships with mentors, elders, great and famous people. The list of those with whom Gardner has worked closely and to whom he can turn for advice is probably unmatched among his contemporaries. He has benefited enormously from the help and support of powerful people.

Gardner earned the respect and admiration of those who became his friends and mentors through an extraordinary work ethic, astonishing knowledge within and across disciplines, and a demeanor that can be diffident and solicitous when appropriate. Long before he became famous, Gardner was on familiar and friendly terms with many of the elite of his profession, helped no doubt by his position (however tenuous) at Harvard; with his temperament and character, he seemed well suited to the milieu within which he made his way.

In February of 1980, Gardner said to the research team: "This year is intended to tell us what are the promising leads for talking about human potential. We hope to have a model by summer, a second-generation model a year later" (Feldman's van Leer project notes, February 21, 1980). When my last notes were recorded in mid-July of 1980, no model was in sight. If a model was produced, it appeared after I left the project in August. These notes tend to support Gardner's recollection that he did not know what form his report on human cognitive potential was going to take. Yet, there were important guiding principles and goals that framed the effort even during that early period (including a reference to interpersonal and intrapersonal aspects of human potential by one of the research assistants on February 7, 1980). What we learned together during our conversations in the spring of 2001 was that Gardner had worked out a model that was very close to the one that became the framework presented several years later in *Frames of Mind*—worked it out and then forgot about it.

Much of the work we did together in the spring of 2001 was an effort to revisit Gardner's earlier writing to discover the genesis of the distinctive ideas and principles that were guiding him at the van Leer project. This took us back as far as his undergraduate term papers (which, incredibly, he still has), to grant proposals at Project Zero, to papers and book proposals that were written from the early 1970s to the late 1970s. Three items proved to be most instructive: a paper written for Stanley Milgram in 1967 when Gardner was a first-year graduate student; some personal notes that describe a series of efforts to construct a set of

TABLE 4.3. Kinds of Minds, circa 1975, and
Frames of Mind, 1983

Kinds of Minds	Frames of Mind
Language	Verbal/linguistic
Music	Auditory
The world of persons	Intrapersonal
	Interpersonal
Mathematics	Logical-mathematical
Bodily space	Kinesthetic
3-D external space	Visual
Visual 2-D world	
	Naturalist (added later)

categories for various "kinds of minds," as he called them; and a proposal for a book (which was rejected) that he wanted to write on the topic of kinds of minds that bears an uncanny resemblance to the framework that emerged several years later as the theory of MI.

In our 2001 discussions, Gardner showed surprise and delight when we uncovered these sources; they were much closer to MI than he remembered, suggesting that he was more directed toward MI than he consciously knew at the time. His sense of discovery was, by his account, not diminished by the apparently unconscious control of the process by a very MI-like set of categories. A summary of the kinds of minds of 1975 and the frames of mind in 1983 is presented in Table 4.3.

The major modifications of the list in Table 4.3 for MI theory were as follows: The world of persons was broken into interpersonal and intrapersonal intelligences, each treated separately, and the three spatial minds (at the bottom of the left column) were divided into kinesthetic intelligence and visual intelligence, making two somewhat differently conceived intelligences where there were three kinds of minds. There are striking similarities between the kinds of minds of 1975 and the frames of mind of 1983. The transformations that were most significant had to do with the latter theory's movement away from the traditional field of cognitive development and toward the field of intelligence.

The Theory and the Field(s)

In my recent discussions with Gardner, I raised an issue that had been of interest to me for some time: the fact that there was very little about *transitions*, or changes from stage to stage, in the theory, in spite of the fact that MI theory is intended to speak to educators and educational concerns. I wondered if Gardner had chosen to finesse the transitions issue in presenting the theory, leaving it to the imagination of the practitioner and policy audiences to come up with ways to encourage and enhance abilities in each of the seven categories. His reply surprised me: He said that he did not consider himself as primarily a developmental theorist and did not think of MI theory as a developmental theory.

I was surprised, because I had always thought of him as having similar interests to mine (with the exception that he has had an abiding interest in the brain and other biological topics). His training was as a developmental psychologist, and he has worked with some of the most prominent developmentalists in the world. In his 1989 book, Gardner tells the story of how he and Ellen went to Geneva the day after they were married in 1966 to see Piaget, their hero, to confer a kind of symbolic blessing on their union (Gardner, 1989, pp. 58–59). And so it took me aback to hear him say that his theory was not intended to be a developmental one.

Of course, the theory uses findings from developmental psychology and adopts some of the core theoretical structures from the field of cognitive development (most notably, stages or sequences of changes with age and end points toward which an intelligence might be going). But Gardner affirmed my sense that the theory is not itself developmental. The claim is that each person has natural potentials in each of the seven (later, eight) intelligences. These potentials develop and transform over time (a claim that sets MI theory apart from the traditional psychometric IQ); the focus of the theory, however, is not on the changes but on the natural endowment that each person receives. To the extent that a set of stages or levels of development has been identified for a proposed intelligence, one of the criteria has provided a source of support for the claim. Using the existence of a set of stages as a source of support for an intelligence did not, Gardner asserted, constitute a developmental theory of that intelligence. Properly speaking, then, MI theory is not a theory about the development of potential. It is rather a theory about the range and variety of potentials that are legitimately thought of as intelligences and the evidence that might tend to support or refute each possible instance.

The field of education (with the partial exception of early childhood education) has not been organized around developmental theories and developmental research. Education (quite correctly) perceives developmental psychology as primarily focused on universals or common kinds of changes, changes that will occur pretty much whether or not a child has the benefit of good educational experience (Feldman, 1980, 1981, 1994). Psychometric theory, however, has been central to education for more than a half century and pervades practice. Testing is something that everyone in education has to deal with; IQ and standard achievement measurement are common currency in the field.

It should not be too surprising that MI theory found a more receptive audience in education than in developmental psychology. It was constructed more in keeping with psychometrics and with educational policy and practice than with the preoccupations of developmental psychology. Although Gardner's initial impetus was to push for a widening of the boundaries of cognitive developmental theory and research (because of his experience in and valuing of music and the arts), when he prepared his synthesis he did so outside the field of developmental psychology. The role played by developmental theory and research is a support role, not the central or starring role, in the theory.

It might seem that Gardner must have been immersed in the field of education, because his academic affiliation for his entire career has been the Harvard Graduate School of Education. However, his department, Human Development and Psychology, is essentially part of the field of developmental psychology. There is no educational psychology program at Harvard, and teacher training was inactive during most of Gardner's time. Thus, his environment, although termed a school of education, was in most respects more closely related to a school of child and human development than to one of education per se.

Gardner has noted that the legendary anthropologist Margaret Mead, commenting on the field of education, said that it can be safely predicted that a new fad will take over education about every 20 years. He has no illusions about the place of MI theory in the field of education and understands that it will have its time in the sun and then, more than likely, will fade into the background as the next craze appears. (It may already have: So-called brain-based education seems to be all the rage, although it could be argued that brain-based education is an extension of MI theory.) Gardner appreciates how remarkable it is that MI has had such an enormous impact on education (and more recently on other fields: business, politics, sports, the military), as well as how likely it is that other theories and other ideas will soon eclipse those of MI and its exponents. He recognizes that his place within his own field, developmental psychology, probably depends as much on his neuropsychology work with brain-damaged patients and his research on artistic development in children as on MI. In what is probably his most revealing off-the-cuff comment about MI theory, Gardner quipped, "Chomsky it's not" (personal communication, March 2001), meaning that MI theory is a less powerful, less important theory than Chomsky's, which revolutionized the field of linguistics nearly 50 years ago (Chomsky, 1957). Chomsky comes up frequently in discussions with Gardner, and it seems to be a marker for the kind of work that he holds in the highest esteem. Chomsky, for Gardner, may be as Einstein tends to be for the wider community: a shorthand way of referring to scientific work of the highest order. Chomsky almost singlehandedly ended the hegemony of behaviorist frameworks in the field of psychology, even as he set the field of linguistics on a new footing by proposing that there are universal grammars or rules that underlie the production of speech in all languages. The goal of the study of language is to specify the rules that generate the production of all speech forms. Some of the conclusions that Chomsky reached have been controversial, especially as to the sources of the rules of grammar and of speech more generally. Still, the magnitude of Chomsky's achievement is perhaps unparalleled among contemporary social scientists.

By Gardner's own account, MI theory, although it has been enormously in-fluential in education and to a lesser degree in fields such as business and poli-tics, and although it delivered another blow against the IQ preoccupation of psy-chometric theory, it has not revolutionized the social sciences nor has it moved the field of developmental psychology in a new direction. The most powerful theories are those that fundamentally alter the structures of a domain at the deepest level in ways that guide inquiry and generate possibilities in the future. Piaget's theory of genetic epistemology was one such, Lévi-Strauss's theory of myth another, Vygotsky's theory of cultural/historical development appears to be yet another. Gardner's mentor Erik Erikson provided a theory of ego devel-opment that approached this level, as did the cognitive developmental theory of another of his mentors, Jerome Bruner. Given who he is and the circles within which he has carried out his work, Gardner has maintained the humility to see his work in relation to the work of the great minds of the field and to believe that its importance does not match theirs.

Although Gardner himself might not equate his work with that of such indi-viduals, its powerful effects on the field of education is arguably equivalent. As our colleague Csikszentmihalyi has taught us (Csikszentmihalyi, 1988, 1996; Nakamura & Csikszentmihalyi, this volume), the actual value of a contribution is set by a field. In this instance, the importance of MI theory in education has been conferred by the gatekeepers and leaders of the field. Certainly in the 20 years since *Frames of Mind* was published, MI theory has established itself as perhaps the most important new contribution to education of the day. It appears that MI or something very much like it will be a permanent part of the conver-sation in educational theory, research, policy, and practice, but experience teaches us that the influence of any contribution rises and falls with time; very likely MI theory will do so as well. The long-term effects of the theory may also be more subtle and less obvious as time passes. Even the great Piaget's work is often not acknowledged by contemporary scholars as the source of changes in the field of cognitive development; the changes have become so much part of the field that their source has faded into history (see Damon, Kuhn, & Siegler, 1998; Gelman, 1979).

It helps to explain Gardner's humility and modesty about his theory to know that, in his own estimation, he has done some important work, work that without question has had impact, but work that is not of the highest order in the field with which he most identifies. I remember that when I first read a draft version of *Frames of Mind* in the months before it was published, I thought that it was going to be very influential. I said as much to Gardner in a note I sent back with the manuscript with comments. But I also remember being surprised that the book was about psychometric issues primarily, issues that seemed far afield for Gardner. Now, nearly 20 years later, I understand better that *Frames of Mind* was another foray into new territory, territory that needed to be organized and categorized, like so many others Gardner had encountered. The fact that his efforts to make sense of the material led him to question the premise of *g* intelligence as the central organizing principle of the field of psychometrics was simply a matter of interpreting the data as he saw them. It was also, of course, another manifestation of his long-standing aversion to a simplistic and narrow interpretation of intelligence and his willingness to take on the psychometrics establishment.

If not precisely his passion, attacking traditional IQ was certainly not a challenge to be avoided. Given his history of finding existing theories (including both psychometric and Piaget) limited and limiting, especially with respect to the arts, Gardner was primed to become a crusader in the intelligence wars. The role was not an altogether comfortable one for him; his preferred mode was discussion, exchanging views, conversation, scholarly mutual respect, and a certain deference to his elders. But, by his throwing down the gauntlet by co-opting the term *intelligence* for his seven proposed abilities, the die was cast.

MI THEORY AND MY THEORY: HOW TO DEAL WITH DATA THAT DON'T FIT

Having presented a summary of MI theory, its creator, the context within which the work was done, and the processes of construction used to build the theory, I now turn to the matter of how well the case material fits the theoretical framework for creativity outlined early in the chapter.

Recall that the core idea of my approach to creativity is an analogy to the process of stage-to-stage change in cognitive development. Creative advances in thinking can be thought of as unusual instances of qualitative, irreversible reorganizations of a body of knowledge, which when communicated are recognized as novel and important within a significant field. Cognitive developmental stage transitions, in contrast, are universally occurring instances of creative thinking. In my view, explaining one kind of qualitative advance goes a long way toward explaining the other (Feldman, 1989).

Armed with this view, when I sat down with Gardner for a series of discussions about MI theory, I was guided by the idea that he must have gone through some form of cognitive developmental transition as he constructed and reconstructed his view of intelligence that became MI theory. My questions and probes were designed to elicit from him those ideas and experiences that were early predecessors of what was to become the theory, the possible catalysts and crystallizing experiences (Feldman, 1971; Walters & Gardner, 1986) that helped to give form to the emerging synthesis, and some recollections about the happy moment when the solution or theoretical structure emerged from his reflections on the mass of empirical and theoretical material.

For several hours, I tried to get him to provide a story that might fit my theory about creative thinking, but to no avail. Eventually, I told him what I was looking for, and he shrugged his shoulders as if to say, "Sorry, that's not the way it happened." The experience made me recall the famous quip by Konrad Lorenz: "It is a good morning exercise for a research scientist to discard a pet hypothesis every day before breakfast." I found myself with a new problem: how to explain the fact that my subject was not conforming to my theory.[1] Here is the solution (such as it is) to the fact that the process of creating the theory of MI seems not to fit my own theory of creativity.

There are several possible reasons why my data did not seem to support my theory:

1. I might not have gotten as much data as necessary for my theory, or I might have gotten the wrong data. Gardner may have been hiding something, so that despite my best efforts he was able to finesse and evade my questions. If I had just been better at interviewing him, I might have the information I need.

2. This particular case might be anomalous or peculiar and can therefore be ignored. After all, Gardner and I are very close colleagues and have been friends for many years. We also are both scholars in the same field, and the field is the one we are trying to study.

3. The theory might just be wrong: Gardner's creative processes may require me to change my theory, to confront the fact that my theory may be beautiful and elegant (at least to me), but its beauty can only be maintained if I ignore empirical reality.

4. As mentioned, developmental shifts are not necessarily recognized by those undergoing them. Thus, perhaps Gardner underwent such a transformation without recognizing it as such.

Finding myself in this situation reminded me of Piaget's early experience in the field of philosophy, when he was frustrated with the field because it never systematically tested its claims against the realities of the world. In many of his writings, Piaget criticized philosophy because it could never settle a scientific question but could only generate more and more systems of ideas (see Bringuier, 1981). One of the great contributions that Piaget made to Western thought was the idea that understanding is always reached through the interplay of existing systems of interpretation as they deal with new and unexpected data from the empirical world. Finding the right balance between theory and fact was at the heart of Piaget's genetic epistemology (Feldman, 1999).

Here I was, happy enough with my theory of the development of creative thinking, being confronted with empirical data from someone with whom I thought I was in near perfect agreement—data that required adjustment in my interpretive structures. Whatever differences may exist between us (and there are some), I always thought that Gardner and I were similar in how we interpret things of mutual concern. We almost never disagree on major points of theory, interpretation, quality, or significance. We seem to be about as close as two scholars can be.

How to resolve this problem? There are certain leads to pursue. On the process side, we need to reexamine the ways that Gardner works, recognizing that, from his perspective, the work done on MI theory was more continuous than discontinuous with other projects. The consequences of the process were different, to be sure, but much about it were refinements and extensions of an approach to challenging topics that he had been studying for more than a decade when he took on the challenge of the van Leer project.

The second lead is the issue of the domain that was transformed as a consequence of MI theory. What I had overlooked was that the major impact of MI theory has been *outside* Gardner's own domain, in the scholarly field of psychometrics and the field of practice having to do with education. Neither of these was Gardner's primary identification when he began the project at van Leer; he was a developmental psychologist whose main interests were cognitive development, brain damage and its relevance to cognition, and development in the visual arts. We need to look more closely at the domains that were transformed in our efforts to understand MI theory as an instance of creative reorganization. When we do so, we find that we may indeed be dealing with an anomalous case, one that still challenges some of the claims of my cognitive developmental perspective on creativity but that also leaves some of them arguably still in place.

It is also a very real possibility that more information about the process through which Gardner created the theory of MI would have yielded a better story for my theory. Even though I have known Gardner for many years, have taught his theory for more than a decade in my courses, have read most of what he and his group have written on the topic, have seen a fair sampling of the writing of others about MI, and have spent several hours interviewing him about how he did the MI work, I may have missed crucial data. Gardner may well have experienced a cognitive developmental transition before 1975 (see note 1); this possibility should be explored. If the evidence supports such a transition in Gardner's thinking, I would be able to avoid Konrad Lorenz's practice of discarding a pet hypothesis for at least another morning or two.

The key point seems to be the one having to do with the domains that were most impacted by MI, these being ones that were not central to Gardner's training, experience, or ambitions. My own theorizing does not encompass a situation in which a person causes a revolution in a field that is not his or her own. The theory of creativity as cognitive developmental transitions best fits situations in which a person moves through the levels of expertise of his or her field to the point of becoming a master of the domain, finds that there are certain questions that cannot be answered adequately using the domain's existing knowledge structures and techniques for gathering and analyzing information, and sets off quite intentionally to construct new means or new techniques or new forms of explanation, so as to better answer an important question or re-solve an unresolved issue. Canonical cases that seem to conform to the con-tours of my theory of creativity as transition are Kekulé's discovery of the ben-zene ring in chemistry, Newton and the proverbial apple, Einstein's solution to the time/space problem, Andrew Wiles's solution to Fermat's last theorem problem and, truth be told, my own theory of creativity as cognitive develop-mental transitions.

When Gardner said, "Chomsky it's not," he was telling me that he knew that MI theory was not a contribution that might lead to the deep-structure reorgani-zation of a domain through targeted effort to solve an unresolved issue or to place the domain's knowledge base on a qualitatively different set of conceptual structures. As Gardner saw his task, it was similar to other efforts he had made. He sees himself as a writer as much as a scholar/researcher/theorist, and the work on MI was in many ways similar to earlier (and subsequent) science-writ-ing projects.

The differences between MI and Gardner's previous efforts seem likely to largely account for the huge differences between MI theory and its predeces-sors. And so, reluctantly, we must conclude that what happened with MI theory is an anomaly in the context of Gardner's career, an anomaly that may raise questions about my own theory and other theories of creativity. It is therefore necessary, finally, to look a bit more closely at the continuities and discontinu-ities in Gardner's work as compared with his other efforts. These may reveal with greater clarity than we have been able to achieve to this point just why MI theory has had such enormous impact in the fields of education and psychomet-rics, and why his other works, (although influential, to be sure) have had much less impact.

Continuities and Discontinuities

Recall that the major differences between Gardner's work for the van Leer proj-ect and his work on other major projects were two: This project was substan-tially better funded, longer in duration, and avowedly more ambitious than any previous effort, and the project was an applied effort from the beginning, inten-tionally aimed at educators and policymakers around the world. The project had been created in part to help Gardner and his young colleague Harry Lasker stay at the Harvard School of Education during a period when tenure was not being given, in part to provide a catalyst for Gardner to move upward and outward as a scholar, and in part to carry out the mission proposed by the van Leer Founda-tion to Paul Ylvisaker, then dean of the Harvard School of Education.

Gardner felt that he was being given a mandate to make a major statement and the resources to make it with authority, backed by the considerable institutional power of Harvard. Being both a dutiful, responsible young man and a risk-taking scholar who did not hesitate to cross boundaries and challenge conventional wisdom, he was well primed to take on this major challenge. He also had few other prospects at the time in the way of support, security, or career direction. At age 36, he was about a decade into his career, a point that his own creativity theory (Gardner, 1993) would later predict to be a likely turning point. What made the situation uniquely well suited for someone like Gardner was that he could remain the loyal junior colleague at Harvard while at the same time issuing a challenge to those whose fields were not the source of his own identity and well-being. He was not challenging his mentors; he was challenging people and ideas distant and peripheral from the center of his world.

The techniques that Gardner applied to the problem of assessing what is known about human intellectual potential were similar to those he had used in his other major projects: his studies of children's artistic development (Gardner, 1980; Gardner & Perkins, 1989), the neuropsychology of brain damage (Gardner, 1974), and, perhaps most important, his studies with Dennie Wolf on early symbolization (Gardner & Wolf, 1983). In each of these projects, the first step was to gather together a full sampling of the available information on the topic—ranging across scientific disciplines, historical studies, consultations with world-class experts, and nonscholarly sources such as drama, dance, criticism, and literature.

Gardner possesses an unusual gift in the amount and the variety of information he is able to productively organize. Going back at least to his graduate student days (e.g., the 75-page paper he wrote for a psychology class), he has been able to rapidly and systematically construct organizational frameworks to cover widely disparate data and other forms of information. It is, in his own mind, a kind of typological and relational process that drives him to want to impose a better order on various phenomena. Human intellectual potential in this respect was no different from artistic development, brain damage, symbolic development, or even creativity (the topic of that undergraduate paper).

Gardner simply turned his protean gifts for hierarchy, order, and relationship to a new task, one for which he was not specifically trained. One of his special abilities might be described as a very high-level science-writer's gift such as that of Robert Kanigel (1991), who wrote *The Man Who Knew Infinity*, the story of the Indian mathematician Ramanujan. This science-writer gift, plus his world-class disciplinary training in psychology and his research/scholarly ambitions—combined with his composer's tendency to create new patterns and transform existing ones—provided him with a unique combination of qualities to meet the challenges that the van Leer project was to impose. Finally, Gardner is a prodigiously hard worker, putting in 10 or 12 hours per day, 7 days per week, for as long as I have known him, and he is a natural writer. Such are the continuities that were brought to bear in the van Leer project. The discontinuities are no less striking and were the catalysts that probably gave rise to the aggressive, even occasionally combative, undertones that run through *Frames of Mind* and much of Gardner's subsequent writing about intelligence.

Two discontinuities seem to have been most important: the amount of money that was given to the project, which was much greater than anything Gardner had seen, and the mandate of the project—to try to impact educational policy and practice throughout the world. Gardner used the resources to travel around the world; to inform himself of what it meant to be a high-level policy operative, for example, with the World Bank or UNESCO; and to train himself to speak the language of policy. As had been the case in other contexts, Gardner was able to move comfortably into the world of high-level, international policies for children and education—forging mentorships, friendships, and colleagueships that were to play major roles in the work of the van Leer project. As we have seen, a special gift of Gardner's is to impress remarkable people and have them take him under their wing as a younger colleague. Befriending Willem Welling of the van Leer Foundation and bureaucrats and agency heads was a challenge that Gardner readily met.

The chapters of *Frames of Mind* that most explicitly reflect the changes in emphasis dictated by the van Leer Foundation agenda are chapters 13 and 14. When I read the manuscript of the book before it came out in 1983, I remember thinking that these two chapters seemed different in tone from the rest of the book. There was a bit of a stilted quality to them, a sense that they were there not there because the author felt that they needed to be, but rather because they needed to be there to satisfy the funders.

Gardner confirmed this impression in our meetings in the spring of 2001. He stated that he knew, when writing the book, that he was moving into unfamiliar territory, and that he felt somewhat uneasy about it but did his best to write in a tone and at a level transparent enough for his targeted audience to read. And in this he was more successful than I predicted. In reading and rereading *Frames of Mind*, I hold the education and the policy chapters to be the least successful from the point of view of a theorist and scholar. Compared with the other chapters in the book (which are well written and clear but technically quite complex and often theoretically more subtle than one might imagine from a superficial encounter with MI theory), the policy and education chapters are less subtle, less complex, and less technically sophisticated. This was an intentional attempt on Gardner's part to reach a broader audience.

The table on page 339 of *Frames of Mind* (reproduced here, in part, as Table 4.2) is something of a tour de force nonetheless, typical of Gardner's work in its conceptual clarity, its extension into its targeted domain, and its ease of interpretation. In characteristic fashion, Gardner first organizes his conceptual territory, gives its categories straightforward labels, provides brief but clear summaries, and then builds his text around the tabular presentation. The use of examples from non-Western cultures and the increasingly common use of non-Western perspectives as a source of support for MI approaches to educational issues clearly reflects the many sessions at van Leer with anthropologically oriented colleagues in child development, most notably Robert LeVine.

Intelligences, Not Talents

As touched upon earlier, the most critical decision that Gardner made was to call his seven categories of human potential intelligences. This decision was made very late in the process, and it was a strategic one. Gardner knew that if he labeled his areas of potential *talents* or *abilities* or anything else, the field of psychometrics would have likely ignored *Frames of Mind*. In choosing the term *intelligences* (plural, of course), Gardner was throwing down a gauntlet to the traditional field of psychometric assessment and psychometric theory. He understood that calling his potentials *intelligences* was necessary if his work would have a chance of becoming an important topic of discussion, of debate, and (eventually) of reform.

There were a number of opportunities to back away from his claim that the evidence pointed toward seven relatively independent areas of intelligence, including olive branches from prominent psychometrically oriented colleagues such as Robert Sternberg and Sandra Scarr. Sternberg, for example, proposed that Gardner relabel the intelligences as *talents*, thus neutralizing his concerns about the theory. But in each instance, Gardner stuck to his guns, and in doing so kept the heat on psychometrics and its business-as-usual attitude. I know that Gardner was able to sustain his stance in part because the stakes were so high for the book but so low for him personally. He was not so greatly concerned that he would offend important colleagues that he risked much by taking the stand that he did. On the other hand, had he not taken that stand, and had he not been able to withstand the pressures to recant his heresy that were to come, the present chapter would very likely not have been written, because MI theory would not have been influential enough to justify it.

Finally, it is abundantly clear that the choice of terms was critical to the success of MI theory, because Gardner was given the ultimate opportunity to cross over to the other side. The makers of the mother-lode intelligence test, the Stanford-Binet IQ test that was the single greatest source of the success of the psychometrics movement, offered Gardner the opportunity to participate in the construction of the fifth edition of the test. The original 1916 version of the instrument, created by Lewis Terman and his associates, has gone through several revisions, never changing its basic focus but moving with the times to reduce perceived cultural bias, gender bias, and the like. In a letter dated June 12, 1997,

Gardner was asked by John D. Wasserman, Ph.D., the director of psychological assessments at Riverside Publishing, to participate in the fifth edition, scheduled to be released in 2003.

Gardner sent me a copy of the letter and his brief reply, in which, although courteous (as always) to a fault, he made it clear that any official association with the Stanford-Binet was not a possibility. In a handwritten addendum to the note he sent me with copies of the letters, he wrote: "This brought back memories of conversations 10 years ago," as indeed it did. I remember sitting with him in 1982 as we began our collaboration on Project Spectrum (see Chen, Krechevsky, & Viens, 1998), discussing our mutual apprehension and concern about the tyranny of psychometric testing, I with no idea that he was about to launch the most powerful antidote to IQ to have appeared in the history of the field. When I first encountered the theory of MI in 1982, I wrote words to that effect in the blurb that appeared on the cover of the first edition of *Frames of Mind*.[2]

He said that he was surprised by the strong words I wrote for the cover and doubted that there would be a big response to the book. On the other hand, he knew that he had made certain strategic decisions that made it likely that controversy and debate would follow the appearance of the book. He has now written eighteen books, and none before or since *Frames of Mind* has caused the extraordinary reaction that followed its publication. A nineteenth book on creativity as good work has just been published (with Mihaly Csikszentmihalyi and William Damon as coauthors), and we will soon have another opportunity to see what the impact of this latest project might be. His wide-ranging talents have been most recently turned toward the corporate world, where he is trying to understand how leadership and ethical behavior can be made to flourish, another example of Gardner's willingness to embrace an unconventional challenge.

PROPAEDEUTIC REFLECTIONS AND FINAL THOUGHTS

My aim in this chapter has been to try to take advantage of the fact that I have known and worked with my subject and thus would be able to contribute to the little we now know about the inner workings of the creative mind. I hoped that, by knowing the person, domain, and field intimately, I would be able to explore the subtleties of Gardner's thinking as he moved toward constructing the set of ideas that would become MI theory (Csikszentmihalyi, 1988, 1994, 1996). Recognizing that the individual mind is but one of the several crucial levels of explanation needed to explain high-level creative work, it is as important—if not more important—a source of information than are domain, field, culture, history, and evolution (Feldman, Csikszentmihalyi, & Gardner, 1994; Csikszentmihalyi, 1988).

I was guided in this effort by a theoretical framework that claims that creative reorganizations of bodies of knowledge are instances of cognitive developmental transitions, similar in some ways to Piagetian stage-to-stage shifts (Feldman, 1974, 1980). To test this claim, I spent several hours with Gardner during the spring of 2001 exploring his (reconstructed) thinking during the time preceding, during, and following construction of his theory. Gardner was also kind enough to share documents (term papers, grant proposals, letters and memos) that might shed further light on the process that led to MI theory. Having been a participant in the research group during the period that Gardner was actively building his theory, I thought I might be able to confirm or disconfirm some of my own recollections of the very active 9 months I spent in residence at the van Leer project, the context within which MI theory was constructed.

I found that my cognitive developmental claims about creative advances in thinking were not well supported by the evidence gathered thus far. There seemed to be no moment of insight, no noteworthy shift in thinking, to mark the emergence of the new theory. Gardner's reconstruction of the process placed more emphasis on continuity than discontinuity, on small increments of change that led to a synthesis of information. Once the interviews were concluded, I tried to explain why my results were not in keeping with my theory's claims. Several of the readers of an earlier draft of this chapter (Susan Butler, Vera John-Steiner, Keith Sawyer, Iris Stammberger, Kat Steere, and especially Ellen Winner) believed that my interpretation that a cognitive developmental shift had not occurred was overly pessimistic. Encouraged by their reactions, I have rethought my initial conclusions and offer the following reflections as points for further discussion. Toward this end, I will briefly discuss three points that emerged in the process of preparing this chapter. These points are as follows: (1) the possibility that a major qualitative shift can occur in a *domain*, whether or not such a shift occurs in the theorist; (2) the possibility that a major cognitive developmental shift did indeed occur in the theorist, but *earlier* than the period that was investigated; and (3) that a major qualitative shift did indeed occur in the theorist, but that it was an *emotional* rather than a cognitive one.

The Domain

A point that deserves to be carefully considered is the fact that MI theory's impact was an *outside-the-domain* advance. That is, Gardner's disciplinary home was, and still largely is, in cognitive developmental psychology. MI theory's influence was felt primarily in the fields of education theory, policy, and practice, and to a lesser degree, in the field of psychometrics. Although the impact of the theory has been undeniably enormous, qualifying it as a high-level advance by criteria common in the field (e.g., that it had major influence on a well-established domain; see Morelock & Feldman, 1999), the domain transformed was not the one with which Gardner most identified. He was not trained in education or psychometrics, did not identify himself as an educational psychologist, and had little contact or affiliation with people in the field of education before he began his work on the van Leer project in 1980.

A possibility that must be considered, then, is that the domain itself might have undergone a major developmental shift because it was ready to do so. MI theory was the catalyst for that shift and served as the main source of it, but an understanding of the domain's history and structure would have revealed that a major change was imminent whether or not MI theory had come along when it did. The domain or domains transformed therefore need to be understood on their own terms as part of the effort to understand why MI theory was so influential. Domain analysis is still in its infancy as a developmental science issue, but it merits serious attention as the field moves forward (Feldman, Csikszentmihalyi, & Gardner, 1994). We are now quite sure that a satisfying explanation of creative contributions involves close analysis of the history, conceptual structure, and development of the unique domain that has been transformed. Particularly in the higher range of creative works, domain analysis is likely to be an essential component of any explanation. For those who emphasize the context of creativity, this of course comes as no surprise (e.g., Csikszentmihalyi, 1988; Moran & John-Steiner, this volume).

Cognitive Developmental Transition

The argument for cognitive developmental advance as a source of explanation for high-level creative works does not depend, of course, on a flash of insight as a marker. My own experience with reorganizations of thought includes examples of both sorts: earth-shaking moments of deep insight, as well as major shifts in thinking that came about in subtle, largely unnoticed ways (Feldman, 1988). It is not the lack of an abrupt change that is so problematic for my theory, but the fact that Gardner insists that there was no major shift at all.

Several reviewers of this chapter, especially Keith Sawyer, have argued that the evidence for a cognitive developmental shift exists in the proposal that Gardner sent to a book publisher in December of 1975. In that proposal, a set of minds was proposed that bears striking resemblance to the seven intelligences that were to appear several years later. It may be that the critical period for the theory was from 1970 to 1975 rather than from 1980 to 1982, when the van Leer project was launched. Gardner was working with Dennie Wolf on a symbol systems approach to cognitive development during those earlier years. A more detailed examination of the collaboration of those years might reveal evidence bearing on the processes of change in Gardner's (and Wolf's) thinking as they forged their distinctive perspective on the nature and development of symbolic capabilities during the opening decade of life.

Emotional Developmental Shift

My focus on the cognitive, the thoughts and ideas that gave rise to MI theory, may have obscured a significant emotional shift that occurred just before Gardner began to write *Frames of Mind* in 1982. Gardner was awarded one of the first MacArthur grants to individuals of exceptional promise, a no-strings-attached, unsolicited award that provided financial support as well as great visibility. Coming when it did, the MacArthur award was a catalyst for a large increase in his confidence and security as he faced an uncertain future. Ellen Winner, in her response to an earlier draft, first raised the possibility of a noncognitive developmental shift as critical to the creation of MI theory. When Winner and I asked Gardner if it seemed plausible to him that such a shift had occurred, he agreed that it was, because the MacArthur award gave him the needed confidence to use the term *intelligences* for his seven kinds of minds.

If the critical period for the development of MI theory was indeed earlier in the 1970s, when Gardner was working with Wolf at Project Zero, a rich source of data about the nature of collaboration might be productively mined by studying documents and interviewing those who were participants. When John-Steiner was working on the book *Creative Collaboration* (2000), she considered using a collaboration between Mike Csikszentmihalyi, Gardner, and me. It may be that she had the right idea but the wrong set of collaborators, because by the time we began working together, our individual paths were largely mapped, possibly limiting the degree of impact that collaboration might have.

With these three possibilities now in the mix, we have engaged several contemporary themes in the field of creativity studies. Yet another theme in contemporary thinking about creativity that might be pursued through further exploration of this case is the interplay between thought and emotion in creative work (see Nakamura & Csikszentmihalyi, this volume; Sternberg, this volume). There is also the need to consider multiple levels of analysis in a systematic and coordinated way if a rounded, subtle, and satisfying account of creative advance is to be achieved (again, see Sternberg, this volume). The approach most likely to be successful, given this expanded and more complex set of challenges for the field of creativity studies, is some form of dynamic systems framework, although it is too early to say just which one it will be (see Gruber & Wallace, 1989; Moran & John-Steiner, this volume; Sawyer, this volume).

As the field of creativity studies has developed, it has moved from a preoccupation with the individual creator as hero toward a richer, more multifaceted framework for considering the person as one part of a complex process of transformation (Csikszentmihalyi, 1988). This is a positive and productive direction for the field and one that seems most appropriate as we move forward in our efforts to understand one of the most challenging aspects of human experience. The unique tendency of human beings to transform their world even as they transform their thoughts is a worthy topic of study in the context of the overall approach (Feldman, Csikszentmihalyi, & Gardner, 1994).

The individual and those with whom the individual struggles toward new vistas of understanding and experience will always be central players in the creativity drama. In Gruber's masterful study of Charles Darwin's thinking as he struggled toward the great synthesis that would become the theory of evolution by natural selection, it was clear that the unique qualities of Darwin's mind and character made a difference at all points in the creative process (Gruber, 1981). Although Alfred Wallace's version of the theory was formally the same, there were many instances of nuance and gist that had Darwin's unique stamp on them.

After more than half a century of active work in creativity studies, we still know amazingly little about the real people who do the work of creativity day to day (although see Wallace & Gruber, 1989). Without falling back into the tendency to overemphasize the role of the individual in the creative process, we need to make sure that we also do not diminish that role. To try to capture the developing thoughts and emotions of individuals who are going to change the world is one of our most challenging tasks. Along with the study of developmental domains, the analysis of fields that sustain and support those domains, and the coordination of levels of the process from evolutionary to historical, the study of individuals and their development should receive its share of scholarly attention. If so, we may anticipate a long and productive future for our nascent field.

NOTES

1. Keith Sawyer (along with Ellen Winner) suggested that I reconsider my conclusion that my theory of transitions was not supported in the present study; their argument was that Howard's cognitive developmental transition took place earlier, sometime in the 1970s, when he was working with Dennie Wolf on symbol systems development. I hope they are right.

2. Looking from the perspective of 2003, it appears that MI theory, powerful though it may be, has not had much success in reducing the preoccupation with psychometric testing in this country. If anything, testing as the preferred means of educational assessment and evaluation has an even stronger hold on the educational establishment. One can only hope that, with time, the merits of alternative approaches, perhaps along the lines of our own Project Spectrum, will begin to have a more prominent role in education.

REFERENCES

Albert, B. (1988, February 14). Student competency test engenders anxiety. *The Indianapolis Star,* pp. 1, 18.

Albert, R. S., & Runco, M. (Eds.). (1990). *Theories of creativity*. Newbury Park, CA: Sage.

Amabile, T. (1983). *The social psychology of creativity.* New York: Springer-Verlag.

Amabile, T. M. (1996). *Creativity in context.* Boulder, CO: Westview.

Bloom, B. (1985). *Developing talent in young people.* New York: Ballantine.

Boden, M. (1999). Computer models of creativity. In R. J. Sternberg (Ed.), *Handbook of creativity* (pp. 351–372). Cambridge, UK: Cambridge University Press.

Bornstein, M., & Krasnegor, N. A. (Eds.). (1989). *Stability and continuity in mental development: Behavioral and biological perspectives.* Mahwah, NJ: Erlbaum.

Breuer, J. T. (1999). *The myth of the first three years: A new understanding of early brain development and life long learning.* New York: Free Press.

Bringuier, J. C. (1981). *Conversations with Jean Piaget.* Chicago: University of Chicago Press.

Chen, J. Q., Krechevsky, M., & Viens, J. (Eds.). (1998). *Building on children's strengths: The experience of Project Spectrum.* New York: Teachers College Press.

Chi, M., Glaser, R., & Farr, M. J. (Eds.). (1988). *The nature of expertise.* Mahwah, NJ: Erlbaum.

Chomsky, N. (1957). *Syntactic structures.* The Hague, Netherlands: Mouton.

Cole, M., Gay, J., Glick, J., & Sharp, D. (1971). *The cultural context of learning and thinking.* New York: Basic Books.

Csikszentmihalyi, M. (1988). Society, culture, and person: A systems view of creativity. In R. J. Sternberg (Ed.), *The nature of creativity* (pp. 325–339). Cambridge, UK: Cambridge University Press.

Csikszentmihalyi, M. (1994). Memes versus genes: Notes from the culture wars. In D. H. Feldman, M. Csikszentmihalyi, & H. Gardner (Eds.), *Changing the world: A framework for the study of creativity* (pp. 159–172). Westport, CT: Greenwood/Praeger.

Csikszentmihalyi, M. (1996). *Creativity: Flow and the psychology of discovery and invention.* New York: HarperCollins.

Damon, W., Kuhn, D., & Siegler, R. S. (Eds.) (2000). *Cognition, perception, and language.* Volume 2, *Handbook of child psychology.* 5th ed. New York: John Wiley.

Ericcson, K. A. (1996). *The road to excellence: The acquisition of expert performance in the arts and sciences, sports, and games.* Mahwah, NJ: Erlbaum.

Feldhusen, J. H. (1997). Secondary services, opportunities, and activities for talented youth. In N. Colangelo & G. A. Davis (Eds.), *Handbook of gifted education*, 2d ed. (pp. 189–197). Boston: Allyn & Bacon.

Feldman, D. H. (1971). Map understanding as a possible crystallizer of cognitive structures. *American Educational Research Journal, 8,* 485–501.

Feldman, D. H. (1974). Universal to unique. In S. Rosner & L. Abt (Eds.), *Essays in creativity* (pp. 45–85). Croton-on-Hudson, NY: North River.

Feldman, D. H. (1980). *Beyond universals in cognitive development.* Norwood, NJ: Ablex.

Feldman, D. H. (1981). Beyond universals: Toward a developmental psychology of education. *Educational Researcher, 11,* 21–31.

Feldman, D. H. (Ed.). (1982). *Developmental approaches to giftedness and creativity.* San Francisco: Jossey-Bass.

Feldman, D. H. (1986). *Nature's gambit: Child prodigies and the development of human potential*. New York: Basic Books.

Feldman, D. H. (1988). Creativity: Dreams, insights, and transformations. In R. J. Sternberg (Ed.), *The nature of creativity* (pp. 271–279). Cambridge, UK: Cambridge University Press.

Feldman, D. H. (1989). Creativity: Proof that development occurs. In W. Damon (Ed.), *Child development today and tomorrow* (pp. 240–260). San Francisco: Jossey-Bass.

Feldman, D. H. (1994). *Beyond universals in cognitive development* (2nd ed.). Norwood, NJ: Ablex.

Feldman, D. H. (1999). The development of creativity. In R. J. Sternberg (Ed.), *Handbook of creativity* (pp. 169–186). Cambridge, UK: Cambridge University Press.

Feldman, D. H., & Benjamin, A. (1998). Creativity and gifted education: An unsettled relationship. *Roeper Review, 21,* 82–84.

Feldman, D. H., Csikszentmihalyi, M., & Gardner, H. (Eds.). (1994). *Changing the world: A framework for the study of creativity*. Westport, CT: Greenwood/Praeger.

Feldman, D. H. (with Goldsmith, L. T.). (1991). *Nature's gambit: Child prodigies and the development of human potential*. New York: Teachers College Press. (Original work published 1986)

Ferrari, M., & Sternberg, R. J. (1998). The development of mental abilities and styles. In D. Kuhn & R. S. Siegler (Eds.), *Handbook of child psychology* (Vol. 2, pp. 899–946). New York: Wiley.

Flavell, J. H. (1963). *The developmental psychology of Jean Piaget*. Princeton, NJ: Van Nostrand.

Gardner, H. (1972). *The quest for mind*. New York: Vintage Books.

Gardner, H. (1974). *The shattered mind: The person after brain damage*. New York: Knopf.

Gardner, H. (1978). *Developmental psychology: A textbook*. Boston: Little, Brown.

Gardner, H. (1980). *Artful scribbles: The significance of children's drawings*. New York: Basic Books.

Gardner, H. (1982a). *Art, mind, and brain: A cognitive approach to creativity*. New York: Basic Books.

Gardner, H. (1982b). Giftedness: Speculations from a biological perspective. In D. H. Feldman (Ed.), *Developmental approaches to giftedness and creativity* (pp. 47–60). San Francisco: Jossey-Bass.

Gardner, H. (1983). *Frames of mind*. New York: Basic Books.

Gardner, H. (1989). *To open minds*. New York: Basic Books.

Gardner, H. (1993). *Creating minds*. New York: Basic Books.

Gardner, H. (1999). *The disciplined mind*. New York: Simon & Schuster.

Gardner, H., Csikszentmihalyi, M., & Damon, W. (2001). *Good work: When excellence and ethics meet*. New York: Basic Books.

Gardner, H., Kornhaber, M. L., & Wake, W. L. (1996). *Intelligence: Multiple perspectives*. Fort Worth, TX: Harcourt Brace.

Gardner, H., & Perkins, D. (Eds.). (1989). *Art, mind, and education: Research from Project Zero*. Urbana: University of Illinois Press.

Gardner, H., & Wolf, D. P. (1983). Waves and streams of symbolization. In D. R. Rogers & J. A. Sloboda (eds.), *The acquisition of symbolic skills* (pp. 19–42). London: Plenum.

Gelman, R. (1979). Why we will continue to read Piaget. *Genetic Epistemologist, 8,* 1–3.

Getzels, J. W., & Jackson, P. W. (1962). *Creativity and intelligence: Explorations with gifted students.* New York: Wiley.

Gould, S. J. (1981). *Mismeasure of men.* New York: Norton.

Gruber, H. (1974). *Darwin on man: A psychological study of scientific creativity.* Chicago: University of Chicago.

Gruber, H. (1980). Afterword. In D. H. Feldman (Ed.), *Beyond universals in cognitive development.* Norwood, NJ: Ablex.

Gruber, H. (1981). *Darwin on man: A psychological study of scientific creativity* (2nd ed.). Chicago: University of Chicago Press.

Gruber, H., & Wallace, D. (1989). *Creative people at work.* New York: Oxford University Press.

Guilford, J. P. (1950). Creativity. *American Psychologist, 5,* 444–454.

Guilford, J. P. (1967). *The nature of human intelligence.* New York: McGraw-Hill.

Guilford, J. P. (1970). Creativity: Retrospect and prospect. *Journal of Creative Behavior, 4,* 149–161.

Heller, K. A., Monks, F. J., & Passow, H. A. (Eds.). (1993). *International handbook of research and development of giftedness and talent.* Oxford, UK: Pergamon.

Howe, M. J. A. (1989). *Fragments of genius: The strange feats of idiots savants.* London: Routledge.

Howe, M. J. A., Davidson, J. W., & Sloboda, J. A. (1998). Innate talents: Reality or myth. *Behavioral and Brain Sciences, 21,* 399–407.

Hunt, E. (1997). Nature vs. nurture: The feeling of vuja de. In R. J. Sternberg & E. Grigorenko (Eds.), *Intelligence, heredity, and environment* (pp. 531–551). Cambridge, UK: Cambridge University Press.

Jensen, A. (1969). How much can we boost I.Q. and scholastic achievement? *Harvard Educational Review, 39,* 1–123.

Jensen, A. (1980). *Bias in mental testing.* New York: Free Press.

John-Steiner, V. (2000). *Creative collaboration.* New York: Oxford University Press.

Kanigel, R. (1991). *The man who knew infinity.* New York: Pocket Books.

Lemann, N. (2000). *The big test: The secret life of the American meritocracy.* New York: Farrar, Straus, & Giroux.

Lubinski, D., & Benbow, C. P. (1995). An opportunity for empiricism [Review of *Multiple intelligences: The theory in practice*]. *Contemporary Psychology, 40,* 935–940.

Miller, L. (1989). Musical savants: Exceptional skill in the mentally retarded. *Psychological Bulletin, 125,* 31–46.

Morelock, M. J., & Feldman, D. H. (1999). Prodigies. In M. A. Runco & S. R. Pritzker (Eds.), *Encyclopedia of creativity* (Vol. 2, pp. 449–456). San Diego, CA: Academic Press.

Morelock, M. J. F., & Feldman, D. H. (2000). Prodigies, savants, and Williams syndrome: Windows into talent and cognition. In K. A. Heller, R. J. Sternberg, & R. Subotnik (Eds.), *International handbook of giftedness and talent* (2nd ed.). Oxford, UK: Pergamon.

Olson, L. (1988). Children "flourish" here. *Education Week,* pp. 1, 18.

Piaget, J. (1971). The theory of stages in cognitive development. In D. Green, M. Ford, & G. Flamer (Eds.), *Measurement and Piaget* (pp. 1–11). New York: McGraw-Hill.

Piaget, J. (1975). *The development of thought: Equilibration of cognitive structures.* New York: Viking/Penguin.

Plato. (2002). *Phaedrus.* New York: Oxford University Press.

Ramey, C. T., Lee, M. W., & Burchinal, M. R. (1989). Developmental plasticity and predictability: Consequences of ecological change. In M. Bornstein & N. A. Krasnegor (Eds.), *Stability and continuity in mental development: Behavioral and biological perspectives* (pp. 217–233). Mahwah, NJ: Erlbaum.

Resnick, L. B. (Ed.). (1976). *The nature of intelligence.* Mahwah, NJ: Erlbaum.

Ross, P. O. (Ed.). (1993). *National excellence: A case for developing America's talent.* Washington, DC: U.S. Department of Education.

Sanford, N. (1966). *Self and society: Social change and individual development.* New York: Atherton.

Shaw, G. L. (2000). *Keeping Mozart in mind.* San Diego, CA: Academic Press.

Simon, H. A. (1988). Creativity and motivation: A response to Csikszentmihalyi. *New Ideas in Psychology, 6,* 177–181.

Simonton, D. K. (1984). *Genius, creativity, and leadership.* Cambridge, MA: Harvard University Press.

Simonton, D. K. (1988). *Scientific genius: A psychology of science.* Cambridge, UK: Cambridge University Press.

Simonton, D. K. (1999). *Origins of genius: Darwinian perspectives on creativity.* New York: Oxford University Press.

Snyder, S. S., & Feldman, D. H. (1977). Internal and external influences on cognitive developmental change. *Child Development, 48,* 937–943.

Snyder, S. S., & Feldman, D. H. (1984). Phases of transition in cognitive development: Evidence from the domain of spatial representation. *Child Development, 55,* 981–989.

Sternberg, R. J. (Ed.). (1982). *Handbook of human intelligence.* Cambridge, UK: Cambridge University Press.

Sternberg, R. J. (1988). *The triarchic mind: A theory of human intelligence.* New York: Viking.

Sternberg, R. J. (Ed.). (1999). *Handbook of creativity.* Cambridge, UK: Cambridge University Press.

Sternberg, R. J., & Lubart, T. I. (1996). Investing in creativity. *American Psychologist, 51,* 3–15.

Sternberg, R. J., & Lubart, T. I. (1999). The concept of creativity: Prospects and paradigms. In R. J. Sternberg (Ed.), *Handbook of creativity* (pp. 3–15). Cambridge, UK: Cambridge University Press.

Thurstone, L. L., & Thurstone, T. G. (1941). *Factorial studies of intelligence.* Chicago: University of Chicago Press.

Torrance, E. P. (1966). *Torrance tests of creative thinking.* Princeton, NJ: Personnel.

Torrance, E. P. (1988). The nature of creativity as manifest in testing. In R. J. Sternberg (Ed.), *The nature of creativity* (pp. 43–75). Cambridge, UK: Cambridge University Press.

Traub, J. (1998, October 26). Multiple intelligences disorder. *New Republic*, pp. 20–23.

Treffert, J. (1998). *Extraordinary people: Understanding "idiot savants."* New York: Harper & Row.

Wallach, M. A., & Kogan, N. (1965). *Modes of thinking in young children: A study of the creativity-intelligence distinction.* New York: Holt, Reinhart, and Winston.

Wallach, M. A., & Wing, C. (1969). *The talented student: A validation of the creativity-intelligence distinction.* New York: Holt, Reinhart, and Winston.

Walters, J., & Gardner, H. (1986). The crystallizing experience: Discovering an intellectual gift. In R. J. Sternberg & J. E. Davidson (Eds.), *Conceptions of giftedness* (pp. 306–331). Cambridge, UK: Cambridge University Press.

Ward, T. B., Smith, S. M., & Finke, R. A. (1999). Creative cognition. In R. J. Sternberg (Ed.), *Handbook of creativity* (pp. 189–212). Cambridge, UK: Cambridge University Press.

Weisberg, R. W. (1999). Creativity and knowledge: A challenge to theories. In R. J. Sternberg (Ed.), *Handbook of creativity* (pp. 226–250). Cambridge, UK: Cambridge University Press.

CHAPTER FIVE

Creativity in Later Life

Jeanne Nakamura and Mihaly Csikszentmihalyi

Every biography of a creative person tries to explain the achievements of its subject in light of a more or less implicit dynamic theory of life-span development. The interest, curiosity, and enduring engagement of the artist or scientist are seen to follow from a series of meaningfully connected experiences stretching from childhood to maturity and old age. For instance, in his classic biography of da Vinci, Freud (1947) traced Leonardo's lifelong curiosity, masked by a dispassionate analytic detachment, to the earliest years of his life, when as an illegitimate child he was left motherless in his father's household. In his biography of Martin Luther, Erik Erikson (1958) hinted at the roots of Luther's stubborn rebelliousness to authority by tracing them to an unforgiving father and a loving but powerless mother. Among more recent psychological monographs that follow the life course of creative individuals are Gruber's (1981) detailed analysis of Darwin's work, and the contributions of Gardner (1993) and Howe (1999).

It is not only psychologists who attempt to trace a series of continuous links between the various stages of the lives of the great men and women about whom they write. Every biographer feels the need to explain creators' outstanding achievements in terms of a series of connections between outstanding events in their lives. Despite this unanimous agreement, however, there is at present no widely accepted model that compares, for instance, with the explanatory reach of the Freudian framework that was so often used in the past century.

A more recent approach to life-span investigations of creativity is based on the historiometric method pioneered by Lehman (1953), Dennis (1966), and recently expanded by Simonton (e.g., 1988). These approaches typically involve arranging the achievements of a scientist or artist in chronological order and plotting them along the life-span axis of the creator. In a recent review, Simonton (1999) claimed, "Illustrious creators can be examined from the moment of conception to the very instant of death, plus everything that takes place within this long interval" (p. 120). The historiometric approach allows its practitioners to analyze a large amount of data, obviously at the expense of the depth and insight that biographies provide.

The combination of these two methods has made it possible to come up with some generalizations about the life spans of creative people. Simonton (1999, p. 122) cites six such findings: that creative individuals tend not to be first-born, that they are intellectually precocious, that they suffer childhood trauma, that their families tend to be economically and socially marginal or both, that they receive special training early in life, and that they benefit from role models and mentors. Although we have some reservations about the robustness of these findings—for instance, according to our investigations, neither precocity nor early trauma seem to be that frequent among creative individuals (Csikszentmihalyi, 1996)—one might expect this kind of evidence to be increasingly more accurate and hence useful in the future.

But no matter how much biographic or historical data is accumulated, the emerging patterns will not reveal the causal links between external events and acts of creation, without a conceptual model that mediates the two phenomena. It is our position that to understand the creative process, one must adopt a systems model that takes into account the interaction of three variables. The first is the *person*, who is predisposed by genetic endowment and early experience to become interested in a particular realm of art or science. The second is the *domain*, which is the set of rules and procedures that constitute the realm in question. Finally, the third component is the *field*, which consists of the gate-keepers to the domain and either encourages or rejects the person's innovations to the domain (Csikszentmihalyi, 1996, 1999; Csikszentmihalyi & Robinson, 1986; Nakamura & Csikszentmihalyi, 2001). Simonton (1999) implies the need for this perspective in one of his five conclusions: "The overall age functions, including the placement of the first, best, and last creative contribution, are contingent upon the specific domain of creative activity" (p. 1220). To understand questions such as "Why do mathematicians and lyric poets do their most original work earlier in life than, say, architects or philosophers?" one cannot simply consider the operations of the creative person's mind. One must also explore the interaction between the mind and the symbolic system of the domain, and the social constraints and opportunities of the field. For example, in domains that are very well integrated, such as mathematics, chess, or musical performance, it is relatively easy for a talented person to move quickly to the cutting edge of the domain and thus be well positioned to innovate in it. In domains that are less logically ordered, such as musical composition, literature, and philosophy, there is less agreement as to what the most urgent issues are. Specialized knowledge is not enough; one needs to reflect on a great amount of experience before being able to say something new. Therefore, one would expect important new contributions in these domains to be made late in life.

THE SYSTEMS MODEL AND ITS RELATIONSHIP TO AGING

The study of creativity in the United States has been almost exclusively confined to psychologists studying individual traits (Wehner, Csikszentmihalyi, & Magyari-Beck, 1991). Even though some psychologists have taken seriously the importance of the culture, the domain, the social context, and other systemic variables (e.g. Feldman, 1980; Gruber & Davis, 1988; Harrington, 1990; John-Steiner, 1985, 2000; Martindale, 1990; Simonton, 1997; see also the edited volumes by Montuori & Purser, 1999; Sawyer, 1997), it is safe to say that these supraindividual variables have been seen as facilitating conditions, not as in any way constitutive of the creative process itself.

One gets a broader perspective if, instead of looking at creativity, one looks at the broader concept of "cultural production," of which creativity is a special case. Although some sociologists have written extensively on this topic (e.g., Becker, 1974, 1976; Zuckerman, 1977) their work has never found its way in the psychological literature. Nor have the writings of the two main theorists of cultural production, Pierre Bourdieu and Michel Foucault, left much of a trace in the work of psychologists. In what follows, we try to draw parallels between the systems model and their approaches, arguing that viable changes in cultural production (i.e., what we ordinarily call *creativity*) can only be understood through a perspective that integrates individual experience with social forces within a symbolic context provided by cultural opportunities.

Bourdieu has taken a radical position that denies any inherent value to cultural productions, including the ones we call *creative*. The value of a poem, symphony, or scientific theory, in his opinion, is decided through struggles within a field constituted by economic and power relations among cultural practitioners (Bourdieu, 1993). Thus, it is useless to look for the value of a Picasso painting in the painting itself. Its value is attributed to it by the recognition bestowed on the painting by other artists, critics, and especially collectors who pay for it—all of these constituting the field of art. Our own use of the term *field* in the systems model largely overlaps with Bourdieu's.

To simplify matters, it is possible to set Bourdieu's paradigm in opposition to the one associated with the early work of Michel Foucault.[1] Immersed in the structuralist philosophical tradition, Foucault (1968) explains cultural production primarily in terms of the natural development of symbol systems, or the "strategic possibilities of conceptual games" (p. 37). In other words, a new poem or theory is made possible by the state of the art in the particular literary or scientific genre, which suggests the next logical steps that need to be taken. In this sense, Foucault's *épistémé*, or cultural order, is equivalent to our use of the concept of domain in what follows (also see Sawyer, 2002).

Instead of stressing the differences between these two approaches, we endeavor to reconcile them. Although it is clear that the substance of any creative act comes from the strategic possibilities provided by the domain, it is also the case that whether the act is going to be recognized as creative or not depends on the outcome of the struggles within the field's network of power relations. Moreover, we try to reconcile these two superindividual approaches—one cultural, the other social—with the third necessary ingredient, namely, the personal experiences of the creator and of the audience, because creativity cannot be understood without the joy it provides. Bourdieu argues that new paintings and scientific discoveries arise solely out of grim struggles between artists and scientists, whereas Foucault holds that new works arise inevitably as a result of tensions within the medium. One can read hundreds of pages by either author that contain no mention of the deep enjoyment that the creative process entails. Yet as anyone who has spent some time with creative individuals knows, working within a medium that allows for novelty to be discovered is one of the most exhilarating experiences life has to offer. The attraction of this challenge is what makes some people willing to immerse themselves in art or science throughout their lives, even when much easier and more remunerative options are open to them. The field of strategic possibilities provided by the domain and the contested arena provided by the field only set the stage on which creativity may unfold. But nothing would happen on that stage unless certain individuals were willing and eager to perform.

Characteristics of Creative Individuals

Every person is potentially creative. Fresh perceptions, ideas, and experiences are within anyone's reach. But individuals who actually change the culture, the ways we see and do things, are relatively few. What makes a person able to transform the cultural environment? It is difficult to answer this question because the phenomenon arises from a complex array of factors. For instance, luck is an essential factor. Being in the right place at the right time makes a tremendous difference. It is not enough to have innate talent; it is not sufficient to be relentless in the pursuit of novelty. One must also have access to the necessary social and cultural capital. A potentially creative mathematician cannot contribute anything new if the society in which he lives does not provide access to past knowledge or provides no opportunities to do state-of-the art work. At the dawn of a new technology—the steam engine, electricity, aviation, telecommunication—there are many opportunities for individuals to make important new contributions, but when the technology reaches a steady state, it is much more difficult for a potentially creative person to introduce a significant novelty.

Although creativity depends as much on the social and cultural contexts as on the individual, it is still true that some persons are more likely to contribute to this process than others. What are the characteristics of such people? First of all, we cannot exclude the possibility that there are genetic differences involved. Certainly great geniuses in some fields, such as music or mathematics, seem to be born with talents that cannot be explained by learning or environment alone. Being innately more sensitive to sounds, for instance, a child might enjoy listening to music and so develop finer skills as a composer and performer. But most child prodigies never seem to do anything creative as adults (Feldman, 1986/1991; Howe, 1999). Whatever the initial genetic contribution to creativity might be, it needs intense cultivation and support, as well as luck, for it to result in a noteworthy achievement.

Although the person is only one of three factors that determine creativity, it is the most important one from a psychological perspective, and it is the one about which most is known. We review three aspects of creative persons: their cognitive processes, their personalities, and their values and motivations.

For most forms of creative accomplishment, a certain amount of intelligence is a prerequisite—a 120 IQ threshold is often mentioned (Getzels & Jackson, 1962). However, the relationship of IQ to creativity varies by domain, and above a relatively low threshold, there seems to be no further contribution of IQ to creativity. The first and longest study of high-IQ children (Sears & Sears, 1980; Terman, 1925) found little evidence of adult creativity in a sample whose mean IQ as children was 152, or even in a subsample with IQs above 170.

The most obvious characteristic of original thinkers is what Guilford (1967) identified as *divergent thinking*, which has been popularized since as lateral thinking or thinking outside the box. Divergent thinking involves unusual associations of ideas, changing perspectives, and unusual approaches to problems, in contrast with *convergent thinking*, which involves linear, logical steps. The crucial step from divergent thinking to creativity involves *problem finding*—i.e., the discovery of a gap or contradiction in the domain that suggests a whole line of work that needs to be done (Getzels & Csikszentmihalyi, 1976; Runco, 1994).

Correlations between divergent-thinking tests and creative achievement tend to be low, and some scholars even claim that the cognitive approach of creative individuals does not differ qualitatively from that of normal people except in its speed (Simon, 1988) and quantity of ideas produced (Simonton, 1988b). The further conclusion some draw is that computers, which are much faster and more prolific than the human mind, will be able to achieve great creative solutions. This can only happen, however, if the computers are linked to a domain that provides questions interesting to humans, and to a field that can evaluate the computers' conclusions.

But most creative achievements are not the result of a linear problem-solving process. They involve numerous iterations of the problematic elements that often result in drastic changes in the formulation of what the problem is and how it should be represented. Creative thinking involves keeping attention focused on the developing process and keeping an open mind so as to take advantage of unforeseen possibilities. Although at times a painter may approach the canvas with a clear idea of how the finished painting should look, in most cases original pictures evolve during the process of painting as the combination of colors and shapes suggest new direction to the artist (Getzels & Csikszentmihalyi, 1976).

How do life-span changes relate to creativity? This question is difficult to answer, because there is a tremendous individual variability in how age affects the body and the mind. One of the answers most often given by older creative persons to the question as to what made it possible for them to continue working in old age was some variant of Linus Pauling's answer. When asked how he could keep up his intense involvement with research at age 89, he quipped that he had chosen his grandparents well. But good genes are not the entire story, because many productive senior creators had serious childhood illnesses and chronic health problems earlier in life, which they seem to have overcome, at least in part, through single-minded dedication to their work.

There is no question that, beginning in the seventh decade of life, creative individuals report a waning of energy and troubles with memory and sustained effort, especially in tasks requiring what has been called "fluid intelligence" (Cattell, 1963). However, age decrements in intellectual functioning appear to be less severe than they were once held to be (Schaie, 1996), and they may be more than compensated for by increased wisdom that accrues with life experience (Baltes & Staudinger, 2000).

A great deal has been written on the personality characteristics and emotional life of creative individuals, especially during the heyday of Freudian psychoanalysis (Csikszentmihalyi & Getzels, 1973; Csikszentmihalyi & Csikszentmihalyi, 1993; Freud, 1908/1955; Gedo, 1990; Kris, 1952). This is not the place to summarize this extensive literature. For our purposes, it is enough to stress two points. The first is that although certain personality traits—for example, curiosity, independence, self-confidence, attraction to complexity, risk-taking—are generally found to be strong among creative individuals in all domains and eras (Barron & Harrington, 1981), many other traits seem to enhance or obstruct creative achievement differently in different domains and historical periods. For example, in some domains, creativity may be linked with mental illness (Andreasen, 1987; Jamison, 1989). The sensitivity required of poets and playwrights, for instance, makes them vulnerable to stress that can result in depression, alcoholism, and other addictions—especially when the field is very competitive or is neglected by the wider society.

The second point, suggested by our study of creative individuals in later life (Csikszentmihalyi, 1996), is that the signature of a creative personality is the ability to function along the entire gamut of human potentialities. Such a person can be very introverted at certain points of the creative process, but when the need inevitably arises to share and evaluate the product, the same person is able to seek out and to communicate with relevant members of the field. When the need arises, creative men can display feminine traits such as empathy and sensitivity, and creative women can be assertive and competitive. In other words, whereas most of us tend to remain at one end or the other of various personality continua, creative people are able to move along the full range of possibilities as the situation demands.

More than physical or mental decrements, what may decrease with age is the motivation to pursue the difficult and often fruitless efforts to create novelty. However, to our knowledge, there has been no systematic study so far of attitudinal changes toward creativity through the life span. It should be remembered that Charles Darwin spent almost his entire adult life developing the theory of evolution (Gruber, 1981), and Lorenzo Ghiberti spent 50 years perfecting the Gate of Paradise for the Baptistry of Florence. During such an extended creative process, the phases of preparation, incubation, insight, evaluation, and elaboration (Wallas, 1926) recur and alternate a great number of times, making it possible for the novel idea or product to slowly emerge from the hazy confusion in the creator's mind.

For a person to be motivated and to persevere enough to sustain such a long immersion in the insecurity that a novel accomplishment entails, it helps to have some very strong internal values (Getzels & Csikszentmihalyi, 1976) and strong intrinsic motivation (Collins & Amabile, 1999). In addition, creative individuals who keep working until the end must have seamlessly integrated their careers into *vocations*, creating unique "life themes" that are enjoyable and meaningful at the same time.

Domains of Creativity

A culture consists of thousands of separate domains such as farming, carpentry, music, mathematics, religion, and gourmet cooking. Each of these comprises instructions for behavior organized into a set of symbols related by rules. Most human activity involves following the rules of some domain or another. Domains are relatively stable and are passed down without change from one generation to the next, through learning. However, there are individuals who are always trying out new ways to farm, new songs to sing, new methods to compute quantities. If these are deemed to be better than the old ways, the novelty will be called creative and added to the domain.

From this, it follows that access to a domain is essential to creativity. A person cannot be creative in the abstract, but only within the rules of some practice or idea system. It is impossible for a child living in an isolated tribe or urban ghetto to become a creative mathematician, or for an athletic young man to become a creative basketball player if that game is unknown in his culture. Domains change with time; creativity in physics, for instance, might be easier in certain periods of growth and more difficult when the organization of the domain has become so complete that no new discovery seems possible.

Droughts in novelty may not be caused by the lack of potentially creative individuals, but rather by the fact that there are limits as to how much novelty any culture can absorb. To use the jargon of economics, the scarcity of creativity is rarely due to lack of supply but must be attributed instead to lack of demand. This is because, in order to maintain their stability, cultures protect themselves from change. A good example is the slowness of the United States to adopt the metric system; the expense of changing tools, specifications, and measurements is so great that it has frustrated all efforts of the advocates of the more efficient system. But material investments are only one obstacle to the adoption of novelty; even more important is the scarcity of attention, which results in our reluctance to add new information to the mind and to change habitual ways of thinking. The average American is only able to name between one and two living painters, even though there are 500,000 persons who identify themselves as artists on census forms. Of the 100,000 or so new books published each year in the United States, few are read by more than a fraction of the population—and those that are widely read follow old conventions rather than adding anything new to the collective consciousness.

Another impediment to creativity has to do with periodic exhaustion of the symbolic system constituting the domain. For instance, Czeslaw Milosz comments on the situation in literature, where the evolution of language may make writing good poetry easier at some times and almost impossible at others: "A genuine poet is able to invest a commonplace sentence with charm. But genuine poets are rare, and there are periods in history when such an operation is impossible, because the use of a 'common style' is then beyond the reach of even the great poets" (as quoted in Davie, 1990, p. 46).

As a person ages, some domains—those, for instance, that depend on physical performance, like dance, or on very rapid mental processing of information—may become less and less easy to innovate in. Domains that change very rapidly, like computing, may also become increasingly difficult to operate in as a person matures and is disinclined to keep up with continuous change. On the other hand, there are domains where age is no handicap; indeed, older people have the opportunity to become increasingly knowledgeable in domains that are relatively stable, complex, and dependent on life experience. Thus, it is not surprising how many great achievements were made by individuals past retirement age. For instance, Michelangelo painted the Pauline chapel at the Vatican when he was 89, Benjamin Franklin invented the bifocal lens at 78, Giuseppe Verdi wrote *Falstaff* at 80, and Frank Lloyd Wright completed the Guggenheim Museum in New York when he was 91 years of age. So although performance in many areas of life may peak in the 20s, the capacity to change a symbolic domain and thus contribute to the culture increases with age in several domains.

Fields of Creativity

Without a group of experts who are involved in the practice of a domain, the domain might just as well not exist. For example, although there are still texts written in the Etruscan language, nobody can read them because the field that knew what the letters meant became vacant many centuries ago. Fields not only preserve domains, but they are also the gatekeepers deciding what novelty should be added to the domains. In the visual arts, for instance, the field comprises active artists, art teachers, gallery owners, museum curators, art critics, and collectors. It is they who decide which of the 500,000 or so self-styled artists in the United States are worthy of recognition, support, and remembrance.

Members of a field can harm creativity in two ways: either by admitting too many novel ideas into the domain, which is likely to create chaos in the system, or by being so strict that most good new ideas are rejected. Of course, fields can err also by making wrong decisions, such as neglecting artists like Van Gogh whom later generations will recognize as having been creative. Now museums show his works, collectors pay millions for his canvases, and art historians write extensive monographs on his oeuvre. It is important to note, however, that the reason we now appreciate Van Gogh is that the field has changed its criteria. Without such a change in the judgment of the field, Van Gogh's canvases would by now be forgotten. It is a moot question whether Van Gogh was creative all along even though he was not recognized, whether he became creative only after his paintings were appreciated, or whether he was never creative and posterity was mistaken in its attribution (see Csikszentmihalyi's comments in the "Creativity in Domains" section of chapter 6, this volume). Creativity is a judgment passed by society through its fields, and it is a relative judgment that holds only as long as a particular set of values lasts.

How do conditions in the field interact with a person's aging process? The answer varies depending on the domain and the historical period. Generally, to the extent that a person's network of contacts increases with time, age should be directly correlated with the ability to affect creativity—gatekeepers tend to be elder statesmen who control the journals, grants, professional associations, and institutions. This is rarely a smooth process, however. As Bourdieu (1993) vividly states, "The history of the field arises from the struggle between the established figures and the young challengers. The ageing of authors, schools, and works is far from being the product of a mechanical, chronological slide into the past; it results from the struggle between those who have made their mark . . . and who are fighting to persist, and those who cannot make their own mark without pushing into the past those who have an interest in stopping the clock" (p. 60).

Direct involvement in domain-related work usually becomes restricted with age: Older scientists may stop doing bench work in the lab to take on administrative positions, and established creators—who tend to be older—may become distracted from the voice of the muse by their lionizing audiences. A good example of some of these extraneous demands was given by the Canadian writer Robertson Davies, who at age 80 commented, "One of the problems about being a writer today is that you are expected to be a kind of public show and public figure and people want your opinions about politics and world affairs and so forth, about which you don't know any more than anybody else, but you have to go along or you'll get a reputation of being an impossible person, and spiteful things would be said about you" (as quoted in Csikszentmihalyi, 1996, p. 206). An identical situation is noted by the physicist Eugene Wigner (1992), describing the sudden change in status of physical scientists after the harnessing of nuclear power at the end of World War II: "By 1946, scientists routinely acted as public servants . . . addressing social and human problems from a scientific viewpoint. Most of us enjoyed that, vanity is a very human property. . . . We had the right and even perhaps the duty to speak out on vital political issues. But on most political questions, physicists had little more information than the man on the street" (p. 254).

Thus, a person's creativity can be affected by age in several ways. Slowing down of physical processes and ailing may substantially limit the novelty a person produces, especially in some domains that depend on energy and quick thinking; other domains may be more suited to persons with experience and judgment. Fields may restrict opportunities for creative contributions (through retirement, demotion, and so on). And finally, the social system in which the fields are embedded may distract successful creative individuals by diluting their focus of attention from the tasks they are best qualified to perform.

These conditions associated with aging militate against producing and bringing to completion novel ideas. It is essential for a person who wants to continue being creative through later life to forge a personally meaningful, enduring engagement with the domain of his or her choice.

VITAL ENGAGEMENT IN LATER LIFE

Some creative persons maintain full involvement or participation in their domains as they grow older (cf. Rowe & Kahn, 1998). A *relationship* with the domain comes to exist in the sense that the domain's hold on attention and energy has endured over many years, rather than being a transient state. Work in the domain occasions experiences of absorption, or *flow* (Csikszentmihalyi, 1975/2000). In addition, through periods of flow but also through periods when work is difficult or tedious, the individual experiences as important both the domain and the aspects of the self that are invested in the relationship with it; the relationship holds meaning.

Vital engagement describes this absorbing and meaningful relationship with art, science, or any other domain (in the study of creativity, cf. the concept of *creative intensity* or continuity of concern: John-Steiner, 1985; Roe, 1952). The notion locates experience (the self-world interaction; Dewey, 1934) and its subjective phenomenology within the context of lives over time. To emphasize the extension across many years, we also will refer to aging creators' lifelong relationship with their work as *enduring engagement*. A person may instead remain involved with a career or activity through life not because it is enjoyable and meaningful, but because of external constraints: financial or status reasons, or simply because of habit.

The usual way of accounting for creative lives is to look to origins. However, as noted earlier, we have been impressed by the compatibility of creative achievement with a variety of origins. We have not identified a set of specific experiences or conditions that universally characterize creators' early lives (trauma, precocity, etc.). If a common thread exists, it may not be a trigger or catalyst early on, but rather a manner of regulating the relationship to the domain all through life via the selective investment of attention and energy in the endeavors that the individual finds vitally engaging at the time. Vital engagement with a domain may originate in experiences of enjoyable absorption or in a sense that the relationship is meaningful (e.g., that through it, the artist or scientist serves a larger purpose or can overcome some personal trauma), or it may originate in a fascination with the object that encompasses from the outset both enjoyment of the immediate interactions and a sense that the relationship is intrinsically meaningful.

The subsequent development of vital engagement is a process of forging a relationship with the domain and field over time. Along with the strong connection between self and domain, meaning derives from the connection of the individual to a network of enterprise, a tradition, and a community of practice that lie beyond the self. Elsewhere, we have discussed some of the ways in which membership in a field grows to be an important source of meaning (Nakamura & Csikszentmihalyi, 2003), rather than the site of conflict portrayed by Bourdieu. In the pages that follow, we focus more heavily on the individual's relationship to a domain of art or science. In contrast to Foucault, we do not see this evolving relationship as some derivative phenomenon driven by the progress of ideas. Furthermore, though we draw on Gruber's fruitful notion of a network of enterprises in describing how vital engagement endures into later life, our focus is not the "cognitive career," the "process of thought as it moves through time" (Gruber, 1984, p. 12) that Gruber (1981) analyzed so painstakingly in the case of Darwin. Instead, we explore the ways in which the relationship to the domain continues to hold meaning and enjoyment for the creator.

For scientists or artists who are still engaged in creative pursuits late in life, the problems of the domain remain compelling, and interactions with the field continue to be stimulating. Indeed, their years of work have created layers of meaning that enrich how they experience work in old age. In contrast, less engaged peers have ceased to experience the domain in which they work as important and exciting and may be marking time until they can retire. They may feel that they have exhausted the possibilities of their particular lines of endeavor and are just repeating themselves, or they may feel obligated to projects that they no longer believe will or should be accomplished.

Some of the negative changes that artists and scientists encounter as they reach later life include changes in the individual with age (e.g., diminished energy), age-related changes in access to the domain and ease of functioning within it, and changes in the field's or larger society's stance toward the aging practitioner and gatekeeper (e.g., shifts in opportunities and normative expectations). That is, the systems approach to creativity highlights that it is not just the biopsychological aging of the individual that affects creativity in later life.

During the past quarter century, we have stopped associating the early years with growth and the second half of life with inevitable erosion. Baltes (1993) has described aging in terms of a shift over the adult years in the balance of gains and losses in adaptive capacity, and optimal old age as "restricted but effective" living in the face of this shift. His view of positive or "successful" aging focuses on the management of this shift through an intensified and increasingly complex deployment of strategies that people use throughout the whole course of life: selection, optimization, and compensation (p. 590). Baltes has described how, with advancing age, people seek to *optimize* their functioning by becoming more *selective* about the domains of activity in which they invest energy and attention and developing means of *compensating* or substituting for lost capacity. In the remainder of the chapter, we touch on but do not dwell on age-related losses and creators' ways of compensating for them, both of which tend to vary by individual and domain. We focus more heavily on the challenge of selective optimization in the face of limited time and waning energy, which all aging artists and scientists confront.

The strenuousness and uncertainty inherent in a life of creative work do not discourage continued involvement among long-term engaged creators. One might ask why aging creators continue to invest their time and energy in endeavors that are so strenuous and uncertain, even as these resources grow more limited. One important answer lies in their many years of artistic or scientific engagement prior to late life.

Those who note the rigors and sacrifices of creative work nevertheless accept them as an integral part of their chosen way of being meaningfully related to the world. As one novelist in her 70s concluded, "This is the structure of your life." Creators who are still engaged focus upon the work's continuing excitement rather than being deterred by its difficulties or uncertainty of success. Some creators' most demanding work lies in the past, and some who have always preferred moderate risk continue to do so in old age. However, for others, the projects being tackled in old age are the most difficult of their careers. Furthermore, rather than seeking to minimize risk with age so as not to waste precious time, some creators feel that age and eminence have freed them to accept *more* risk—to tackle the problems experienced as most significant. A chemist in his 70s explained, "The amount of what I would call really 'high risk research' that I would do when I was younger is less than it is now. In other words, I feel that I can take big risks. And if I fail, I fail. But at least I will not have just spent my time on what I would consider more mundane problems."

Given creativity's uncertainties, it is not surprising that many creative individuals explicitly profess positivity, optimism, or hope (cf. Colby & Damon, 1992), both as a general attitude and in their creative work (e.g., in scientists' provisional assumption that the solution to a problem exists). It is unclear to what extent this positivity contributed to past persistence and achievement and to what extent it was born of, and sustained by, an engaged and successful life. But in the later years it supports continued engagement, allowing the provisional assumption that time and capacity exist to complete projects. A distinguished social scientist acknowledged, after outlining several ambitious works either in progress or awaiting attention, "I have got all of these projections like I have got all of the time in the world. You know, I don't know how much time I have. When you get to be 75 you can't count on much." He nevertheless concluded by affirming, "But those are the main things that I am going to do."

One might also ask how aging creators decide to devote their increasingly precious attentional resources to one project rather than another, after making the decision to selectively invest attention and energy in creative work rather than in other activities. Age might be expected to alter the phenomenology of project choice, making it more difficult. The distinguished literary critic Wayne Booth, now in his 80s, commented, "In one way, it's a little harder [to make those decisions], because you feel time is running out. Before, you could say, 'If I put it over here on the back burner, I can come back to it.' The back burner is not burning as brightly." In fact, however, eminent creators who continue to be deeply engaged in their work express little stress or strain about selecting the projects they will tackle. Though many commented on the shrinking time that remains, they described eagerly throwing themselves into one endeavor rather than another without expressing doubts about the choice. In fact, the phenomenology of attentional allocation appeared dramatically altered during the late career only for the creators *most certain* of their goals, such as those striving to complete a long-standing work. Predictably, they described an increased sense of focus and urgency.

Several characteristics support lifelong creators' unhesitating engagement (cf. Zuckerman & Cole, 1994). First, they have established clear selection criteria. Second, many claim to be able to judge the promise of prospective projects. Finally, central to the discussion here, they have adopted as a primary principle of selection the extent to which a prospective project promises to vitally engage them. For example, for Wayne Booth, vital engagement is a self-conscious criterion: "I think the basic drive is always what produces both the combination of doing something for the world and the best personal feelings of joy or bliss or love. What do I really want to do, to make this life now the life worth living?"

The creators' goals are *emergent*, arising out of their interaction with the world and regulated by the quality of their subjective experience of the activity (Csikszentmihalyi & Nakamura, 1999; Nakamura & Csikszentmihalyi, 2003; Sawyer, this volume). Booth described very clearly the process of investing time and attention based on the feedback arising from the evolving experience of the work itself: "I settle down and try to do some work on [a project]. And if it turns out to be fun and challenging, then that will hook me. . . . You finally decide, 'Is this really a good book of its kind? Let's try it. If it's not, let's drop it. The initial idea wasn't good enough.' But also, the idea of the fun of working on it is very decisive for me."

Three Patterns of Late-Life Engagement

We will consider three different, emergent motived pathways that may have different implications for creativity in later life. In the first and most common pathway, a history of engagement presses for *continued activity in a domain, into late life*. In the second pathway, *a change of domain* may arise out of shifts in how vitally engaging a long-standing domain comes to be, relative to other possible spheres of activity. Finally, life-span changes may lead to *a broadening of focus within or beyond domains*.

Scientists and artists differ from people in most other domains in that they must invent their own careers; the career paths are not structured by institutions. They must create the physical and temporal structures of their work and determine what work they will do. Thus, when older artists or scientists reach what for others may be an unstructured phase of life (old age), the lack of structure is not new; they have spent a lifetime actively shaping their own experience. A second difference is that they generally have an opportunity to stay engaged even after retirement, whereas older businessmen, for example, may not. Both domain and field are closed to retirees in many fields, even if they wish to stay engaged and continue pursuing creative work. As a result, the first way of sustaining engagement that is described here—continued pursuit of projects within the same domain—is not universally possible in later life.

Continued engagement with one domain.   The most basic aspect of vital engagement that fosters continued involvement in later life is the very fact that the endeavor has become, over time, a central source of flow and meaning in the person's life. That is, the relationship with the domain has continued to be absorbing and has come to locate the individual in the world in a way that matters. Many endeavors lack the complexity to provide enjoyment and meaning throughout life. But cultural domains such as the arts and sciences have the capacity to occasion both absorption and meaning. First, they integrate concrete goals (e.g., pursuit of specific problems or projects), which occasion flow, and higher order goals or more enduring sources of connection with the world (e.g., answering a call, contributing to a valued tradition and community), which give a sense of purpose to life (cf. Emmons, 1999).

For example, a poet in her 70s professed the concrete goal of "making good poems." Doing so was a route to flow for her; she observed, "My personal experience has been that writing in itself is exciting and pleasurable. And that I only wish I were doing it all the time, or more of the time." This concrete goal was connected to an overarching sense of purpose that defined her enduring relationship to the domain: "Poetry is an art, and art is not a matter of a career. It's a matter of a vocation. And you serve an art."

As mentioned, our conversations with lifelong creators highlighted not the role of contentious relations and opposition as in Bourdieu's framework, but instead the degree to which individual creators' interactions with the field grow to be a central source of meaning that supports their continued involvement with the domain. Artists and scientists differ in the following way (John-Steiner, 2000; Mockros & Csikszentmihalyi, 2000): Scientists' work is more strongly enriched by their intense participation in a community of practice, including relationships with teachers, students, collaborators, and colleagues. In contrast, the meaningfulness of artists' work is often enriched by formation of a sense of fellowship with peers from other places and times. The poet just quoted, musing on aging and mortality, conveyed this source of meaning when she voiced the desire that, through her work, she might "join the rest of the poets of the other centuries that do go on living [through their work] and whom I have lived with, and from, and by, all my life." Enjoying the pleasures of writing and the meaningfulness of life in a calling, she could not conceive how any poet could outlive involvement with the domain: "Language and the sort of translation of perception into language for a poet. . . . You never—you do not sort of come to the end of it and . . . turn your attention to something else. So it just goes on as long as you live." The incomprehensibility of disengaging—this notion that one "can't not" continue—recurs throughout the accounts of older creators and other engaged individuals (cf. Daloz, Keen, Keen, & Parks, 1996).

In addition to an integrated goal hierarchy, vital engagement is fostered by the temporal integration of the individual's present work with both a history, from which the current relationship to the domain has emerged, and a horizon defined in part by the possibilities that the ongoing work suggests. That is, enduring engagement with art or science is fostered by the lifelong creator's formation of a *network of enterprise* (Gruber, 1981; Wallace & Gruber, 1989)—an evolving set of goals—that connects the individual to the past and the future. Indeed, creators' lives seem to be defined most by the intrinsic rhythms of these networks of enterprise rather than by the family life course or career trajectory.

Consider in more concrete detail this forward momentum of vital engagement with a domain. Enduring engagement with one artistic or scientific domain creates an experiential structure that *actively presses* for continued involvement. The domain is experienced as being full of possibility in a general sense; typically, in addition, the promise of particular projects draws the creator on. This has several aspects.

First, the creator is in the midst of something. Most simply, one or more projects are actively being pursued and are pressing to be completed. Creators, especially artists, may describe thematic concerns to which they return over and over again throughout their careers. Apparently, these concerns do not get worked through once and for all, and they may sustain a hold on the individual's imagination into later life. An inability to set a fascinating topic aside accounts for the continuity of focus.[2] If the creator has followed one line of inquiry over an extended period of time, the compelling problems may become more demanding later in life; they may involve integrating a larger body of knowledge, or tackling trickier or more complex questions. Over the course of extended engagement with a domain, unfinished business (i.e., interrupted or suspended work) accumulates. Gruber and Wallace (2001) have described the creator "repeatedly returning to the hard work of a beloved but exasperatingly intractable project or task" (p. 348). Problems may simply be difficult, or the state of the domain may prevent closure. Creators describe turning anew to a problem after months or years, when some discovery or new technology renders the problem soluble. Alternatively, the field may be an obstacle; a creator may resuscitate an idea that fell on deaf ears earlier, rethinking and presenting it to what is, in effect, a new field. Unfinished business may exert a strong grip on creators even as they enter the late career.

Second, particularly in domains where projects take a long time to complete, inventories or backlogs of project ideas accumulate over the course of an individual's life. These create a pool of already existing possibilities that are waiting to lay claim to the creator's attention whenever a project is winding down. Artists and scientists describe ideas collecting in drawers, files, journals, notebooks. By his early 80s, the inventor Jacob Rabinow had filled a bookshelf with "nine volumes of my ideas. I just record ideas. I don't care whether they're old or new, when I think of an idea, I record it. Then later I decide whether it's worth pursuing or not, and then I decide later whether it's worth patenting. . . . There are some 2,000 of them in there."

Third, this inventory is continually expanding because the network of enterprise is "self-renewing" (Gruber, 1984, p. 17). New project ideas emerge out of the ongoing work and then press for the creator's attention. These include not only subsidiary or derivative projects, but also fresh lines of inquiry generated by the continued learning that is a necessary part of all creative work (Gruber & Wallace, 2001). Enduring engagement is fostered by an evolving set of goals that connects the individual to the past and the future, giving current work a rich sense of personal meaning. Even as it does so, however, it is fed by new developments in the domain and by the emergent goals that arise out of the current work. That is, the network of enterprise may require continued learning within the creator's domain at any phase within the creative process. In the problem-finding or formulation phase, for example, scientists describe "auditing" the literature and attending seminars to hear their colleagues present "hot new findings," as well as devising more informal means of staying current within their area. Some scientists cope with retirement by adopting the role of student, despite the fact that this may violate normative expectations concerning the conduct of distinguished older members of the field. This mode of instrumental late-life learning was illustrated by an eminent physicist still active in his 80s who sought out younger experts at other universities to learn about new work in his area: "I realized that there is a development in general relativity that I ought to learn about and I did not know the people who had done the work, or if I knew them it was just a casual meeting, and I would have to go and get acquainted. So I got up on my hind feet and phoned and made an appointment and went."

The engaged artist or scientist acquires new knowledge and masters new technologies in the subsequent phases of the creative process, as well. Ideas for new projects may emerge at any point in the course of this continued learning, which might be called *centripetal* because it tends to hold attention within existing channels of interest. In these ways, a lifetime of vital engagement with a domain tends to propel creators on into an engaged future even in later life; at least, this is true in the arts and in many sciences, where domain and field tend not to prevent continued activity in old age.

As noted earlier, the eminent older creator plays roles other than innovator, including gatekeeping and teaching. We have stressed how these roles can obstruct sustained creativity, but they also can occasion exposure to new knowledge and, in that respect, may contribute to creativity in later life. Gatekeeping roles, such as editing professional journals, may have this impact. Teaching, in particular, can be a way either of staying current within a domain ("Students in a sense are telling us what's going on at the frontier") or of broadening one's knowledge ("The heterogeneity of inquiry and interest that come with teaching give you more backburners to opportunistically develop"). In these ways, age and eminence may be consistent with, even conducive to, continued learning and creativity.

To return to Baltes' notion of positive aging, we have been suggesting that most older creators who remain engaged do so by selectively investing their attention and energy along the same general lines as in the past, continuing to devote themselves to artistic or scientific work and to work in the same domain, though on ever-changing projects. In addition, being vitally engaged can (a) lead creators to overlook negative age norms that otherwise might lessen creative efforts, and (b) make it possible, in at least some cases, to overcome age-related losses.

The later years are thought to be accompanied by increased reminiscence about the past as part of coming to terms with the life that has been lived (Cohler, 1982; Neugarten, 1969). In this view, objects increasingly are valued and vitalize the self because of memories they embody rather than because of action possibilities they hold (Csikszentmihalyi & Rochberg-Halton, 1981; Galatzer-Levy & Cohler, 1993). Old age is thought to encompass concerns with the legacy to be left behind, pleasure in reflecting upon it, and a more philosophical and accepting stance.

However, caught up in ongoing enterprises and looking ahead to others, many aging creators appear to have their attention focused primarily on the present and future (cf. Goodman, 1981; Rowe, 1976). For example, after detailing a current line of investigation, a 71-year-old chemist noted, "I will continue doing more of this for a while, but it probably won't be too many years before I gradually slide over to another problem." Creators may explicitly articulate an awareness of their temporal orientation:

> I think of things not yet done. That's what preoccupies me, rather than any feeling of satisfaction with what I've done. I see it all as part of a process, part of a journey, not a series of destinations, you might say. . . . Someday I may think that way, but I don't yet. (Biologist, 76)

> I am interested that my wife thinks back about this and that, and what she might have done. . . . She has much more perspective on the past than I do. I am always thinking about the next thing. (Physicist, 81)

This temporal orientation is consistent with moving into the later years focused not on the past, but instead on the evolving network of enterprise in the domain.

Not only does enduring engagement diminish attention to negative age norms, in some cases it also provides a weapon against the negative effects of aging. For example, the centrality of engagement in a creator's life may inspire the strenuous effort required to compensate for, or even to recover from, age-associated losses. Jazz pianist Oscar Peterson suffered a stroke in his late 60s. He spent an arduous year recovering, and at the time of the interview had returned to performing and recording. He explained, "I just wanted to be able to play again. . . . I wanted to sort of unshackle myself. If I could. I didn't know if I could, but I believed I could. . . . Piano's been my life. And I guess will always be some part of my life. And the thought of not being able to talk to it the way I had been able to talk to it, seemed incomprehensible."

In a more familiar use of the medium of art to come to terms with age-associated losses, a second musician, also in his late 60s, described becoming frozen creatively in the wake of his wife's death. After many months, he was suddenly inspired to compose a work that memorialized their life together. The experience itself was one of intense engagement, compounded with a sense of relief that he was working again. The composition was a source of solace because it connected him with his wife. It also reconnected him to the creative work in which he continued to find absorption and meaning. Its power as a work of art earned a Pulitzer Prize.

The basic condition for remaining engaged via this first late-career path is that the individual continues to see meaningful and enjoyable possibilities for action in the domain. For a variety of reasons, however, creators may experience diminished enjoyment of their work or feel that it has lost meaning. Changes at any locus within the system—the person (e.g., reduced capacities), the domain (e.g., stagnation, technological changes), the field (e.g., changes in access), or the relationship of the discipline to the wider society (e.g., isolation from or negative impacts on culture and society)—might be factors. Faced with diminished vitality of engagement, some eminent older creators might continue to work merely out of habit. Others might retire. However, in two alternative pathways to late-career engagement, the aging creator *actively reshapes* the relationship to art or science in response to loss of enjoyment, on one hand, and loss of meaning, on the other.

A common denominator across all three pathways is the decisive role played by *emergent motivation*. In the two patterns to which we turn next, as in the first, creators actively appropriate their own experience and shape the network of enterprises in line with an emergent sense of what will be interesting, absorbing, and meaningful to do; that is, a particular kind of experiential structure characterizes the engaged artist or scientist, one that permits its own transformation (cf. Colby & Damon, 1992). Engaged creators experience emergent motivation in the sense that the experience of vital engagement is their key compass in defining direction. They are attuned to the meaningfulness of their experience and to its capacity to provide flow. This one compass accommodates or even encourages change at the level of specific projects and goals for those who follow the first pathway, and more dramatic change for those who follow the two paths considered next. Emergent motivation accounts for the self-regenerative character of an evolving network of enterprises within a single domain, but also for the capacity to sustain vital engagement if the long-standing relationship ceases to be enjoyable or meaningful.

Shifting to a new domain.   The most common pathway into late-life engagement is an evolving network of absorbing and meaningful enterprises within a single domain. However, some lifelong creators shift their focus beyond the domain in which they have worked when they reach old age, in either of two ways: (1) by changing domains of creative endeavor, or (2) by moving beyond innovation in a circumscribed domain in response to new concerns associated with later life.

First, some creators make a wholesale change of direction because they have lost their enthusiasm for the domains that have vitally engaged them for many years. Though they may continue to feel that those domains are important, they no longer experience the same intense absorption and enjoyment in their work. In later life, when retirement is an option, moving into a new domain provides an alternative to simply disengaging from creative work. For example, a social scientist decided to exchange basic research—in an intellectual community to which he still felt strongly connected—for applied work in a different institutional setting. His motivations were experiential: "At first I resisted, saying I couldn't leave this university or this department. But on the other hand, I've been at this university now a long time. This is my 27th year. And I do feel I'm growing stale. Although it's an exciting place to be, every year it's the same place. And the kinds of problems I work on are starting to feel very similar from year to year."

Some individuals establish a pattern of changing domain or subdomain prior to late life. They may describe the pattern as a conscious strategy for sustaining engagement and thereby creativity. For example, this social scientist went on to explain, "The way I keep my energy going is that every couple of years, I change the field I'm doing." In a similar vein, a scientist in his 60s who had become a writer at age 55 reflected that he had "always jumped around very easily from one field to another." He contended that "it is a good idea to change careers every 10 years or so" as "a way of keeping young and vigorous."

When the relationship between a person and a domain ceases to occasion intense absorption, how does the person identify a new domain that might be vitally engaging? The scientist-turned-writer advocated maintaining broad interests: "Most of the people who burn out tend to be those who are very specialized. And after they have exhausted their particular narrow specialty, there is nothing more for them to do and they lose interest. If you can manage to avoid that and stay broad, you will have much more chance to be able to keep active and go into new things." The social scientist described a deliberate strategy of constantly exploring new areas of knowledge that might inform future creative work: "I learn something new every year. I mean a major area, like I'll learn a new mathematics. . . . Last year I studied anthropology a lot. . . . That's the other philosophy I have, which is to learn something about everything and have a wide variety of experiences, because you never know."

We distinguish between two kinds of learning. In discussing evolving networks of enterprise, we discussed the centripetal learning that is an integral part of pursuing an existing line of inquiry. Among engaged artists and scientists even in their later years, centripetal learning is pervasive and contributes to sustained creativity. Other acquisition of knowledge is more diffusely or uncertainly relevant to a person's ongoing or planned work. It has a *centrifugal* impact on attention; it can suggest the direction for major shifts in the network of enterprise and can support the kind of domain integration that characterizes many major creative insights (Sternberg, this volume). Some creators reduced their investment in this form of learning as they aged but for others, as we have seen, this second kind of learning continued to be evident. Centrifugal learning may be pursued as a deliberate strategy, as in the two cases described previously. In addition, individuals can be exposed to unfamiliar domains more haphazardly, through a variety of roles and experiences. These include the roles of teacher and gatekeeper mentioned earlier, as well as travel, accidental encounters, and social relationships outside one's field.

Note that from the standpoint of subjective phenomenology, changing subdomains may resemble a more dramatic shift across *domains*. That is, many lifelong creators change *subdomains* when they experience a waning of interest in the territory they have been exploring for some time, combined with rising excitement about some new area of inquiry appearing on the horizon. In addition, they may experience their histories as full of change, even if they also identify some unifying thread that runs through their careers. In both patterns, change is prompted by feedback from subjective experience; motivation is emergent. The distinction between the two is important to retain, however. The sacrifice entailed by crossing disciplinary boundaries may be high on multiple fronts—knowledge, expertise, reputation, and other resources may not transfer. As a result, subdomain and domain shifts can have different implications for creative achievement, a point we return to later.

In seeking to restore their enjoyment of art or science, creators who change domains sacrifice long-standing connections to the world that have become a source of meaning for them. For example, the social scientist mentioned earlier initially resisted change because of existing ties to a valued community of practice. Creators who change domains also sacrifice the identification with a particular specialization that can become an important source of work's meaning in the enduring engagements described in the previous section. However, lifelong engagement in creative work can be understood in multiple ways. Depending on how it is construed, its subjective meaning can accommodate significant shifts in the person's focus of energy and attention. An individual who changes domains may actively construct a sense of identity as a lifelong explorer, learner, creator, or witness, rather than (or as well as) someone who has been engaged within one particular specialization or characterized by a particular history or past achievement. Creators may define themselves in terms of changefulness, as do the scientist and social scientist just described, or they may identify an underlying continuity beneath the changes. This includes changes occurring during the late career, such as those encouraged by age-related limitations.

Deriving meaning from a sense of identity not tied to a specific domain carries its own advantages in relation to staying engaged and sustaining creativity. For example, the personal meaning of one's relationship to a domain might reside in an identity as a certain kind of artist or scientist. The naturalist E. O. Wilson described an identity as a synthesizer or "pattern hunter" that has distinguished his decades of intense engagement with the natural world: "I enjoy most learning all sorts of new things, all the time, and putting them together and looking for the pattern. And then defining the pattern, and then proving its existence by experiments and innovation. . . . It's an altogether honorable way of doing science. That's the way Darwin did science. That's a good predecessor. You know, he gathered everything he could possibly do, and then he looked for a pattern, how to explain it all, and so on."

In his 60s, Wilson became interested in the social sciences. Although this constituted a dramatically different focus of attention, he retained his sense of identity as a synthesizer. He recounted how he had

> listened spellbound [to an eminent economist discussing] economic theory, which I've begun to enter in my exploration. And I was grabbing concepts the way I collect ants, and storing them, and putting them together, and classifying them, and evaluating economic theory in a way that would allow me to come back and hopefully build a synthesis. You see the metaphorical equivalency. In other words, I can't literally keep going into rainforests. For various reasons, I can't continue to be literally a physical explorer. But I *can* explore the wildness—the wild, distant reaches—of anthropology, economics, and sociology, and other subjects in my effort to synthesize them.

Because Wilson's new project was physically less demanding than conducting fieldwork, this shift successfully compensated for age-related limitations. Alternatively, we might emphasize how continuity of engagement is aided by the individual's active making of meaning.

Broadening one's concerns. A third pathway can be contrasted both with shifting from a familiar domain to an unfamiliar one and with continuing to move from one engaging project to the next in the same domain. In both of those cases, one circumscribed domain or another is vitally engaging. As some creators grow older, however, they become dissatisfied with the narrow questions of a domain and reach for broader questions. Individuals who are open to change on the basis of their subjective experience are more likely to respond to this late-life impulse by changing the focus of their work.

This shift in focus has been recognized in the literature on age and creative accomplishment. For example, in his survey of creative individuals through the ages, Lehman (1953) identified kinds of achievement that appeared to be distinctively associated with the later years, including works organizing individual or disciplinary knowledge (e.g., writing textbooks) and endeavors new to the aging individual (e.g., history, memoir). According to other researchers (e.g., Gardner, 1993; Simonton, 1988a; Zuckerman, 1977), in addition to taking a historicist turn, in the later years some eminent scientists may move toward philosophical, meta-, or reflective perspectives on their domains. In addition, older creators may become increasingly occupied with the interconnections between the domain and the wider world or with sociopolitical concerns. Each of these activities might be undertaken as a kind of retirement activity to fend off idleness, or out of a sense of reluctant obligation. At least for some individuals, however, they represent opportunities for new forms of vital engagement and, at the same time, ways of taking up age-related concerns.

Earlier in their careers, these individuals experienced the domain as a separate reality that provided rich possibilities for action (as others still do). However, for the individuals in question, this separate reality has begun to seem limited. The very self-sufficiency that makes it a good "game" tends to exclude other aspects of the world and other aspirations that come to seem more important. Why some individuals and not others tire of the game and are drawn to larger concerns is unclear. Some possible factors include individual differences in life history (e.g., early role models of the late career), social encounters during adulthood (e.g., a spouse or colleague motivated by broader concerns), opportunities presented by the field (e.g., the role of "social sage"; Zuckerman, 1977), and sensitivity to age-related psychological shifts (e.g., generative concerns).

A scientist in his 80s provides one kind of example. He described working on a broad-scale issue for which he was immersing himself in philosophy. In contrast, in middle age he had been "more bogged down in mathematical questions—how do you solve such-and-such an equation?" The scientific enterprise currently represents, for him, a quest for truth that springs from the same source as religious quests: "To me, the effect it will have on all of humankind, when we find out how this strange and wonderful world has come to be, is worth so much that that's, I feel, the greatest contribution I could make. 'This world: How come?' . . . People are still searching for it, as you can tell from interest in religion. . . . the ultimate truth. People want to know, 'Where am I in this great scheme of things?'" Similarly, an engineer and inventor in his 60s had grown increasingly concerned with sustainable development. He contended that, with age, "You think about a lot bigger subjects than you did when you were 26 and just trying to get the next project that you'd be working on, which might also be fun but it didn't have such global [aspects]."

If a scientist moves beyond the accepted framework of the domain, seeking answers to deeper questions, he or she may be deemed a "deep-ender" by those absorbed in domain problems. It is probably safe to say that these scientists are accepting a lower likelihood of creative success than those who have continued to pursue more circumscribed problems, whether in a long-standing or even a new domain—if for no other reason than the skepticism of many scientists toward philosophical or meta-inquiries.

Better supported by normative expectations about the late career is movement into established metadomains (e.g., philosophy of science). For example, for one 75-year-old physicist-turned-historian, the shift to writing a memoir and history of science allowed him to give expression to an interest in the past that is normatively associated with growing older. It also became vitally engaging as a form of creative work in its own right, and the individual's writings won recognition in this new field.

The same impulse to move toward a broader perspective, or engage broader concerns, may motivate an increased sense of custodianship: nurturing the formation or progress of a domain, field, or particular individuals. Two illustrations from our interviews are an anthropologist's dream of training anthropologists from Third-World countries and a biologist's battle to place his domain on an equal footing with others in the history and philosophy of science. Even though these efforts do not result in creative products, they may be creative in the systems sense because they may transform fields or domains. By the same token, interactions with the general public that are made possible by eminence—for example, efforts to publicize and promote the role of women in science—may result in wider societal interest in the domain and thereby have significant downstream effects on the vitality of the field.

Although age norms support some of these changes of focus, counterpressures exist. This is particularly true in the sciences, because the ethos of science places highest value on original research within a circumscribed domain of knowledge. Nevertheless, for a handful of creators, there is a clear shift away from the details of specialized problems toward concern with larger questions or wider perspectives.

Comparing the Three Pathways

In the first and second late-career paths, aging individuals remain vitally engaged within creative work in one cultural domain or another. These individuals are so intently focused on the domain that they may seem unaware of normative expectations, including ones that might encourage either withdrawal from creative work or concessions to age that are inimical to engagement and creativity (e.g., reduced access to new ideas). Additionally, they may seem unaffected by psychological transformations of later life that might lead them toward concerns beyond the domain (e.g., a shift in temporal focus, an increased concern with legacy).

Both the first and second late-career patterns may simply extend into later life the ways that individuals have sustained engagement throughout the adult years. Those who change domains in the second half of their careers may have explored multiple pathways or cultivated side interests earlier in their careers. As noted, it is less clear why some aging creators appear to be more sensitive than others to psychological shifts with age, ceasing to find the challenges contained within any circumscribed domain, old or new, sufficient to deeply engage them.

Our main point is that one underlying dynamic characterizes all of the individuals who continue to work with intensity in later life: a willingness, or need, to regulate their decisions about the investment of attention and energy primarily on the basis of vital engagement—what is meaningful and absorbing to do—despite the many other possible considerations, such as reputation, certainty of success, and normative expectations. It may be more important to clearly recognize this common dynamic than to sort out the influences that favor one path rather than another. The array of influences may include differences of temperament (e.g., attraction to depth versus attraction to variety or breadth), differences in a domain's richness as a field of possibilities during a creator's career, and differences in the way the relationship between a particular individual and a domain, as manifested in the network of enterprises, happens to unfold.

Whatever factors are at work, the artist's or scientist's pathway in later life may affect the likelihood of continued creative accomplishment. The majority of late-life creators continue to pursue work in the same domain as they have throughout their careers, experience an unflagging fascination with the object, and remain caught up in a long-standing but continually evolving network of enterprises. The engaged creator's attentive give-and-take with the object is clearly a requirement for any creative accomplishment. In addition, this first path makes optimal use of a creator's accumulated intellectual, reputational, and other resources, which tend to be tied to work in a specific domain and field. Long-term involvement in a single domain carries at least two threats to sustained creative achievement, however. One widely recognized factor is loss of the fresh perspective that appears to be key to many major discoveries. A second factor is the potential for a creator's evolving network of enterprise to diverge from the dominant concerns and paradigms of the field. As the personal line of inquiry gains a momentum of its own, this can lead to work that has diminishing connection to the current domain and therefore becomes less likely to be noticed or judged important by the field.

A smaller number follow a different path, changing domains in later life. Often they have done so throughout the second half of their careers. From the standpoint of contributing creatively, this pathway is riskier than the first because it requires that the individual adopt the status of a novice in later life, with all that entails in terms of new learning. However, making a significant change in the object of one's attention (topic or theme, medium or even domain) may prove fruitful. Periodically changing research topics has been identified as a way of sustaining scientific creativity precisely because it allows the individual to acquire a fresh perspective (Gardner, 1993; Root-Bernstein, Bernstein, & Garnier, 1993). As we have seen, aging creators may embrace domain change very deliberately as a strategy for maintaining creativity. The likelihood of creative achievement in the new domain is affected by the interaction of age-related changes in capacity, if any, with the particular demands of the new domain. Some domain changes exemplify selective optimization with compensation, such as the transition from theoretical physics to the neighboring domain of astrophysics (Stephan & Levin, 1992). A lifetime's accumulated knowledge of physics retains relevance, but the demands on fluid intelligence are less great.

Finally, late-career movement toward broader concerns is favored by age-related psychological transformations and by shifts in the opportunities accorded to eminent creators as they grow older. Change of this kind has varying consequences for creativity, depending on the nature of the shift. When it comes to the content of an individual's work, the arts generally are more amenable than the sciences to a turn toward larger questions, simply because the latter fall within the established scope of the arts. In the sciences, lines of inquiry that challenge existing disciplinary boundaries may be regarded skeptically, given the specialization and the rewarding of technical virtuosity that increasingly characterize many disciplines. On the other hand, age and eminence create opportunities for historical, philosophical, general science, and other metacontributions that may be better received than efforts to broaden the boundaries of the domain itself. Some individuals successfully migrate from scientific or social-scientific research to metadomains, making original contributions by drawing upon multiple talents. Finally, experience and eminence also provide resources that may support an older creator's efforts to change the field or the domain's role in the wider culture.

CONCLUSION

In conclusion, when viewed from our systems perspective, the life course presents a shifting landscape of obstacles and opportunities for continuing creative accomplishment. Advanced age, in particular, can have negative effects on creative work because of decreasing energy and other physical decrements, because of loss of support from the field as one has to relinquish laboratories and academic positions, and because of inability to keep up with advances in the domain—or disinterest in doing so. Nevertheless, there is ample evidence that creativity can be sustained late in life. We have accounted for the ability to sustain valuable contribution in advanced age with the notion of vital engagement. Individuals who are still involved in pushing the boundaries of a domain in their 80s and 90s are those who both enjoy their work and find a deep meaning in it. There are three main ways that older persons continue to be vitally engaged.

The first and most widespread is simply to continue producing and learning within the boundaries of one's domain. The second is to shift into a neighboring, or even somewhat removed, domain. The third, and in some ways the most risky, development is to move to a metalevel in which the person seeks to connect the domain with broader cultural or social issues. These are very different paths in which creativity can be expressed in the last segment of the life course, but they all depend on having identified oneself with the rules of the domain and the coworkers constituting the field, for many years.

The systems model that we used to organize our data shares many of its premises with the constructivist theories of cultural production developed by Bourdieu and Foucault. But in looking at how individuals relate to the field and the domain over the life span, a very different picture emerges from the one described by those authors. True to the conflict-theory perspective they share, Bourdieu and Foucault see cultural production as a process of unending strife. Within and between fields, individuals vie for resources and attention. The content of domains is shaped to protect epistemological boundaries corresponding to power and privilege. In this constant turmoil, age could become a marker for drawing the lines between "us" and "them."

There is a lot of truth to this perspective provided by conflict theory. Yet it also distorts the lived experience of creative individuals in fundamental respects. Fields are not just competitive arenas for gladiatorial combat: They also provide some of the warmest and most sustaining personal relationships—with mentors, peers, students. Domains are not just impersonal cognitive structures forcing people to think and act according to their dictates: They also provide flexible rules for creative, playful action. It is because of this that joyous immersion in one's work is such a central, pervasive aspect of the phenomenology of creativity. Few ways of growing old are as rewarding as continuing to work in the domain of one's choice, in the company of like-minded persons.

NOTES

1. See, for instance, Bourdieu (1993): "Michel Foucault . . . refuses to look outside the 'field of discourse' for the explanatory principle of each of the discourses in the field

... like so many others, Foucault succumbs to that form of essentialism or, if one prefers, fetishism, that is manifested so clearly in other domains, notably in mathematics" (p. 179).

2. The subjective phenomenology is very different when continuity of focus is due to domain factors (e.g., conservatively confining oneself to topics that one already knows well) or field considerations (e.g., giving the audience what it has come to expect).

REFERENCES

Andreasen, N. C. (1987). Creativity and mental illness: Prevalence rates in writers and their first-degree relatives. *American Journal of Psychiatry, 144,* 1288–1292.

Baltes, P. B. (1993). The aging mind: Potential and limits. *Gerontologist, 33,* 580–594.

Baltes, P. B., & Staudinger, U. (2000). Wisdom: A metaheuristic (pragmatic) to orchestrate mind and virtue toward excellence. *American Psychologist, 55,* 122–136.

Barron, F., & Harrington, D. (1981). Creativity, intelligence, and personality. In M. R. Rosenzweig & L. W. Porter (Eds.), *Annual Review of Psychology, 32* (pp. 439–476). Palo Alto, CA: Annual Reviews.

Becker, H. S. (1974). Art as collective action. *American Sociological Review, 39*(6), 767–776.

Becker, H. S. (1976). Art worlds and social types. *American Behavioral Scientist, 19*(6), 703–719.

Bourdieu, P. (1993). *The field of cultural production.* Chicago: University of Chicago Press.

Cattell, R. B. (1963). Theory of fluid and crystallized intelligence: A critical experiment. *Journal of Educational Psychology, 54,* 1–22.

Cohler, B. J. (1982). Personal narrative and the life course. In *Life-span development and behavior* (Vol. 4, pp. 205–241). New York: Academic Press.

Colby, A., & Damon, W. (1992). *Some do care: Contemporary lives of moral commitment.* New York: Free Press.

Collins, M. A., & Amabile, T. M. (1999). Motivation and creativity. In J. R. Sternberg (Ed.), *Handbook of creativity* (pp. 297–312). New York: Cambridge University Press.

Csikszentmihalyi, M. (1996). *Creativity: Flow and the psychology of discovery and invention.* New York: HarperCollins.

Csikszentmihalyi, M. (1999). Implications of a systems perspective for the study of creativity. In R. J. Sternberg (Ed.), *Handbook of creativity* (pp. 313–335). Cambridge, UK: Cambridge University Press.

Csikszentmihalyi, M. (2000). *Beyond boredom and anxiety: The experience of play in work and games.* San Francisco: Jossey-Bass. (Original work published 1975)

Csikszentmihalyi, M., & Csikszentmihalyi, I. S. (1993). Family influences on the development of giftedness. In *The origins and development of high ability* [Ciba Foundation Symposium 178] (pp. 187–206). Chichester, UK: Wiley.

Csikszentmihalyi, M., & Getzels, J. W. (1973). The personality of young artists: A theoretical and empirical investigation. *British Journal of Psychology, 64,* 91–104.

Csikszentmihalyi, M., & Nakamura, J. (1999). Emerging goals and the self-regulation of behavior. In R. S. Wyer (Ed.), *Advances in social cognition: Vol. 12. Perspectives on behavioral self-regulation* (pp. 107–118). Mahwah, NJ: Erlbaum.

Csikszentmihalyi, M., & Robinson, R. E. (1986). Culture, time, and the development of talent. In R. J. Sternberg & J. Davidson (Eds.), *Conceptions of giftedness* (pp. 264–284). New York: Cambridge University Press.

Csikszentmihalyi, M., & Rochberg-Halton, E. (1981). *The meaning of things*. New York: Cambridge University Press.

Daloz, L., Keen, C., Keen, J., & Parks, S. (1996). *Common fire*. Boston: Beacon Press.

Davie, D. (1990). *Slavic excursions: Essays on Russian and Polish literature*. Chicago : University of Chicago Press.

Dennis, W. (1966). Creative production between the ages of 20 and 80 years. *Journal of Gerontology, 21,* 1–8.

Dewey, J. (1934). *Art as experience*. New York: Perigree Books.

Emmons, R. A. (1999). *The psychology of ultimate concerns*. New York: Guilford.

Erikson, E. H. (1958). *Young man Luther*. New York: Norton.

Feldman, D. H. (1980). *Beyond universals in cognitive development*. Norwood, NJ: Ablex.

Feldman, D. H. (with Goldsmith, L. T.). (1991). *Nature's gambit: Child prodigies and the development of human potential*. New York: Teachers College Press. (Original work published 1986)

Foucault, M. (1968). Réponse au cercle d'épistémologie. *Cahiers pour l'Analyse, 9,* 9–40.

Freud, S. (1947*). Leonardo da Vinci, a study in psychosexuality* (A. A. Brill, Trans.). New York: Random House.

Freud, S. (1955). The Moses of Michelangelo. In J. Strachey (Ed. and Trans.), *The standard edition of the complete psychological works of Sigmund Freud* (Vol. 8, pp. 211–238). London: Hogarth. (Original work published 1908)

Galatzer-Levy, R. M., & Cohler, B. J. (1993). *The essential other: A developmental psychology of the self*. New York: Basic Books.

Gardner, H. (1993). *Creating minds: An anatomy of creativity seen through the lives of Freud, Einstein, Picasso, Stravinsky, Eliot, Graham, and Gandhi*. New York: Basic Books.

Gedo, J. (1990). More on creativity and its vicissitudes. In M. Runco & R. Albert (Eds.), *Theories of creativity* (pp. 35–45). Newbury Park, CA: Sage.

Getzels, J. W., & Csikszentmihalyi, M. (1976). *The creative vision: A longitudinal study with artists*. New York: Wiley.

Getzels, J. W., & Jackson, P. (1962). *Creativity and intelligence: Explorations with gifted students*. New York: Wiley.

Goodman, L. (1981). *Death and the creative life*. New York: Springer.

Gruber, H. E. (1981). *Darwin on man: A psychological study of scientific creativity* (2nd ed.). Chicago: University of Chicago Press.

Gruber, H. E. (1984). The emergence of a sense of purpose: A cognitive case study of young Darwin. In M. L. Commons, F. A. Richards, & C. Armon (Eds.), *Beyond formal operations: Late adolescent and adult cognitive development* (pp. 3–27). New York: Praeger.

Gruber, H. E., & Davis, S. (1988). Inching our way up Mount Olympus: The evolving systems approach to creative thinking. In R. J. Sternberg (Ed.), *The nature of creativity* (pp. 243–270). New York: Cambridge University Press.

Gruber, H. E., & Wallace, D. B. (2001). Creative work: The case of Charles Darwin. *American Psychologist, 56,* 346–349.

Guilford, J. P. (1967). *The nature of human intelligence.* New York: McGraw-Hill.

Harrington, D. M. (1990). *The ecology of human creativity: A psychological perspective.* In M. A. Runco & R. S. Albert (Eds.), *Theories of creativity* (pp. 143–169). Newbury Park, CA: Sage.

Howe, M. J. A. (1999). Prodigies and creativity. In R. J. Sternberg (Ed.). *Handbook of creativity* (pp. 421–448). New York: Cambridge University Press.

Jamison, K. R. (1989). Mood disorder and patterns of creativity in British writers and artists. *Psychiatry, 52,* 125–134.

John-Steiner, V. (1985*). Notebooks of the mind.* Albuquerque: University of New Mexico Press.

John-Steiner, V. (2000). *Creative collaboration.* New York: Oxford University Press.

Kris, E. (1952). *Psychoanalytic explorations in art.* New York: International Universities Press.

Lehman, H. C. (1953). *Age and achievement.* Princeton, NJ: Princeton University Press.

Martindale, C. (1990).*The clockwork muse: The predictability of artistic change.* New York: Basic Books.

Mockros, C., & Csikszentmihalyi, M. (2000). The social construction of creative lives. In A. Montuori & R. Purser (Eds.), *Social creativity* (Vol. 1, pp. 175–218). Cresskill, NJ: Hampton.

Montuori, A., & Purser, R. E. (Eds.). (1999). *Social creativity.* Cresskill, NJ: Hampton.

Nakamura, J., & Csikszentmihalyi, M. (2001). Catalytic creativity: The case of Linus Pauling. *American Psychologist, 56,* 337–341.

Nakamura, J., & Csikszentmihalyi, M. (2003). The construction of meaning through vital engagement. In C. L. M. Keyes & J. Haidt (Eds.), *Flourishing: Positive psychology and the life well-lived.* Washington, DC: American Psychological Association.

Neugarten, B. (1969). Continuities and discontinuities of psychological issues into adult life. *Human Development, 12,* 121–130.

Roe, A. (1952). *The making of a scientist.* New York: Dodd, Mead.

Root-Bernstein, R. S., Bernstein, M., & Garnier, H. (1993). Identification of scientists making long-term, high-impact contributions, with notes on their methods of working. *Creativity Research Journal, 6,* 329–343.

Rowe, A. R. (1976). The retired scientist: The myth of the aging individual. In J. F. Gubrium (Ed.), *Time, roles and self in old age* (pp. 209–219). New York: Human Sciences Press.

Rowe, J. W., & Kahn, R. L. (1998). *Successful aging.* New York: Pantheon.

Runco, M.A. (Ed.). (1994). *Problem finding, problem solving, and creativity.* Norwood, NJ: Ablex.

Sawyer, R. K. (Ed.). (1997*). Creativity in performance.* Greenwich, CT: Ablex.

Sawyer, R. K. (2002). A discourse on discourse: An archeological history of an intellectual concept. *Cultural Studies, 16*(3), 433–456.

Sears, P., & Sears, R. R. (1980, February). 1528 little geniuses and how they grew. *Psychology Today,* pp. 29–43.

Schaie, K. W. (1996). Intellectual development in adulthood. in J. E. Birren & K. W. Schaie (Eds.), *Handbook of the psychology of aging* (4th ed., pp. 266–286). San Diego, CA: Academic Press.

Simon, N. A. (1988). Creativity and motivation: A response to Csikszentmihalyi. *New Ideas in Psychology, 6,* 177–181.

Simonton, D. K. (1988a). Age and outstanding achievement: What do we know after a century of research? *Psychological Bulletin, 104,* 251–267.

Simonton, D. K. (1988b). *Scientific genius: A psychology of science.* Cambridge, UK: Cambridge University Press.

Simonton, D. K. (1997). Foreign influence and national achievement: The impact of open milieus on Japanese civilization. *Journal of Personality and Social Psychology, 72,* 86–94.

Simonton, D. K. (1999). Creativity from a historiometric perspective. In R. J. Sternberg (Ed.), *Handbook of creativity* (pp. 116–136). New York: Cambridge University Press.

Stephan, P. E., & Levin, S. G. (1992). *Striking the mother lode in science: The importance of age, place, and time.* New York: Oxford University Press.

Terman, L. M. (1925). *Genetic studies of genius.* Stanford, CA: Stanford University Press.

Wallace, D. B., & Gruber, H. E. (Eds.). (1989). *Creative people at work: Twelve cognitive case studies.* New York: Oxford University Press.

Wallas, G. (1926). *The art of thought.* New York: Harcourt Brace.

Wehner, L. Csikszentmihalyi, M. & Magyari-Beck, I. (1991). Current approaches to studying creativity: An exploratory investigation. *Creativity Research Journal, 4*(3), 261–271.

Wigner, E. (1992).*The recollections of Eugene P. Wigner.* New York: Plenum.

Zuckerman, H. (1977). *Scientific elite: Nobel laureates in the United States.* New York: Free Press.

Zuckerman, H., & Cole, J. R. (1994). Research strategies in science: A preliminary inquiry. *Creativity Research Journal, 7,* 391–405.

CHAPTER SIX

Key Issues in Creativity and Development

Prepared by all authors

We have treated this project as a coauthored volume from start to finish, and we began our collaboration at the early stage of preparing the abstracts. Keith Sawyer and Counterpoints Series Editor Marc Marschark closely examined the abstracts to ensure that each spoke to common volume themes, so that the book would have a coherence and an impact worthy of this important topic. The abstracts were significantly revised in response to this review, and the initial chapter manuscripts were all exciting and important treatments of the book's themes: common theoretical issues in creativity research and in developmental psychology.

This collaborative process continued throughout the project. After receiving first drafts of the chapters in the fall of 2001, Sawyer circulated copies of all manuscripts to all authors. John-Steiner and Sawyer then collaborated to review each manuscript and offered detailed editorial commentary. Each author responded to these comments and to the ideas in the other chapters by generating a substantially revised draft, and these were completed by January 2002. John-Steiner and Sawyer then circulated all of these revised manuscripts to all of the authors, in preparation for the discussion of this final chapter.

A distinctive feature of volumes in the Counterpoints series is that the final chapter brings together all of the authors for an exchange on the ideas presented in the individual chapters. We decided to take advantage of new technology by organizing our discussion as an Internet newsgroup. In March 2002, John-

Steiner and Sawyer prepared a list of discussion questions inspired by the chapters. Sawyer's initial e-mail of April 9 suggested a free-form, open-ended discussion: "Please feel free to suggest additional questions or topics for discussion. Also, feel free to reach down into the list and respond to any one of the questions; we don't have to go in any particular order, and you don't have to wait for me to post a question." We initially circulated the following 10 questions, and as the discussion proceeded, it emerged that our collective interest focused on the first 3 questions:

1. Does society suppress children's natural creativity?
2. Are there different domains in development and in creativity?
3. How does one balance social context and individual psychological process in creativity research?
4. What is the relation between motivation and personality? How does social context interact with motivation (and personality)?
5. What is the role of historical development? Moran and John-Steiner mention it in Vygotsky's theory, but the other chapters are mostly silent. Csikszentmihalyi has often claimed that creativity is defined differently in different periods—that Mendel was not creative until after his death. Is there anything historically universal about creativity? What aspects of creativity are most likely to change over time?
6. What are some developmental precursors to adult creativity? Are there any proven correlations between activities of children (for example, fantasy play) and adult creativity?
7. Theories of qualitative developmental transitions (such as Piaget's) claim that basic mental processes of children are different from those of adults, but we apply the same theories of creativity to both children and adults. Do we need different theories of creativity for children than for adults? If not, then why not?
8. Are development transitions creative, as Feldman and Sawyer suggest? Or is this a case of stretching an analogy too far?
9. Are there creative personalities or individuals (or perhaps domain-specific creative personalities)? If so, what is developmentally unique about them?
10. Contrast Sternberg's investment theory (defy the crowd, buy low) with Csikszentmihalyi's systems theory (which seems to imply going with the crowd). How can we reconcile these?

The discussion took place over a one-month period and concluded by June 3, 2002. Sawyer then edited the postings for clarity and coherence and organized them in topic and sequence.

CREATIVITY AND CHILDREN

The question: Our culture has a folk belief that society suppresses creativity: for example, that formal schooling squashes children's natural creativity. If so, then this would suggest that children are more creative than adults and that normal development is a process of becoming less creative. Is there any truth to this folk belief? If so what's the evidence? If not, then why do so many people believe it?

David Henry Feldman

One of the best ways to get a strong response from my students is to propose to them that children are not creative. This runs directly counter to the belief that children are naturally creative, and it arouses very strong feelings and reactions. Of course, my point is to push them to try to be more precise on their definitions of creativity. In a certain sense, it is true that children are naturally creative, but in another sense, no child has ever added to a culturally valued body of knowledge. Many children are spontaneous, expressive, and unselfconscious in their willingness to say or do unconventional things, but many are not. If by creativity we mean the charming qualities of children, then it is true enough that these qualities tend to diminish with time (although again, not all of them, nor in all children). As a culture, we tend to romanticize childhood, and this is another example of it. The relevance to creativity is real but probably exaggerated.

The question of how important it is to sustain or enhance some of the presumed childish qualities that might be involved in significant creative works is nonetheless an important one. Gardner's (1993) analysis of turn-of-the-century creators focused on some childlike qualities that seemed to be present in the personalities of each of them. But as Gardner pointed out, this may be distinctive to that group of individuals, to a particular moment in time, to the domains within which they worked, and probably to other things as well. The valid issue, which a number of creativity scholars have addressed, is to distinguish among various forms of creative activity. My use of the terms *low-*, *middle-*, and *high-range creativity* (Morelock & Feldman, 1999) is an example of this; Winner (1997) has also proposed a set of helpful distinctions. The point is that the term *creativity* needs to be technically specified and given appropriate parameters. Children often exhibit some of the qualities of what I refer to as low-range creativity, meaning that the transformations and extensions they produce may be surprising and delightful but have no enduring effect on a body of knowledge, skill, or understanding.

It is almost certainly true that the qualities that are so appealing in low-range creativity must be to some degree honed, refined, and even perhaps diminished in order for creative activity of a more enduring sort to take place—what I call middle- or high-range creativity. Essentially, as with many other kinds of development, some things are given up in the service of more focused, powerful, and enduring creative contributions to culture. This may be in some sense regrettable, but significant creative work requires sustained focus, hard work, well-organized knowledge, persistence in the face of failure, and a coherent presentation of the work. One of the most challenging questions for the field is: How can we sustain the childlike spark that ignites the creative process, through the many challenges to its expression, in a form that can be appreciated by others?

Mike Csikszentmihalyi

This question is formulated within a conventional or individualistic perspective on creativity, and it is very difficult to answer this question in terms of my systems model. It is a little like saying that "the air squashes fishes' natural propensity to fly." If you look at creativity in terms of the systems model, it is nonsensical to conceive of creativity as separate from society. This is an epistemological issue; in my view, it is society that constitutes creativity; therefore you can't say that a child has any creativity to be suppressed until a certain segment of society—the *field*—construes it as such. I don't know what it means to say that children are creative or that they display creativity. Usually what people mean by these terms is that children often appear to adults to be original, imaginative, or nonconforming. One could just as well interpret such behavior as ignorance of rules, or inability to follow them. There is really no evidence that this relates to adult creativity, as we usually think of it—that is, as an original response *that is socially valued and brought to fruition.*

It could be argued that children's spontaneous, original productions are indeed socially valued, because the children's mothers and teachers value them. In this restricted sense, one can indeed say that children are *creative within the domain of children's art* or what have you. But such domains are peripheral to every culture, except perhaps in developmental terms (it's good for the children to practice art, etc.), but the creativity of such productions is not very relevant.

Of course, society and its institutions may be more or less effective at co-constituting creativity in certain places and at certain times. Thus, for instance, schools are not very well equipped to make creativity happen, and for good reasons: Schools are institutions designed to transmit the *domain*, the results of past creative achievements that have become part of the culture. They are not supposed to enhance creativity, but to prepare the grounds for its happening by introducing each generation to the information needed to live in that culture, and if they so desire, to change and add to it—thereby making creativity happen. So schools are primarily conservative, and they should be so, even if in being so they frustrate many young people who are potentially creative.

Similarly, there are many societies that are not very open to novelty, nor do they encourage change and innovation. Asian cultures especially see themselves in this light. But I wouldn't say that a social system that prefers tradition to innovation squashes or suppresses creativity, for the reason given above: There is no such thing as individual creativity to suppress to begin with. It is more appropriate to say that such a system does not *encourage, support, stimulate,* or *reward* creativity, because these terms all comment on the social system rather than the individual.

Vera John-Steiner

The way in which society, and most particularly schools, respond to children's playful and innovative behaviors is a serious issue in our contemporary climate. Children differ in the intensity of their imaginative and artistic endeavors. Some longitudinal studies—for instance, the Mills Longitudinal Study (e.g., Helson & Pals, 2000)—suggest that the intensity of these imaginary activities correlates well with later creative productivity. But creative productivity—as Feldman has already pointed out—requires sustained motivation, resilience, the ability to deal with rejection and failure, successful mentoring, and communities that contribute to the support of creative activities. So, although childhood play is definitely an important source for the development of imagination and for the engagement of intrinsically and extrinsically motivated activities, it is but one aspect of the broader social system of creativity as developed by Vygotsky, Csikszentmihalyi, and others.

At the individual level, the processes that contribute to the construction of the novel require the weaving together of imagination, risk taking, domain-specific symbol systems, judgment about one's field of expertise, emotional intensity, and courage. These factors never develop in isolation from the social system of creativity, which includes socially constructed artifacts such as language, musical notation, computers, choreographic notation, scientific equipment, and activity systems such as collaborative communities, symphony orchestras, and laboratory teams. In our focus on the relationship between creativity and development, we need to discuss more fully society's role in contributing or impeding creative practices. I can think of at least three ways that society influences individual creativity.

First, artistic or scientific knowledge of a depth needed to make a creative contribution is not easily accessible to children and young people marginalized by society. Specialized urban magnet high schools have assisted in nurturing young artistic talent drawn from a variety of diverse backgrounds, but these gifted children are increasingly neglected by a society that values business and scientific endeavors. Related to this trend is the imposition of test-driven education that is narrowing, rather than broadening, imagination and fantasy; the emphasis is placed on finding correct answers at the expense of valuing the processes that lead to discovery and the development of creative new questions. Together with this trend is a reduced emphasis on teaching about artists and poets in the schools; yet, learning about these figures has long inspired young learners to trust their creative interests and hone their skills.

Second, the well-documented high school art classes that Wilson (1977) described as *communitas* provided an environment in which students had the freedom to experiment with a variety of resources (such as live models and art supplies) after school, whereas, at the same time, they were not under any coercion to produce. Art classes are domain-specific activity systems that provide a historically changing context for the development of creative practices. Their presence is one aspect of the cultivation of creative activities. The fact that these environments are not currently valued in most public schools illustrates my fundamental argument: The nurturing of individual and group creativity is highly dependent on societal policies and resources. This argument is similar to the one made by Csikszentmihalyi (1988) about the important role of the field, as we are both emphasizing how society may stimulate the emergence of new ideas or artworks.

The investment in domains highly valued in a particular society—for example, ballet and chess in the former Soviet Union, or visual arts in France—can change dramatically with shifting historical circumstances. From a systems perspective, children's playful explorations are but a small part of a life constructed around creative endeavors. Their development requires family, community, and societal support, as these provide a range of opportunities to master domain-specific knowledge and help in overcoming the difficulties of constructing a creative life. Thus, I see society as a historically changing context for suppressing or cultivating creativity.

Third, as Feldman and Csikszentmihalyi have suggested, in order to answer this question we need to become more precise about our definitions of creativity and the various components of creative processes. Similarly, we need to explore in much greater detail what we mean by *society*. This is a task that, as psychologists, we can do only in a very limited way. A full treatment of this topic requires a stronger reliance on sociologists of art and science.

In conclusion, to answer this question, we need to focus on theoretical issues as well as on the contemporary challenges facing young people who aspire to a life devoted to creative activities. In bringing a historical perspective to these issues, we need to take into account that this is a period in the United States that is inimical to the nurturance of artistic creativity. And although this is a situation of considerable concern to creativity scholars, we also need to acknowledge that, within the larger society, there are smaller thought communities that resist societal pressures and can provide some support for the struggles of creative individuals. If these communities find ecological niches to maintain the relationship between the creative individual and the broader social context, then it may be possible for them to survive periods of time when broader social forces are negligent in fostering these efforts.

Mike Csikszentmihalyi

I agree with John-Steiner that schools in general could do a much better job to stimulate and nurture "playful and innovative behaviors" in children. Children need playfulness and the opportunity to express themselves in order to become whole persons, to develop self-confidence, and above all, to enjoy their lives. There is ample evidence, for instance, that kids who have access to extracurricular opportunities in their schools (art, music, theater, athletics, etc.) do much better later in life, academically and otherwise, controlling for all sorts of other variables that might facilitate coping.

Yet from my perspective, none of this speaks to whether schools stifle creativity, mostly for the reasons John-Steiner cited. What I would add to those reasons is my usual epistemological and ontological caveat: Because creativity does not exist until it produces a change in the culture, it cannot be observed or measured in children (unless children do change some domain of the culture, which hasn't happened yet, to my knowledge). This distinction is so simple that 99.99% of the people can't understand it, yet, in my opinion, it's absolutely fundamental.

Why do people refuse to abandon the idea that the novelty of children represents creativity? In my opinion, it is due to a gradual sea change in our culture. We have lost trust in most of the virtues that, in the past, supported our self-esteem as human beings. Sexual innocence was laid to rest by Freud; the conviction that we are good, altruistic persons, by Marx; the belief that we are made of godlike stuff, by Darwin; and so on and so on. One of the last bastions of superiority is the belief in creativity. We are too realistic to pretend that we are all Einsteins or Michelangelos, but we can assume that each of us has a spark of their "divine" nature. As Pareto and many others since have said, a belief does not have to be true to be helpful—in fact, perhaps the opposite is often true. So I am ready to accept this last bid for decorating humans with a superior endowment as therapeutically valid, but given the fact that my calling is scholarship, I cannot support its truth.

Seana Moran

From a Vygotskian perspective, children are not more creative than adults, because they have not mastered themselves or their skills. Integration of the functional systems of subjective imagination, objective imagination, and thinking in concepts—and conscious control of these systems—must occur for true creativity to be possible. Yet even schoolchildren think that preschool children are more creative than they are. In a fifth-grade classroom I was observing, a student told me that kindergarteners come up with all kinds of wacky ideas, such as tree leaves talking, but that she knows reality better and knows that leaves can't really talk. These fifth graders think there is a tension between reality and creativity; they think that writing nonfiction is not creative because it is about reality.

We think of our adult lives now and sigh; we remember that it was simpler when we were younger. We could draw pictures that looked like nothing and be called talented; do little experiments that showed no results but a big mess and be called clever; write stories with no plot and be called creative. Just about anything productive we did earned us kudos from the people who loved us. As we got older, our drawings needed to look realistic; our experiments needed to work; our stories needed to have structure. Some of us absorbed these rules— socially agreed-upon conventions—and just stuck with them. Some of us rebelled against them and found that we had trouble getting jobs or communicating with others: We were just eccentric. And some of us absorbed the rules as tentative boundaries that could be reconfigured in certain cases and perhaps became what creativity researchers call creative: We changed the way others saw and knew about the world. Creativity needs social conventions, rules, and operations, not only as a backdrop, but also as an integral part of how creativity arises.

I think this folk belief about childhood creativity prevails because of our nostalgic view of childhood as a carefree time. One problem is that childhood isn't so carefree as we like to remember; children are subjected to many rules and constraints. And, once we are adults, I think we underestimate children's generative abilities and so are more surprised when they say something original than if an adult says it.

Creativity does not suddenly spring to life in adulthood, and that's why looking at childhood might be fruitful. But I don't think it is fruitful to categorize whether children or adults are more creative. I think there are developmental pathways, as Gruber (1988) has mentioned in his case studies and evolving systems approach. The question should be how do children's activities become transformed into the creativity of adulthood?

Jeanne Nakamura

Let me add one more voice to the chorus on the two central points. First, the rejection of the premise that creativity is located in the individual: For those of us who have been studying big *C* Creativity—the significant products that transform a culture—from a systems perspective, the notions of childhood creativity, and of creativity as a native quality of the individual, make little sense, although some theorists consider this to be a small *c* form of everyday creativity. From a systems perspective, society and culture play constitutive roles in any accomplishment defined as creative. Rather than ask whether culture squashes creativity, it would make more sense to ask whether and how a culture (or one of the creative fields within a culture) rewards the reproduction of culture rather than its transformation, discouraging novelty in favor of virtuosity. Second, the cultural diagnosis: I agree that the folk notion under discussion, and U.S. students' near universal recoil at nonindividualist views of creativity, are rooted in deep cultural beliefs that others have already elaborated in their replies to this first question.

At the same time, our emphasis on the extraindividual is obviously a product of our location in the field of psychology and responds to psychology's tendency toward hyperindividualism. I suspect that many sociologists of culture and historians of art would scratch their heads, wondering what all the fuss is about, if they overheard us insisting on the cultural and social constitution of creativity. And, in fact, we might wind up sounding a lot more like other psychologists in an exchange with sociologists, as we rushed to argue that the individual also makes an essential contribution to creativity and isn't just Art's way of making another artwork.

Big *C* Creativity itself is not a personal quality. However, as others' comments suggest, one kernel of truth in the folk belief is the fact that some personal qualities are conducive to big *C* Creativity, and these qualities may be suppressed by society (even as other personal qualities conducive to big *C* Creativity may be fostered by society). Already mentioned in this exchange are expressiveness, spontaneity, imaginativeness, and defiance (or ignorance) of convention. To this list, I would certainly want to add an eager curiosity about the world.

The eminent artists and scientists in the creativity in later life study (Csikszentmihalyi, 1996) talked a great deal about their own intense inquisitiveness about the world around them, which they viewed as a contributor to their lifelong pursuit of art or science. And they worried quite a lot about society's current impact on childhood curiosity and on the child's room to indulge it. Here's a typical comment, from a grandparent who happens also to be an eminent astronomer:

> I really worry whether we are doing something awful to our grandchildren because when I think about my childhood, I was enormously curious. I mean, I can actually think of questions that—I don't know how old I was, I certainly wasn't 10, I might have been 6—things that puzzled me about the physical universe. I mean I can remember asking questions like why, when we drove down the road, the moon was following us. . . . I could give you five questions that bothered me as a child. And now I see these kids whose lives are so filled with "things" that I just really wonder whether

they have any time to be curious. Maybe they will turn into scientists anyway? Maybe they will go to college and they will study math or physics and decide that they like that, and they'll become a scientist?

Developmental psychologists can legitimately study the origins and dynamics of this curiosity about the world, its contribution to creativity, and its fate, including whether and how it is cultivated or discouraged by society in a given time and place. Here the question of the impact of formal schooling does seem appropriate. In what ways does formal education discourage curiosity, as folk beliefs might argue, and under what conditions does it spark curiosity, as the quoted astronomer hopes it might do? A related question is: Through what means other than formal schooling is curiosity nurtured in those who go on to become influential artists and scientists? For many of the eminent artists and scientists we interviewed, including this astronomer, schools were not remembered as playing a significant role in their initial attraction to the domain or subsequent immersion in it.

Keith Sawyer

Does society suppress creativity? I agree with everything said above. I expected Csikszentmihalyi to say that children aren't really creative anyway, because in the systems model, they don't effect a change in any domain. I was more surprised to find that Feldman essentially agreed—that children are not all that creative, that we think so only because we romanticize childhood. I suppose I was surprised because, based on Feldman's (1986/1991) book about child prodigies, I thought he would find those prodigies creative, even though Csikszentmihalyi would not. However, Feldman said that creativity requires "sustained focus, hard work, well-organized knowledge," and I suppose you could say that prodigies have those qualities even if they don't effect a change in any domain.

Csikszentmihalyi said that there is no evidence of a relation between children's original playful activities and adult creativity. I would at least agree that the evidence is inconclusive. There have been studies that have identified small correlations between, for example, children's fantasy play and later measures of divergent thinking (see the introduction to this book). Under some definitions of creativity, children might be said to be creative. For example, we could define creativity as an unexpected or original response to a task or problem; children often do something unexpected—although as Csikszentmihalyi and John-Steiner pointed out, that's probably only because they haven't internalized the rules of the domain yet. If we define creativity as ideational fluency, then preschool children probably wouldn't score as highly as primary school children. But I can't think of any measure of creativity that would show a gradual, monotonic decline with age, as implied by the notion that society suppresses creativity.

Students in my creativity class typically think that anything that constrains the individual in any way is an interference with creativity and is thus inherently bad. When I teach them about domains (Csikszentmihalyi, 1988) or about the languages and conventions necessary in a creative domain (Becker, 1982; John-Steiner, 1985) they absorb it just fine, but they still think everyone would be more creative if they could only break out of those rules and constraints. I think that this stance is one result of our culture's ingrained individualism: The free, unfettered individual is the greatest good, and the best society is one that just gets out of the way. It's very hard to teach my students that no one could be creative *at all* without these rules and conventions, a point that Becker makes very effectively in his book *Art Worlds* (1982), which I use in this class.

This individualistic anticonventions attitude, I think, leads to the idea that children are more creative *exactly because* they haven't yet internalized a domain. It also leads to what Csikszentmihalyi pointed out with frustration—that 99.99% of the people can't accept the idea that creativity can only be defined in a system that includes the domain and the field.

That's why I've spent so much time analyzing the social-theoretic topic of the relation between the individual and society (as I do in chapter 1, using the notion of emergence; also see Sawyer, 2001). Translating Csikszentmihalyi's systems theory into my terms, I would say that creativity is an emergent property of the group, field, or society, rather than a property of individuals. However, I don't think we have to choose one or the other; I think it would be possible to define creativity as both a property of groups and of individuals, although the two definitions would not necessarily be the same. For example, one can say of both a society and a person that they are functional or well integrated, although these clearly could not mean the same thing at both levels of analysis.

CREATIVITY IN DOMAINS

The question: The conflict between *domain-general* and *domain-specific* has been central in both developmental psychology and in creativity research since at least the early 1970s. But these parallels didn't receive much attention in our individual chapters. What is your position on this issue? Where do you fall on this spectrum? I assume that everyone will say, "Somewhere in the middle," and if you do, then get specific: Exactly how do you fall in the middle? What is domain-general and what is domain-specific about both development and creativity, and why do you think so?

David Henry Feldman

The domain-general/domain-specific issue is certainly a central one for creativity studies, but it is a long way from being clearly conceptualized. Most of the work that we (individually and collectively) have done in the past decade has been with extreme cases of creative accomplishment. This has allowed us to finesse the question of how much or in what ways a work is done using universal or general processes versus unique or more specific ones. To some extent the big *C* Creativity and little *c* creativity distinction recognizes that creativity can be thought of as those culture-transforming products generated by a small number of exceptional individuals (big *C*) or can be thought of as an everyday quality that is shared by all humanity (small *c*). An argument can be made for both claims. It is unlikely that we are all equally capable of composing Bach's *St. Matthew's Passion* or drawing up the plans for Frank Lloyd Wright's Falling Water. With these examples of extreme creativity, the need to posit unique qualities, capabilities, talents, and ideas seems overwhelming. On the other hand, there is a case to be made that we are all capable of taking liberties with what exists, transforming the world in ways that seem compelling to us.

I find that, when I teach creativity, my students are most interested in the domain-general form of creativity, feeling that it is more immediately relevant to their lives than the great creativity examples that we tend to study. The more they know about the extremes, the more they want to distance themselves from them. As most of us who have studied extreme cases have discovered, great creativity is rarely a pretty sight when viewed at close range.

I think that Sternberg has made a major contribution to the field in chapter 3, because he has helped to provide order and pattern for the several forms that creative contributions might take. All the examples that Sternberg provides are domain-specific, to be sure, but some of the examples undoubtedly utilize domain-general as well as domain-specific capabilities. By providing more specific descriptions of the varieties of creative contributions, Sternberg has helped move us closer to being able to parse what kinds of qualities of the individuals, groups, institutions, fields, and context tend to be implicated in each of the kinds of creative contributions. Gardner started this process in his wonderful 1993 book, and Sternberg has taken things further.

In several of my writings, I use a metaphor of a piano keyboard as a way of differentiating various creative processes. Those that everyone has the ability to do regularly are in the low range at the left; those that are potentially done as an expression of one's craft or profession are in the middle range of notes; and the extreme kinds of transformations that only rarely occur are represented by the high notes. The keyboard metaphor is intended to put a wide range of creative activities on a continuum (a tendency I have) that does not place more value on one than another. They all have their place on the keyboard, and great music (i.e., a rich, vital, rewarding culture) requires sustained activity across the range. This is simply another in what is now becoming a series of attempts to transcend the either/or of big *C*/little *c*, domain-general/domain-specific, and the like and get down to the specifics of what is involved in each of the several ways in which creative work manifests itself.

My own sense is that we need to focus some of our efforts in the middle range, where very little research on creativity has been done.

Seana Moran

Exactly what is a domain? Some definitions I have heard include *symbol system*, *knowledge structure*, and *rule set*. So something that is domain-specific is constrained by the symbolic content, organization, and functioning of some bounded body of knowledge. Domains are distributed across many people's minds, filing cabinets, computer hard drives, Web sites, books, boxes of paper scraps, theatrical or musical performances, and conversations. In Sawyer's terms, domains are emergent properties of complex systems. A domain is not a closed system; its boundaries are fuzzy, and its content, structure, and function change over time as knowledge is gained, lost, or changed. At any given point, a snapshot of the domain would find different elements of it changing as meanings and functions shift. Domains can die as they fall out of use and there is no one left to interpret their symbols or rules (e.g., alchemy, phrenology).

Can we say that a pure domain exists out there, or is the domain only what is filtered through individuals and internalized? This is a question related to social emergence (Sawyer, 2001). Vygotsky would say that it is filtered by and distributed across people differently on the basis of their varied experiences with interacting in the world, and that these differences are what lead to creative contributions. Like Durkheim's social fact, the internalization of a domain in each individual's mind is only a subset of the domain and only partially overlaps with others' internalizations. These different internalizations lead individuals to interact with the domain in different ways, and as a result, different properties of the domain may be brought to the fore by different people. The manifesting of these latent or developing properties—bringing new configurations to the attention of oneself and others—can lead to what is called creativity.

If creativity is defined as a product that transforms a domain, as in Csikszentmihalyi's model, then such products are by definition domain-specific. Ideas that are imported from another domain can also be handled by such models; even though the borrowed idea is itself specific to its own domain, the creative act that relied on the borrowing can be thought of as multiple-domain-specific, but still not necessarily universal.

If creativity is an individual trait—like playfulness or tolerance of ambiguity—then I think it may cross domains but still is not universal. During the personality era of the 1950s and 1960s, when creativity was thought to be the generation of novelty, such definitions were still domain-specific because the assessment of novelty is consensual, as Amabile (1983) first argued. One must know what already exists to determine what is new in relation to what is already known. People just getting started in a domain may be very "creative" in generating aberrant responses because they don't know any better. But as they come to internalize the rules and structure of the domain, they may become more rigid, as their activity is increasingly appropriate to their domain. Only when they reach the highest levels of expertise do they again generate novelty, as they explore the margins of the domain.

I agree with Feldman that continuum thinking helps us avoid dichotomies. Some products are creative at the domain level, perhaps by creating a new artistic style or scientific methodology or theory; others are creative at the cultural level, because their domain-specific contribution metaphorically spills over into other domains, such as the way in which biological or genetic metaphors are spilling over into psychology right now. Finally, an elite few are creative universally, because their ideas become worldviews or paradigms, such as Einstein's relativity and Darwin's evolutionary theories—both filtering into everyday activities from business to education to marriage counseling.

Mike Csikszentmihalyi

[Question 5 was circulated but not explicitly addressed by our discussion. It suggested that Csikszentmihalyi would say that "Mendel was not creative until after his death."]

Perhaps I have been unclear about this in the past, but, strictly speaking, Mendel was not creative either before or after his death. His work became recognized as creative after his death—and therefore we attribute creativity to Mendel posthumously. The same is true of everyone—Bach or Van Gogh were not creative while they were alive because no one thought so, nor did they mysteriously become creative in the grave—what changed was our perception.

As psychologists (and as folk theorists) we are wedded to the belief that, because we attribute creativity to Michelangelo, therefore Michelangelo must have had something in his brain that made him creative. This is not necessarily so, but if you want my candidates for the traits shared by people who are able to change the domain in significant ways, here's my list:

1. Cognitive abilities: None; at least, none that are general across domains. Perhaps problem-finding qualifies, but that may be more a motivational construct—see below.
2. Motivational traits: Curiosity, interest, and perseverance are all essential and cut across domains (even though *what* you are curious, etc., about is

of course very domain-specific). With these traits, you are likely to enjoy working for its own sake, exploring, and pushing the envelope.

3. Personality traits: It helps to have access to the entire range of human behavioral repertoire (e.g. masculinity *and* femininity, extraversion *and* introversion, etc.). Most of us are trained to operate in one narrow space along this continuum and thus fail to perceive the full range of possibilities.

4. Background characteristics: Marginality (ethnic, social, financial, etc.) helps a lot to break down the taken-for-granted worldview. Usually, the early childhoods of future creators are either quite awful or very enriching; the large "normal" population tends to be underrepresented.

Concerning whether there is anything historically universal about creativity: It seems to me that having the above four traits helps one to introduce novelty into any domain—thus, these qualities are candidates for what it takes to become known as creative in any domain, provided that (a) you have access to a domain you are deeply curious about, and (b) you can convince the relevant gatekeepers that what you came up with should be noticed and remembered.

SOCIAL CONTEXT AND THE INDIVIDUAL

The question: In our chapters, we all agree on the importance of social context. Is it safe to say that this is now a new consensus in the field? How can we reconcile this with the continued methodological individualism of mainstream experimental psychology? Do you think our explorations of the social context–individual relation could have broader implications for the field of psychology more generally?

Robert Sternberg

I think there is an emerging consensus among many in the field that creativity cannot be understood outside its context. Csikszentmihalyi has been saying this for a long time, and at some level, it must be true. Even if one were a great composer of Mozartian kinds of classical music, it might be viewed as not very creative in our time.

As we all agree on this issue, I think, I would like to bring up the issue of the other side of the coin. In 1996, Elena Grigorenko and I edited the book *Intelligence, Heredity, and Environment*; it contains chapters by people who emphasize both genetic and environmental (contextual) views. Earl Hunt wrote a concluding chapter (I had to get a second one because he was so critical in his first draft) stating that the problem with the social contextualists is, in essence, that their work is scientifically vacuous. They talk about context, but it is fuzzy talk, and there are rarely any compelling data.

More generally, I think a problem that psychology faces is how to talk about context in a scientifically rigorous way. I realize that the types who populate the Psychonomic Society or Division 3 of the APA (experimental psychology) or the Society of Experimental Psychologists may not be an audience that my coauthors care about. (As a member of all three groups, I care, and I would hope to convince you that you should, too.) Whatever one thinks of such groups, it is an audience that is important if we want work on creativity to have the kind of reception—at least in the field of psychology—that perhaps we want it to receive. If the work is perceived as unscientific, then it tends to be taken as not serious. Ultimately, I think, it also has less impact. It may take a long time, but the work tends to die out because there is little or no evidence that meets the standards of scientific psychology. It is not a question of method, but rather of perceived scientific rigor. Are the concepts clearly defined? Do they make predictions? Are there converging operations to support the claims being made?

I think there is room in psychology for all kinds of work. But sooner or later, one must subject one's ideas to a scrutiny that meets the general scientific standards of the field—or one will be marginalized. Of course, there are some who will pick on what we do, regardless. For example, I doubt that there is any work that any of us or at least that I could do that would satisfy Linda Gottfredson (a defender of IQ testing who has frequently criticized my work). But she is at the extreme of the right wing. Others are more willing to look with a fully open mind.

At the same time, I think the field of scientific psychology is headed, in many ways, in the wrong directions. For example, there seems to be a belief among many that simply doing functional magnetic resonance imaging (fMRI) work makes the work worth doing, regardless of the question asked and regardless of whether there is any theory behind it. The "biologization" of the field, often at the expense of taking into account contextual variables, is most troubling. This points out, all the more, the need to do contextually-based work in a way that provides an alternative road for young scientists who want to be contextual but who don't want to be marginalized. As some of you know, I recently edited a book called *Psychologists Defying the Crowd*. It is great that there are crowd defiers, but most young people prefer to join the masses, and so we need to provide a means whereby those who want to join the masses nevertheless can study creativity. It is a sad commentary that Division 10 of APA, which is concerned with creativity, is one of APA's smallest divisions. The question, then, is what can we do about it? Can we become more mainstream without selling out? If so, great. If not, it's not worth it.

Howard Gardner

I am really an eavesdropper on this conversation, but let me put in a few cents. I believe that the conversation about creativity always must oscillate between what is unique to the individual and his or her circumstances and what can be generalized to a domain, a subdomain, a population, a subpopulation, and so on. In some of my writings, I have talked about building a bridge between the Gruberian idiographic approach and the Simontonian nomothetic approach; for example, that's what I tried to do in *Creating Minds* (1993) and *Leading Minds* (1995). Put another way, Creativity (with a capital *C*) may be one of those topics that truly benefits from a blend of humanistic study (the detailed mastery of cases) and scientific study (the search for patterns, when observable and appropriate). Perhaps creativity research needs to insist on its special status as a "border" study that can't be carried out if one wants to take an exclusively humanistic approach (à la Leon Edel on Henry James, 1953–1972) or an exclusively scientific approach (à la the more physics-centric psychology journals). And if we could succeed in making this case, it could be important to many other disciplines/domains/problems that struggle to satisfy these two masters.

This is in some sense a continuation of the debate that Sternberg and I have had (not in conversation but on paper) about the future promise (Sternberg) and limitations (Gardner) of scientific psychology.

David Henry Feldman

Context has certainly asserted itself as a critical aspect of creativity. It is hard to imagine anyone doing cutting-edge work in the field and ignoring the context in which creative efforts are being pursued. Consensus may be too strong a word for where we are, though, because there are still a number of scholars who pursue their work in the traditional manner, particularly those who are psychometrically or clinically inclined.

In chapter 4, I take something of an individualistic approach in trying to learn how a unique human being was able to construct and present a novel perspective on intelligence. I have no doubt that certain unique qualities of Howard Gardner played critical roles in how multiple intelligences theory was crafted. After all, there were formally similar theories proposed a number of times in the decades prior to Gardner's 1983 work. I think that Gardner's training as a contemporary cognitive developmentalist (as a student of Bruner, Piaget, and the like) was important to how he looked at things, as was his work in the VA Hospital in Boston with brain-damaged patients. Gruber (1974) has made a similar argument with respect to Charles Darwin as compared with Alfred Lord Wallace. The theory of evolution by natural selection had certain unique qualities that would not have been part of the theory had it been Wallace's version that was accepted. So my effort in this book has been to keep the consensus about environment and contexts from overwhelming the vital role that individual creators (or groups of creators) have on what gets put into the world.

That said, it is equally clear to me that multiple intelligences theory was powerfully influenced by the context within which it was constructed, particularly the broad sets of social and cultural changes associated with civil rights, feminism, gay rights, and the like that preceded its appearance. Gardner has said that the impact of the van Leer project—a more local context—on his confidence, boldness, and willingness to confront controversial issues was profound.

A more systems-like, dynamic, emergent perspective does seem best suited to the complexities and subtleties that are manifest in any significant creative process, as Sawyer argued in chapter 1. The Vygotskian perspective of chapter 2 is also valuable in reminding us of the importance of shared effort, collaboration, and a goal or purpose within a social/cultural context. Csikszentmihalyi was perhaps the first to try to generate a framework that gives voice to the complexity of individual, domain, field, and culture that all must be reckoned with for creative works to be explained in a satisfying way. Sawyer (2003) has focused on the processes of interaction that play themselves out as the various elements interact, with amazing outcomes from time to time. I recall that the wonderful science writer and physician Lewis Thomas (1975) wrote, in *Lives of a Cell*:

> The real surprises, which set us back on our heels when they occur, will always be the mutants. We have already had a few of these, sweeping across the field of human thought periodically, like comets. They have slightly different receptors for the information cascading in from different minds, and slightly different machinery for processing it, so what comes out to rejoin the flow is novel, and filled with new sorts of meaning. Bach was able to do this, and what emerged in the current were primordia in music. In this sense, the Art of the Fugue and the St. Matthew Passion were, for the evolving organism of human thought, feathered wings, apposing thumbs, new layers of frontal cortex. (1975, p. 169)

Other than too little consideration for intentionality and a sense of guiding purpose (in most instances), Thomas captures the dynamic processes wonderfully well. He even goes so far as to say that the cumulative benefit of all of this activity may make us less dependent upon producing so many "mutants" in the future. I'm not so sure about that.

Seana Moran

I think we are near consensus that we must consider social context in our models of creativity, but we are not near consensus regarding what context actually means, whether it is a backdrop or an active player, or whether it can change, both affecting and being affected by the individuals that comprise it.

What is the social context of creativity? Is it the resources and constraints within the painter's studio or inner circle of friends? Is it the field? The market for the painter's works? The political or geographical landscape in which he or she works? The past, present, and future? These questions bring to mind concentric circles of contexts. This idea is nothing new; still, we grapple for methods to study how these different contexts interact with each other and with the individual to bring forth new ideas and artifacts.

I don't see how we can do justice to creativity without dissolving the boundary between the individual and the social. Within the systems model of creativity, individuals comprise the field, and within that field's domain, part of the domain is within each individual's mind. I think a helpful metaphor is metabolism: Individuals draw resources from their environments—social and material, use them, and return them in a different form. The new form is absorbed into the ecology of the environment, used by other individuals in the environment, and returned in a different form. It is not just that society judges what is creative at any given point; it's that different individuals within the social network need each other to be creative, to garner resources to do potentially creative things, to help others produce, and to decide courses of action through their life spans. As Vygotsky would say, the social and the individual are dialectically intertwined in personal and historical development.

So we are back to a change over time, an ecological perspective: not just developmental pathways for the individual, but also for the field and domain. Feldman's theory discusses how domains evolve. Kuhn, Martindale, and others have looked at how certain fields evolve. It seems that what we need is a developmental or historical conception of creativity, as the connection between current and future reality. I think that we do not take time into account explicitly enough. Perhaps part of this is that most creativity studies—psychometric, gestaltist—have been cross-sectional. Only in the last 15 years or so have idiographic approaches allowed time and multiple contexts to play a role in creativity theory. This is where I think emergence and system dynamics theories and approaches will be increasingly important, because they incorporate both time and contextual parameters (see chapter 1). Still, even powerful computers are limited in the number of variables that can be at play in one model. So one must always decide—which variables are most important to the development of creative work? Are they individual, social, or both at once? When is their influence felt?

Vera John-Steiner

One of the most important things we have learned in the last 30 years is that creative contributions are labor-intensive and time-consuming. It is for this reason that researchers addressing creative phenomena are likely to be few but passionate about their interest in the subject. In this book, contributors share a commitment to a systems approach, which requires that context be included. The concept of a system includes input from and output to the broader surrounding field. Where we differ is in the tools we use for specifying the relationship to the larger system. These include Csikszentmihalyi's field, Feldman's cultural organism, and Vygotsky's cultural historical processes. Although we have not, as a community of scholars, jointly and clearly defined what we mean by creativity, we have adopted certain working definitions that many of us find sufficiently clear so that we are able to differentiate between big *C* and little *c* creativity. But these distinctions may not meet the operational definitions demanded by some of our colleagues. There are many sciences (including astronomy, geology, and evolutionary biology) in which some predictions can be made but control groups are not available. In other fields (for instance, pharmacology), the role of control groups is central. There is no universal scientific method. It is precisely for that reason that context is so crucial. Before you can make rapid progress in a field, it is important to become deeply familiar with the phenomena. Sternberg urges us to skip ahead in our exploration of creativity without the longitudinal methods of study that have been so productive in developmental psychology and that I believe are needed in the study of creativity. He wants precision and efficiency, whereas the field is really calling for laborious, lengthy studies of long-term creative activity.

An effective methodology for creativity research was first proposed by Jonas Salk (1987), who suggested the construction of a shared archive of data about creative projects, individuals, and discoveries. After we have access to each other's collected materials and are able to analyze these with shared theoretical frameworks, we can then hope to establish a sufficiently cohesive understanding of creative processes to allow us to influence the field of psychology.

If we are to make progress as a group of scholars, we need to negotiate our use of terminology. To me, *context* does not fully capture the profoundly social nature of creative processes. In Vygotsky's cultural historical framework, the emphasis is on socially constructed meaning, the impact of creative outcomes on the culture, and the role of artifacts such as musical instruments, computers, and imaging techniques. These aspects of context are broader than the immediate surroundings of the creative person. A full study of these is an interdisciplinary (rather than a narrowly psychological) approach. A second important task facing creativity researchers is the examination of major concepts in the field. For example, Sawyer proposes that emergence might provide an effective paradigm for the joint study of development and creativity. Although I agree that the emergence of new levels of reality, understanding, and complex adaptive systems is a critical aspect of creative phenomena, this formulation must be careful not to ignore the central role of purposeful human activity in creativity.

One of the recurrent questions about the relationship between the individual and the social is how are these two linked? In my research, I found complementarity, namely, the way in which individuals with different temperaments, working habits, and training expand each other's resources and together create new phenomena beyond the arithmetic sum of their individual contributions.

Seana Moran

Ultimately, I think this question is misleading. Chapter 2 has a lot to say about both cognitive processes and social processes, because Vygotsky saw them as dialectical. The social processes and experiences that the individual engages in form his or her mental processes, and those mental processes contribute to the emergence of certain social processes, such as Sawyer's improvisational theater example in chapter 1, or the collective reactions an audience shares after seeing a performance of Hamlet.

This question seems to suggest an object or entity orientation. Science seems to focus an awful lot on entities and their stable properties (such as people and their mental capacities) and not enough on relationships and interactions (such as how certain capacities only manifest under certain socio-environmental conditions, and how certain social contexts arise when a certain combination of people and their capacities are present). Both Piaget and Vygotsky emphasized relationships and interactions, as the first two chapters make clear.

We emphasized emotion in chapter 2 because it is a relationship, a bridging of the inner and the outer worlds, the individual and social. Although the information-processing model has been in ascendance in cognitive psychology, we don't just process information; we also experience the world as embodied minds. We make decisions and engage in social interaction by drawing on tacit knowledge, feelings, and expectations. The role of emotions in creativity is a key place to forge new links and new pathways between the social and cognitive processes that contribute to creativity.

Jeanne Nakamura

To the extent that a consensus has developed about the appropriateness of a systems perspective on creativity, my sense is that its proponents need more methodological tools. We need to develop research approaches that are compatible with this family of perspectives so that the field is able to systematically build knowledge. We are indebted to Howard Gruber and his colleagues for their sustained effort to self-consciously develop and deploy one such approach, the intensive, contextualized study of individual cases. Gardner (1993) extended this approach in his study of multiple cases. What other research strategies might allow us to advance the study of creativity and development from a systems perspective? An affinity exists with both the various systems perspectives in human development and the life-course approach in the social sciences more generally, insofar as both of the latter argue that the individual cannot be understood in isolation from society, culture, and history. Can we learn from them? In her response to this question, John-Steiner advocated longitudinal research, a recommendation that I certainly second; this is one example of an area where we might learn from life-course researchers.

Mike Csikszentmihalyi

Methodological individualism works well as long as what we wish to understand is the behavior of the organism *in vacuo*, so to speak. But if we are to study the organism in its natural and social context (out of which context it cannot survive), we are always better off if we can understand how the two are related—which means, for humans, understanding the mutual interaction between individuals, on one hand, and society and culture on the other. Magyari-Beck (e.g., 1999) has been arguing for some time that creativity studies are impoverished by excessive reliance on the individualistic perspective and has suggested that a new discipline called *creatology* be started. I don't think that would work. So how would we contextualize psychological approaches in a broader perspective? What John-Steiner and Nakamura have suggested makes sense. I would add the idea of having 1- to 2-week interdisciplinary workshops in which we could discuss issues with other social scientists, including historians. I don't think we could expect anyone to get retrained in a different discipline, but at least we would get a fuller appreciation for what these issues entail. The problem is not so much that we can't think as sociologists or historians think, but that it is very difficult to write from a dual psycho/social perspective. Given the ever-stricter rules of domains, it runs the risk of being like a game of chess in which the moves occasionally follow to the rules of checkers, instead. This, of course, is not true only of the study of creativity, but, as the question suggests, it is true of psychology more generally.

Keith Sawyer

There are many parallels between the social-systems views of creativity, on one hand, and sociocultural perspectives in developmental psychology, on the other. Perhaps the defining issue of sociocultural psychology is the individual-social relation (see Sawyer, 2002). Socioculturalists claim that all studies of human behavior and cognition must be conducted with social context a central and indispensable aspect of the inquiry. It's not enough to add a few social variables to the end of the regression equation—educational level, annual income, race or gender—along with the traditional psychological variables (as in the psychometric tradition that Sternberg refers to). Rogoff (1998) referred to this as a so-cial-context approach and explicitly contrasted sociocultural approaches, be-cause the sociocultural approaches argue that the individual cannot be analyti-cally separated from the social and cultural context (in Sawyer, 2002, I call this the inseparability claim). And Moran posted a similar comment: "I don't see how we can do justice to creativity without dissolving the boundary between in-dividual and social."

A big part of me agrees with such statements. But there's a problem with such strong claims: It's hard to see where traditional individualistic psychology fits in. Many of these socioculturalists will readily admit that they think individ-ualistic psychology is wrong-headed and should go into the dustbin of history. When many of my colleagues say *individualistic,* they mean it to be pejorative (I have been guilty of this usage myself). So I agree with Sternberg that we have a problem here in showing how our work can speak to the rest of psychology. The same problem faces both socioculturalists who make strong claims for the inseparability of the individual and the social context and creativity researchers who say that social and cultural context can never be removed from the analysis.

I think all of us have made such statements at one point or another, in print, in the past. But there is an apparent disconnection between the uncompromising tone of such statements and the empirical work that we have all done at various times that focuses on individuals. Feldman correctly noted that his contribution to this volume is individualistic, in that it focuses on what is unique about Howard Gardner. Yes, Feldman also discussed social context, but he thinks that Gardner, the person, is somehow unique; I don't think that Feldman would say that anyone could have done what Gardner did, had he been in the right place at the right time.

So a part of me thinks that of course there are questions for which we can focus solely on the individual. I'm not ready to dismiss the traditional individu-alistic field of psychology completely. Here, I agree with Sternberg that we are marginalized and often perceived to be less scientific. The burden of proof is on us, and we can't afford to ignore what mainstream psychology thinks of our re-search. I agree with Sternberg that we need to create a narrative, to make a case, to show how our work is consistent with the "general scientific standards of the field." One exemplary career is Barbara Rogoff's. Even with her strong claims for the inseparability of individual and context, Rogoff (e.g., 1998) has been very effective at communicating her ideas to a mainstream audience of develop-mental psychologists.

At the end of her posting here, John-Steiner emphasized the complementar-ity of both individual and context approaches, and the importance of an interdis-ciplinary approach. I agree wholeheartedly with both of these points; we really need to be interdisciplinary. That means being both psychologists and sociolo-gists from time to time. Echoing a comment that Nakamura made earlier, I'm surprised that I rarely see any references to the sociological study of art and science among our systems-view theorists. A theory of scientific change like Kuhn's has much in common with Csikszentmihalyi, and there is an entire sub-discipline of sociology focused on art. Becker's book *Art Worlds* (1982) is completely simpatico with systems approaches. I think we need to be more interdisciplinary in drawing on and tying in to these traditions.

CLOSING COMMENTS: KEITH SAWYER

Howard Gardner, who was a legitimate peripheral participant in our discussion, posted a comment near the conclusion that sums up my feeling as well: "I appreciate this continuing conversation. Perhaps it is one of the ways in which 'creativity studies' moves toward becoming a scholarly domain." I believe that our discussion comments focus on key issues in creativity and development.

Responses to the first question (does society suppress a child's natural creativity?) clarified many important definitional and conceptual issues. We came to a consensus that children are not really creative, given the definitions of creativity that are necessary to explain the important and influential innovations that have impacted our lives. Some of us are willing to retain a residual notion of small *c* creativity—the everyday cleverness that makes us smile or makes life easier—for the novel, unusual actions of children, but we all distinguish this from big *C* Creativity, the creation of culture-transforming products that is found only in adults.

The second question—about domain specificity—has been important in both developmental psychology and creativity research, and over about the same time span—roughly since the 1970s, when the notion of development in domains became one of the foci of neo-Piagetian research. Gardner's 1983 book on multiple intelligences represented a full flowering of this new approach, and it was equally influential in creativity theory and in educational psychology (if not developmental psychology proper). Our responses to this question again emphasized parallel theoretical issues in studies of both creativity and development.

The third question—about the role of social context—raised some foundational issues for our field of study, because although we are all trained as psychologists and work as psychologists, we all reject the individualist focus of psychology as inadequate to the phenomenon of creativity. Yet, as Sternberg pointed out, this is a risky strategy, because it threatens to leave us marginalized and ultimately with no scientific impact. As I noted in chapter 1, these same issues are foundational for those developmental psychologists who take a socio-cultural approach. Creativity researchers and developmental psychologists are thus facing similar issues.

Our goal in this volume has been to explore the connections between two traditions of research: the psychology of creativity, and developmental psychology. We focused on theoretical parallels related to the notion of *process*. Although this book is one of the first attempts to explicitly integrate the two traditions, our chapters have shown that there are many indirect and implicit connections. We noted historical parallels between the staged models of creativity and of development in the early twentieth century, and we identified many parallels between sociocultural developmental psychology and social context theories of creativity. From the early twentieth century to the present, both creativity and development have been conceived of as processes of emergence in complex systems; this shared emphasis broadly unifies approaches ranging from Piagetian developmental theory to Csikszentmihalyi's systems model. In the last few decades, both sociocultural psychology and socially oriented theories of creativity have developed a systems approach that incorporates both the individual and the social into the analysis.

These many connections suggest that researchers in both areas could benefit from a greater mutual familiarity. To date, creativity researchers have benefited from these parallels more than developmental psychologists; many approaches to creativity have been based on frameworks originally designed for developmental psychology. In comparison, developmental theorists are rarely familiar with the relevant work on creativity that we have identified here. Theory and practice in both creativity and development should take an interdisciplinary approach; for example, theories could be evaluated to see how well they account for the data on both creative insight and developmental stage transitions, and empirical data could be analyzed using theoretical models from both areas.

REFERENCES

Amabile, T. M. (1983). *The social psychology of creativity*. New York: Springer-Verlag.

Becker, H. (1982). *Art worlds*. Berkeley: University of California Press.

Csikszentmihalyi, M. (1988). Society, culture, and person: A systems view of creativity. In R. J. Sternberg (Ed.), *The nature of creativity* (pp. 325–339). New York: Cambridge University Press.

Csikszentmihalyi, M. (1996). *Creativity: Flow and the psychology of discovery and invention*. New York: HarperCollins.

Edel, L. (1953–1972). *Henry James*. 5 vols. Philadelphia: Lippincott.

Feldman, D. H. (1991). *Nature's gambit: Child prodigies and the development of human potential*. New York: Teachers College Press. (Original work published 1986)

Gardner, H. (1993). *Creating minds*. New York: Basic Books.

Gardner, H. (1995). *Leading minds: An anatomy of leadership*. New York: Basic Books.

Gruber, H. E. (1974). *Darwin on man: A psychological study of scientific creativity*. Chicago: University of Chicago.

Gruber, H. E. (1988). The evolving systems approach to creative work. *Creativity Research Journal, 1,* 27–51.

Helson, R., & Pals, J. L. (2000). Creative potential, creative achievement, and personal growth. *Journal of Personality, 68,* 1–27.

John-Steiner, V. (1985). *Notebooks of the mind: Explorations of thinking.* Albuquerque: University of New Mexico Press.

Magyari-Beck, I. (1999). Creatology. In M. A. Runco & S. R. Pritzker (Eds.), *Encyclopedia of creativity* (Vol. 1, pp. 433–441). San Diego, CA: Academic Press.

Morelock, M. J., & Feldman, D. H. (1999). Prodigies. In M. A. Runco & S. R. Pritzker (Eds.), *Encyclopedia of creativity* (Vol. 2, pp. 449–456). San Diego, CA: Academic Press.

Rogoff, B. (1998). Cognition as a collaborative process. In D. Kuhn & R. S. Siegler (Eds.), *Handbook of child psychology: Volume 2. Cognition, perception, and language* (5th ed., pp. 679–744). New York: Wiley.

Salk, J. (1987). Concluding comments. Paper presented at the Invitational Conference on Creativity, Salk Institute, San Diego, CA, January 11–12.

Sawyer, R. K. (2001). Emergence in sociology: Contemporary philosophy of mind and some implications for sociological theory. *American Journal of Sociology, 107*(3), 551–585.

Sawyer, R. K. (2002). Unresolved tensions in sociocultural theory: Analogies with contemporary sociological debates. *Culture & Psychology, 8,* 283–305.

Sawyer, R. K. (2003). *Improvised dialogues: Emergence and creativity in conversation.* Westport, CT: Greenwood.

Sternberg, R. J. (Ed.). (2002). *Psychologists defying the crowd: Stories of those who battled the establishment and won.* Washington, DC: American Psychological Association.

Sternberg, R. J., & Grigorenko, E. (Eds.). (1996). *Intelligence, Heredity, and Environment.* New York: Cambridge University Press.

Thomas, L. (1975). *Lives of a cell.* New York: Viking.

Wilson, M. (1977). Passage through communitas: An interpretive analysis of enculturation. *Dissertation Abstracts International, 38*(5), 2496-A. (University Microfilm #77–23, 291).

Winner, E. (1997). Giftedness vs. creativity in the visual arts. *Poetics, 24,* 349–377.

Index